Brand Global, Adapt Local

How to Build Brand Value Across Cultures

Katherine Melchior Ray with Nataly Kelly

KoganPage

Publisher's note

Every possible effort has been made to ensure that the information contained in this book is accurate at the time of going to press, and the publishers and authors cannot accept responsibility for any errors or omissions, however caused. No responsibility for loss or damage occasioned to any person acting, or refraining from action, as a result of the material in this publication can be accepted by the editor, the publisher or the authors.

First published in Great Britain and the United States in 2025 by Kogan Page Limited

Kogan Page

Kogan Page Ltd, 2nd Floor, 45 Gee Street, London EC1V 3RS, United Kingdom
Kogan Page Inc, 8 W 38th Street, Suite 902, New York, NY 10018, USA
www.koganpage.com

EU Representative (GPSR)

Authorised Rep Compliance Ltd, Ground Floor, 71 Baggot Street Lower, Dublin D02 P593, Ireland
www.arccompliance.com

Kogan Page books are printed on paper from sustainable forests.

ISBNs

Hardback 978 1 3986 1982 1
Paperback 978 1 3986 1971 5
Ebook 978 1 3986 1981 4

British Library Cataloguing-in-Publication Data

A CIP record for this book is available from the British Library.

Library of Congress Control Number

2025008294

Typeset by Integra Software Services, Pondicherry
Print production managed by Jellyfish
Printed and bound by CPI Group (UK) Ltd, Croydon CR0 4YY

This book is dedicated to marketers, business professionals, and students whose curiosity and drive to connect across cultures shape the future of global business. Your commitment to understanding people, and their evolving needs and desires, inspires us. These stories, insights, and tools are shared with you in mind, to celebrate the work of fostering collaboration, creativity, and commerce. It is through this work that we build not only successful brands but also deeper human connections that transcend differences.

PRAISE FOR *BRAND GLOBAL, ADAPT LOCAL*

"Brands shouldn't strive to be the same everywhere—they should strive to be strong everywhere. Rooted in purpose, fluent in culture—this book will show you how modern brands win."
David Aaker, considered the "Father of Modern Branding" and author of *Aaker on Branding*, 2nd Edition

"The best brands don't just adapt to culture—they help shape it. Katherine Melchior Ray and Nataly Kelly's insights into global branding show how to keep a brand's soul intact while igniting passion across diverse markets. *Brand Global, Adapt Local* is a must-read for marketers and leaders who want to create brands that not only sell but inspire."
Greg Hoffman, former Chief Marketing Officer, Nike and author of *Emotion by Design*

"*Brand Global, Adapt Local* is an essential guide for leaders navigating the complexities of global business. Rich with real-world examples, this book invites us to see the world with fresh eyes and embrace the human dimension at the heart of every successful global brand."
Emmanuel Prat, former Chairman, LVMH Japan

"In the age of AI, speed is easy—relevance is hard. *Brand Global, Adapt Local* illuminates a critical truth: technological reach is meaningless without genuine human understanding. Katherine Melchior Ray and Nataly Kelly offer a vital blueprint for navigating the complexities of global expansion to build digitally scalable, yet culturally nimble, brands. A must-read for leaders wanting to thrive as technology rewrites the rules of engagement."
Miki Iwamura, VP of Marketing, APAC and Japan, Google

"*Brand Global, Adapt Local* is a refreshing take on the long-acknowledged tension between international economies of scale and demand for cultural authenticity. Katherine Melchior Ray and Nataly Kelly address this classic debate between economics and anthropology with an immensely readable perspective that is part branding next practice and part personal travelogue. With intensifying anti-globalization debates, this book could arrive at no better time."
Rohit Deshpande, Baker Foundation Professor, Harvard Business School

"Some books teach marketing. Some teach psychology. In *Brand Global, Adapt Local*, Katherine Melchior Ray and Nataly Kelly teach both—and more. By blending consumer insight, innovation, and masterful storytelling, it reveals how cultural intelligence turns good brands into global powerhouses. Whether you're launching a product, shaping a message, or leading a team, this book will change how you think about influence across borders."
Jonah Berger, Wharton Professor and bestselling author of *Contagious* and *The Catalyst*

"Winning in global markets isn't just about reach—it's about relevance. In *Brand Global, Adapt Local*, Katherine Melchior Ray and Nataly Kelly showcase how brands can stay globally strong while locally agile, ensuring they connect with consumers in a meaningful way, no matter where they are."
Stephan Gans, SVP Chief Insights and Analytics Officer, PepsiCo, and co-author of *The Consumer Insights Revolution*

"In *Brand Global, Adapt Local* we get wisdom from the trenches. Katherine Melchior Ray has earned her stripes in the most demanding industry in the world: fashion. Her insights on cultural differences alone are worth the price of admission. Eye-opening stuff."
Marty Neumeier, author of *The Brand Gap*

"Timely and thought-provoking, *Brand Global, Adapt Local* offers sharp insights on business, branding, and culture—and what it takes to go global today. More than a book, it's an inspiring journey that will leave both the marketer and the traveller in you wanting more."
Elisa Riboldi, Chief Marketing Officer, Nestlé Iberia

CONTENTS

PART TWO Culture, Consumers, and Communication

PART THREE Creating Value across Cultures

LIST OF FIGURES AND TABLE

Figures

Table

ABOUT THE AUTHORS

Katherine Melchior Ray

Katherine Melchior Ray lectures on international marketing and leadership topics at Haas School of Business, University of California, Berkeley and consults with businesses globally. Her expertise results from a 25-year career building the world's best consumer brands through culture-flexing across three continents, four countries, and five industries: fashion, beauty, travel, tech, and television. Known as a catalyst for growth, she held senior executive roles at Nike, Nordstrom, Louis Vuitton, Gucci, Hyatt, Shiseido, and Babbel as they sought entry into new markets and digital or organizational transformations. She was Chief Marketing Officer (CMO) at Shiseido, the $10 billion cosmetics company based in Tokyo, before joining tech startup Babbel as CMO in Berlin. She has lived and worked in Japan three times, under three subsequent Emperors, and has worked with CEOs of eight different nationalities.

As a business leader, marketer, and former on-air reporter, she speaks frequently on topics such as global growth and branding, cultural dynamics, and the power of diversity, authenticity, risk taking, and resilience. She has guest lectured at Stanford, Wharton, Brown, and Portland State University, and been featured on CBS *60 Minutes*, CNN, *The New York Times*, and numerous international media. She has been profiled in *The Wall Street Journal* and was voted one of the "Most Compelling Women in the Travel Industry" by *Premier Traveler* magazine. She can be heard on various podcasts and blogs related to global marketing and leadership, culture and diversity, women's empowerment, and the future of work.

A graduate of Brown University, Melchior Ray served on the Board of Brown's Alumni Association and the Brown Women's Leadership Committee. She is an International Advisory Board Member of EDHEC Executive Education and MBAs in France. She attended Keio University in Japan for a semester of postgraduate study and Stanford School of Business for a Design Thinking program with IDEO.

Melchior Ray and her husband are the parents of two grown children and split their time between the West Coast of the U.S. and Nice, France.

Nataly Kelly

Nataly Kelly is a seasoned tech executive, international business expert, and longtime *Harvard Business Review* contributor on topics of global business and international marketing. She is Chief Marketing Officer at Zappi, a consumer insights platform. Previously, Kelly served at HubSpot as Vice President (VP) of Marketing, VP of International Operations and Strategy, and VP of Localization. Kelly also served as Chief Growth Officer and VP of Marketing for two other software companies in the MarTech space, and previously held the role of Chief Research Officer for CSA Research, where she oversaw the company's subscription-based market research practice.

Her prior books include *Take Your Company Global: The New Rules of International Expansion* (Berrett-Koehler Publishers) and *Found in Translation* (Penguin Random House). Her expertise has also been featured in *The Wall Street Journal*, *The New York Times*, the *Financial Times*, *Forbes*, and many other major media outlets.

Kelly has served as an adjunct professor in the M.A. program in localization management at the Middlebury Institute of International Studies in Monterey, California. An award-winning marketing leader, she was named one of the Top 50 CMOs on LinkedIn, a Top 25 Content Marketer in Enterprise Software, Marketing Executive of the Year by Best in Biz, and a 40 under 40 by Direct Marketing News, among others.

She is a former Fulbright scholar, having studied sociolinguistics under her research grant, while pursuing her Master's degree in Latin American Studies with a minor in Language Policy at the Universidad Andina Simón Bolívar in Ecuador.

She also studied at the Universidad San Francisco de Quito in 1997 and spent a year abroad at the Pontificia Universidad Católica del Ecuador in 1998. She received her bachelor's degree in Spanish with a minor in Intercultural Communication from Wartburg College.

Kelly lived in Donegal, Ireland, during the pandemic with her Irish-born husband, two young daughters, and beloved rescue pup. They remain part-time summer residents of Donegal, and reside in New Hampshire, U.S., during the school year.

List of Brands Featured

Adobe, Airbnb, Apple, Babbel, Braniff, Budweiser, Bulgari, Cartier, CHANEL, Chevrolet, Coca-Cola, Comptoir des Cotonniers, Dior, Dolce & Gabbana, Façonnable, Fast Retailing, Google, Goldman Sachs, Gucci, Hanna Andersson, HubSpot, KitKat, La Perla, Levi Strauss, Louis Vuitton, MAC, Marlboro, Meta, Microsoft, MillerCoors, Natura, Nestlé, Nike, Nordstrom, NARS, NIVEA, Oriflame, Patagonia, Pepsodent, Princesse Tam Tam, Revlon, Rolex, Samsung, 7-Eleven, Salesforce, SAP, Sephora, Shiseido, Starbucks, Starwood, Tata Consultancy Services, Tesla, Tommy Hilfiger, Tory Burch, Toyota, Unilever, Uniqlo, Van Clef and Arpels, Wieden & Kennedy

List of Contributors by Industry

We are able to bring to life real stories and descriptive scenes from dozens of brands in different industries thanks in great part to the hard-earned lessons our incredible contributors volunteered to share. We are very thankful for the unparalleled insights from everyone listed below, as well as many others who helped us in our professional and academic lives. All direct quotes from those interviews and additional sources have been approved for use.

- Beauty
  - Jennifer Anton, **Revlon**
  - Fabio Luizari Artoni, **Natura, Oriflame**
  - Ndungu Wanjohi, **Revlon**
- Consulting
  - John Rowe, **Wieden & Kennedy**
  - Abhinav Kumar, **Tata Consultancy Services**
- Fashion and Apparel
  - Avery Baker, **Tommy Hilfiger**
  - Greg Hoffman, **Nike**
- Food and Beverage
  - Jennifer Anton, **Budweiser**
  - Carlota Casellas, **Nestlé**
  - Takafumi Minaguchi, **Starbucks**

- Financial Services
  - Lisa Shalett, **Goldman Sachs**
- Hospitality
  - Sara Kearney, **Hyatt**
  - Frits van Paasschen, **Starwood Hotels**
- Technology
  - Marvin Chow, **Google**
  - Masakatsu Kosaka, **HubSpot**
  - Morin Oluwole, **Meta**
  - Dmitry Shamis, **HubSpot**
  - Shohei Toguri, **HubSpot**
  - Jean-François Vanreusel, **Adobe**
  - John Yunker, **Byte Level Research**

FOREWORD

I first met Katherine Melchior Ray when she was sitting beside me on a long-haul flight to Asia. She was on her way to Japan, leading Shiseido's luxury brands as CMO, and I was fully immersed in my role leading the Jordan Women's division at Nike. What started as casual conversation quickly turned into a deeper exploration of a question we were both passionate about: How do you build a brand that resonates consistently across borders while honoring the unique character of each place it touches?

Growing up in Mexico and working in markets all over the world, I've seen firsthand how culture shapes people's values, aspirations, and choices. These experiences taught me that you can't simply export a one-size-fits-all brand strategy and expect it to connect. You have to approach each market with curiosity and respect, recognizing that real connection for brands—just like for humans—happens when you adapt without losing your identity. As we flew across time zones and Katherine shared her experiences navigating these complexities, I was struck by her ability to articulate what I'd always felt: The strongest brands balance global vision with local authenticity.

That balance is at the heart of *Brand Global, Adapt Local*. This book is more than a guide to global brand building; it's an invitation to think differently about how we connect with the world. Katherine's approach reflects a truth that has become central to my own career: great brands don't impose themselves on culture—they collaborate with it. They represent universal values that can ebb and flow through the intricate currents of local culture. And as the book demonstrates, this is not just a business strategy; it's an art form.

The world we live in demands a new approach to value creation. Consumers today expect more from brands. They want products and campaigns that reflect their values, speak to their individuality, and celebrate their communities, while at the same time reflecting the diversity of the global audience. The strongest brands thrive by embracing diversity—not as a challenge to navigate, but as an opportunity to add meaning. Katherine doesn't just acknowledge these demands; she equips readers with the tools to meet them. Through stories drawn from international business leaders and her own remarkable career with brands like Louis Vuitton, Nike, and Shiseido, she offers practical strategies for adapting products, services, and communication to local markets while staying true to a brand's core identity.

This effort is elevated by the contributions of Nataly Kelly, whose expertise in digital localization and global B2B strategies adds important perspectives. In a world increasingly defined by digital connections, Nataly shares invaluable insights on how technology can enhance a brand's ability to adapt and thrive across borders. With consumers' preferences evolving rapidly and the pace of innovation increasing, brands require greater agility than ever before. The degree to which brands can adapt and grow alongside the ever-changing lives of their customers will ultimately drive their competitive advantage.

What makes this book so compelling is its humanity. At its core, *Brand Global, Adapt Local* is about more than business; it's about people. Katherine and Nataly challenge us to look beyond short-term wins and focus on what really matters: the relationships brands cultivate with the people they serve. It's an approach that resonates deeply with me, reminding us that the most enduring brands are those that honor and reflect the diverse stories of the communities they touch.

Whether you're a seasoned executive leading international teams, an entrepreneur expanding into new markets, or someone simply curious about the value of global connection, this book will inspire you to see the world through a new lens.

Andrea Perez, Board Director, Global Brand and Business Leader, Former Senior VP at Sony Interactive Entertainment, and Global VP at Nike

ACKNOWLEDGMENTS

Writing this book has been a deeply rewarding experience, and it would not have been possible without the incredible support, guidance, and encouragement of many people along the way. This project was inspired by two sets of experiences and insights as well as countless individuals and organizations who shared their wisdom, stories, and support. The fact that I wrote many of the chapters while teaching a global marketing class created a welcome, inspiring, and productive exchange of relevant insights and stories.

First and foremost, we are deeply thankful to the many individuals and organizations who shared their stories, experiences, case studies, and resources for this book, as your insights add authenticity and depth to these pages. This book would not have been possible without you. Additional thanks to Aperian, Rohit Deshpande, and Esther Perel for generously offering your ideas, resources, and support. For illustrative purposes, certain scenes in the book are descriptive or modified with fictitious names.

We thank the entire Kogan Page team, beginning with our editor, Donna Goddard-Skinner, for your vision in bringing this book to life and helping shape the ideas into a compelling outline. We were lucky to have not one but two developmental editors, Jeylan Ramis and Bobbi-Lee Wright, whose thoughtful feedback and encouragement made this book much stronger.

We want to thank Bree Barton for collaborating on organization and inspiring confidence in the writing. We're indebted to Sarah Vlazny, a former student, who gathered and compiled information alongside course work and a marketing job. Melissa Boles helped by verifying and itemizing references. We are grateful to Guonan Design for the sleek graphics.

To my (Katherine's) family, David Ray, Sabin, and Hunter, Natalie Bennett, and Gabriel Lesser, your ideas, support, and encouragement helped more than you can imagine. Thank you for always cheering me on and for understanding the long hours—your belief in me means everything. To my parents, who taught me to think deeply and consider alternate viewpoints, this book would not have happened without you.

I am grateful to have worked alongside hundreds of people at different brands across countries and industries. So many people have been invaluable sources of insight and inspiration, helping me cultivate the knowledge, skills, and instincts to build brands across cultures. In particular, I want to thank my mentor, Gun Denhart, founder and CEO of Hanna Andersson, whose decision-making and entrepreneurship inspired and shaped my own values as a young working mother. I was lucky to work for the great Yves Carcelle, CEO of Louis Vuitton, whose bold ideas, guidance, and wisdom profoundly shaped my thinking and audacity, as reflected in the stories in this book.

I want to express my deepest gratitude to my co-author, Nataly Kelly, whose experience, contribution, and support encouraged me from concept to completion. What serendipity to discover one another from your *Harvard Business Review* article on the global marketing mistakes companies make. As a fellow executive, global marketer, mom, and family relocator, we've shared not only content but compassion during our busy lives.

I (Nataly) would like to thank my husband, Brian Kelly, and my daughters, May and Eve, for your support while writing this book.

I'm also very grateful to the colleagues who bring great joy to my role as CMO at Zappi: Aaron Kechley, Steve Phillips, George Kadifa, Ruben Mier, Sofija Ostojic, Pejman Pourmousa, Sanjeet Mitra, Pablo Romero Yusta, Melissa Coito, Ana Sordo, Rodrigo Souto, Anthony Lansing, and the entire Zappi marketing team.

Huge thanks to Linda Fletcher, Carla Lourenco Rodney, Beth Dunn, Paula Trigo Blanco, Renato Beninatto, Marcy Schinder, and Elana Konstant for your ongoing support, guidance, and mentorship.

Tremendous thanks to Katherine Melchior Ray, whose career I first read about in *The Wall Street Journal* as a newly minted VP of Marketing. What an honor, years later, to cross paths and be invited to participate in this book and continue to learn from you. You are an inspiration to so many marketers, business professionals, and "globalistas" like me. If only English words could capture the deep embodied respect conveyed in a Japanese bow.

Finally, thank you to our readers. Whether you are navigating your own global brand journey or simply curious about this complex world, we hope this book inspires and informs you. It's been an honor to bring this project to life, and we are grateful for the opportunity to share it with you.

Introduction

Welcome to the Global Village

The sun rises over Surat, India, painting the sky in strokes of saffron and gold. In a small park tucked between concrete buildings, men of different ages stretch their arms overhead and side to side, their breath visible in the morning air. Nearby, a makeshift gym has sprung up in what was once a vacant lot, its metal weights clanking against the rhythm of Bollywood music from a tinny speaker. This scene, replicated across hundreds of India's emerging cities, tells a story of economic transformation.

In 2017, India wasn't just awakening to a new day—it was awakening to a new relationship with fitness, sport, and global brands. Cricket still reigned supreme, as the Indian Premier League had injected glamor and money into the traditional game. Marathons drew thousands to city streets. Parks that once stood empty at dawn pulsed with activity. In this nation of 1.4 billion people, where 19,000 daily newspapers compete across 22 official languages and 380 TV channels beam images into homes from Kashmir to Kerala, the market was brimming with opportunity.

A 14-year-old with cricket dreams in his eyes pushes open the door of a local sports shop. The shelves tower with promises: Nike's technical prowess, Adidas's professional heritage. But Rohit's eyes catch something else first—Puma's flip-flop sandals on display. Standing over them in a poster, Indian cricket captain and Puma ambassador Virat Kohli makes him smile with national pride.[1] He recalls racing with his friends before practice, inspired by eight-time Olympic champion Usain Bolt channeling speed in the Puma campaign *Forever Faster*, and turns to look at Puma's other offerings.[2] An hour later, Rohit emerges with cricket shoes and flip-flops adorned with Puma's fast cat logo, his friends trailing behind with envy as palpable as the rising heat.

How did small, sleek Puma, with global sales of only $4 billion, overtake industry behemoths Adidas and Nike, with global sales of $21 billion and $31 billion respectively, to steal number one market share in India?[3]

The agile German company achieved the difficult duality of global coherence and local connection. Arriving fashionably late to India's market in 2006, Puma overcame the global resources and technical superiority of its daunting competitors to turn that challenge into Olympic gold. The company looked to the market for opportunity. It saw young men and women flocking to fitness. In a nation enamored with Bollywood flamboyance, where open footwear was a part of daily life, Puma recognized that flip-flops could be both practical and aspirational. Through a deep cultural focus on the consumer, Puma understood that style mattered as much as sport. Puma innovated products in new categories like sandals and women's fitness, launched in select retail outlets and online, and invested in brand partnerships from sport to spectacular. The company anchored its global brand in local culture. Those India-specific sandals sold five million pairs annually—a testament to the power of speaking a global language with a local accent.[4]

This is the art of global brand building in the twenty-first century: communicating universal values that can flex and flow through the intricate currents of local cultures. It takes more than market research; it demands a particular kind of vision—one capable of zooming out to align with overarching brand principles while zooming in to express those values authentically within each culture's unique context. This approach calls for both strength and agility, balancing consistency with cultural nuance. With a global mindset, you can navigate this complexity to see a kaleidoscope of opportunities and build connections across borders.

Join us as we explore how successful brands manage these multi-layered priorities. Learn why some global giants stumble while others soar, and how even small brands can build bridges across cultural divides. Visit the sleek Tokyo office of Louis Vuitton Japan, where ancient spiritual principles impact modern business behavior. Drive along dusty roads in South Africa with Revlon, where entrepreneurial men and women selling goods from blankets and small metal kiosks expand the local's national pride and the visitor's humility. At Nestlé's Swiss headquarters, nestled near Lake Geneva, discover the precise chocolate percentages that appeal to different cultural tastes. See how Rome's ancient cobblestones inspire a Gucci love story for Asia. Each scene represents a market opportunity, accessible only after the culture is first unlocked.

But first, let us explain how we learned to see through myriad cultural lenses, so you can too.

We have spent decades building global brands in new markets, learning to understand the foreign or unfamiliar. We are chief marketing officers (CMOs) with long careers building some of the world's best consumer and business-to-business (B2B) brands through culture-flexing across four continents and five industries: fashion, beauty, travel, tech, and television. Many of the stories in this book are culled from our personal experiences and professional networks.

We are American nationals from different backgrounds who both recognize the value of embracing diversity. We each became fluent in at least one foreign language: Katherine speaks French and Japanese; Nataly is fluent in Spanish. We both lived and worked abroad solo and with our families. Our abilities to see things differently across cultures may be, in part, due to being women in a man's world, confronting novel ways others might see and treat us as women operating in their cultures. To figure out how to work with and through those expectations, we had to make the invisible visible. These experiences inform our knowledge and passion for the value of a global mindset for businesses, brands, and anyone open to opportunities. Our hope is to share the knowledge we've gained and the lessons we've learned to inspire others to learn what it takes to build powerful global brands across cultures and to pursue such experiences themselves.

Bringing Your Family to the World (Katherine)

Most recently, I was the CMO in Japan at Shiseido's luxury brands before shifting into the tech world as the CMO of the Berlin-based language app Babbel. Prior to that, I had worked as a senior executive at Nike, Nordstrom, Louis Vuitton, Gucci, and Hyatt, building brands across the U.S., France, and Japan. I was drawn to the growth opportunities I saw each time: building women's-only footwear at Nike in the U.S.; growing Nordstrom's first foreign acquisition in France; helping the world's largest luxury brand, Louis Vuitton, in the world's largest luxury market—Japan; and bringing brand management to high-end hospitality. I've seen firsthand how global awareness increases empathy, inclusivity, and productivity so that innovation can pollinate across industries and cultures. This led to teaching global marketing to MBA students at Haas School of Business, University of California, Berkeley, which helped inspire this book.

I wasn't always this way. I lived for my first 18 years in one city, albeit a diverse and cosmopolitan one: San Francisco. As a first-generation American with a German refugee father, I was raised amid multiple cultures. I attended a French bilingual elementary school and explored regional cuisine variations in Chinatown. I confronted more cultural differences when I moved to the East Coast for college at Brown University. Studying history, I learned to select facts to frame a story—and now a brand—tracing the *fil rouge* or "red thread" of values as they shift alongside culture. Perhaps the challenges I faced as a California girl in New England gave me the skills and flexibility to pursue foreign lands—and pursue them I did. Flying straight to Japan for several years after university, I dove deep into the eccentric and the extraordinary, developing my business and storytelling skills at Fuji Television.

Living and working abroad for 15 years in four countries, with my family in tow for part, wasn't just a career—it was the ultimate embodiment of the principles shared in this book. While building global brands requires understanding and adapting to cultures, living it day to day, especially as a family, adds a profoundly personal dimension. Raising children across borders for eight of those years wasn't always easy, but it was deeply rewarding. Together, we confronted what it means to stand out, to not understand, and to make mistakes. We learned to embrace our minority status and navigate cultural nuances, sometimes clumsily, but always with an open mind. Through it all, we discovered humility, resilience, and a deep respect for the traditions and values that make every culture unique.

Managing this life—spanning countries, companies, careers, two kids and a canine—required an adventurous spirit, a flexible mindset, a supportive spouse, and a sense of humor. For those who wonder whether balancing work and family on a global scale is complicated or crazy, I'd say you can have it all, just maybe not all at once! A life that integrates the professional and the personal, the local and the global, isn't always seamless, but it is endlessly satisfying. For me, the blend of work, family, and culture is inseparable. This isn't just my life—it's my life's work. In this book, I present many of my marketing stories with informative and practical insights, but gaining them was neither easy nor straightforward, so I'm now writing a memoir about the joys, surprises, sacrifices, and lessons of my adventurous career abroad.

Among the many things I've discovered, nine years in Japan revealed the art of service, subtlety, and social cohesion. Six years in France taught me to embrace my instincts as well as my intellect. Two years in Germany helped me refine my reasoning and appreciate a culture that follows the rules during a pandemic. While I now share this wisdom with global clients and business students, I keep learning. Every consulting project, every classroom discussion, every speaking engagement adds new chapters to this ongoing story of how brands create value across cultures.

What I've come to understand is this: Whether interacting with consumers, colleagues, or classmates, they are essentially welcoming us into their world. It's our responsibility to meet them with humility and empathy, to understand and appreciate what makes their lives meaningful. And that, in turn, expands ours.

Bringing the World to Your Family (Nataly)

Growing up in a small rural town with cornfields outside my window, I felt very far removed from the many distant, exotic places I dreamed of visiting. But the world is never quite as far away as we think, and my lifelong mission has been to bring it closer. As a child, I devoured my father's *National Geographic* magazines. I signed up for various pen pal programs, making friends via "snail mail" with people in Turkey, Scotland, and the Philippines. In my hometown of 2,500 people, I admired my piano teacher, a Korean immigrant. I befriended and taught English to local migrant workers while improving the Spanish I was learning in the public school system.

When I got to college, the world seemed even closer. I became friends with students from Tanzania, Malaysia, Pakistan, Cyprus, and Peru. I enrolled in study abroad programs, moving to Ecuador and spending more time overseas than at home. I studied French, Italian, Japanese, Arabic, and German. I knew that languages were a gateway to the world.

I landed my first job after college as an interpreter for AT&T, interfacing between Spanish-speaking consumers in the U.S. and brands such as Comcast, Blue Cross Blue Shield, State Farm, Wells Fargo, Home Depot, and more. Becoming the voice of the immigrants for whom I interpreted made me keenly aware of the power of language to access services, economic opportunities, and human rights, and it marked the beginning of my career in international business. I started consulting for multinational companies such as Samsung, Pfizer, NetApp, Google, and others. Settling in the Boston area and marrying a man from Ireland, I became Vice President (VP) of Marketing at the software company HubSpot, leading teams around the world.

When I started a family in my late 30s, I wanted to bring the joy of being a global citizen to my own children. When they were toddlers, I enrolled my two daughters as the only non-Chinese students in weekend Chinese school. I watched with awe as they learned a language neither of their parents could speak. As they prepared to enter the school system, we relocated to a town with a French immersion program so they could become fully bilingual. When the pandemic hit, we moved close to family in Donegal, Ireland. There, they began learning Irish Gaelic, an important language tied to our family's heritage.

Returning to the U.S., my daughters knew full well what it was like to be the classmate who didn't look or sound like everyone else. They had been that person. They had learned the importance of diversity and inclusion, which they rely on each day in the U.S. Now that they are 8 and 11, we travel the world as a family while spending summers in Ireland to maintain their bicultural identity. Their journey continues to unfold, but it's important to me as a parent that their appreciation of diverse cultures, languages, and economic disparities continues.

I am currently CMO at Zappi, the consumer insights platform used by many of the world's largest multinational brands. Over my career, I have visited every continent and more than 60 countries—some for work assignments, others for pleasure. I have been the voice communicating prices to consumers in their language and the strategist deciding whether the global tagline resonates locally. I've learned that the localized copy on the drop-down menu for the software interface matters every bit as much as the punchline in the expensive Super Bowl ad. My experience has taught me that every single communication touchpoint carries meaning, with the power to build or erode trust between global brands and the local customers they serve. Connecting people across cultures and geography isn't just a career priority. It extends into every aspect of my life. As an executive, a parent in my local community, and a global citizen concerned with our greater world, it's a lifelong pursuit that gives me purpose.

While not everyone has the chance to move abroad or work directly with international businesses, the skills we develop to navigate foreign cultures help us embrace and celebrate diversity at home. In the U.S., for example, over 350 languages are spoken, creating a vibrant tapestry of multicultural and multilingual experiences. Encountering perspectives and cultures different from our own can be unsettling, often tempting us to retreat to the comfort of familiarity. Yet, when we make the effort to understand and embrace these differences, we not only enrich our lives but contribute to a more abundant and vibrant world.

Because beyond the narrow streets of Surat lies a universal truth about our interconnected world: International growth begins with international understanding.

This book is your passport to that journey.

Structure

The book is divided into four parts:

- Part One: The Foundation of Marketing and Branding
- Part Two: Culture, Consumers, and Communication
- Part Three: Creating Value across Cultures
- Part Four: Connecting the Global Dots

Part One: The Foundation of Marketing and Branding

We start with the foundation to define marketing and branding. While these words are often used, they are just as often misunderstood. As this book crosses multiple cultures and languages, we need to be clear. What is marketing anyway, what are its many functions, and how do they collaborate across countries?

We explain how Samsung leveraged marketing to upgrade from a low-level technology maker to a premium brand, delivering much greater value along the way.

We define the what, why, and how of branding, describing how companies like Nike, Louis Vuitton, and Coca-Cola define their brands and bring them to life across cultures and over time. Baseball may resonate in Boston but not in Beijing, so Budweiser conveys its American brand identity one way in the U.S. and in different ways abroad.

We learn about the role history and geography play to understand when and where a brand was born and how it grows alongside culture. Levi Strauss & Co. began by selling durable denim pants with copper rivets to miners in San Francisco during the California Gold Rush in 1853. Nike innovated strong but lightweight running shoes during the fitness boom of the 1970s. Brazil's Natura drew from the Amazon's rich biodiversity to create luxurious cocoa butter soaps, while Japan's Shiseido found its beauty inspiration in the pearly white teeth of European visitors in the nineteenth century.

Brands arise from cultural trends. They survive by remaining relevant to them.

Part Two: Culture, Consumers, and Communication

In a book about adapting to local culture, we can't go far before exploring what culture is and why it's so complex. To unfold the layers, we step into the mindset of young Chinese travelers eager to visit Shanghai's famed dragon boat races. Their needs, concerns, and expectations reveal both the universality of human desires and the subtle, often invisible barriers of cultural differences. We examine how Airbnb grappled with the challenges of building trust with China's digitally savvy, growing middle class, who seek unique, Instagram-worthy experiences but are wary of the foreign and unfamiliar.

In this section, we introduce important concepts and practical tools to anticipate and appreciate cultural differences, reduce misunderstandings, and improve the chances of business success. The key lies in cultural intelligence—the ability to navigate and adapt effectively to cultural challenges. We practice with cultural resources from Aperian and the C.A.G.E. framework of distance.

After laying the base for understanding cultures, we move into communicating across them in Chapter 4. If you've ever played the game of telephone, you know a message gets mixed up even in one language. Add in multiple languages and cultural contexts, and you quickly discover that what works in one country may not translate into another. Language stands as both a bridge and a barrier in cross-cultural communication and marketing; while words convey literal meanings, they also carry immense cultural nuance and subtext that are often hidden. We learn to avoid common pitfalls and introduce helpful tools to get the message right. Since communication takes many forms, we discover how to "read the air" and listen with our eyes. Moreover, in the era of influencers and social media, where trendy marketing channels arise as frequently as new cultural sensitivities, brands must navigate the geopolitical climate around messages they no longer fully control.

For brands to deliver meaningful value, they must first understand the people they aim to serve. Understanding customers in a foreign market begins with learning to truly listen. Chapter 5 explains how to target your audience and how to use the culturally attuned mindset and communication tools from the previous chapters. We introduce frameworks for determining a company's value proposition and competitive advantage. From luxury house Louis Vuitton to Wall Street powerhouse Goldman Sachs, with insights from communication specialist Esther Perel, we learn how cultural research and deep listening inspire innovation that delivers value across borders.

Part Three: Creating Value across Cultures

This section is the heart of the book, featuring many examples of brands adapting their marketing across cultures, with separate chapters on adapting products, services, and marketing. With every brand today striving to engage customers online, we devote two chapters to how technology companies excel not only in marketing online to consumers and to businesses, but also in delivering their products and experiences in digital environments.

Chapter 6 travels to the forests of Borneo, where creative teams design chocolate to satisfy the customer's sweet tooth as well as their cultural pride. We learn how KitKat continuously innovates new candy bars for local preferences while balancing global consistency. We explore how companies from Apple to Coca-Cola and 7-Eleven encourage innovation across markets and industries. The secret of encouraging local creativity while channeling it into one global brand is introduced here as the concept of freedom within a framework.

Services connect brands directly with their customers, so Chapter 7 is devoted to the importance of adapting these most-human touchpoints to local culture. We visit Cartier stores in Paris and Dubai to understand how their retail shops, product offerings, and selling ceremonies dance to those markets' needs. Luxury brands demonstrate how staff training and exceptional customer service double as marketing strategies, emphasizing that retaining customers is more cost-effective than acquiring new ones. We explore how Patagonia and Nordstrom also leverage the full customer service cycle to build loyalty. Building valuable relationships with your customers around the world also requires honoring each country's unique privacy laws.

Chapter 8 dives deeper into the dynamic essence of the book, exploring how brands adapt their positioning, imagery, offerings, stores, communications, and campaigns to create relevance in local cultures. We span the globe, illustrating how brands like Budweiser and Starbucks from the U.S., CHANEL from France, Natura from Brazil, Gucci from Italy, Shiseido from Japan, and others bring their brand values to life differently across markets. We examine how history and provenance provide rich yet complex opportunities to add value, exploring how brands leverage their past to stay relevant in the present. We explain how to harness the marketing funnel to layer multiple messages and introduce the Brand Fulcrum to balance seemingly opposing values. By embracing and celebrating history, culture, and craftsmanship, these brands forge stronger emotional connections with their customers, transforming global entities into cherished local institutions.

Digital companies succeed across markets by adapting online experiences with speed and scale. Chapter 9 highlights HubSpot's website and office expansion into Japan and dives into Adobe's behind-the-scenes efforts to localize websites in over 100 markets. Chapter 10 focuses on the challenges of globalizing B2B brands, featuring Indian tech giant Tata Consultancy Services and its success in crafting a global brand campaign rooted in local engagement.

Part Four: Connecting the Global Dots

Chapters 11 and 12 shift the focus from markets to the cultural dynamics that shape global teams and careers. High-performing, culturally diverse teams are essential to driving innovation, fostering customer-centric cultures, and building globally equitable organizations. Diversity isn't just ethical—it's a proven business strategy that delivers results with broader insights by challenging assumptions and enhancing objectivity. The chapters highlight the importance of aligning teams around shared values and goals, with practical tools to build trust and collaboration. Leading with emotional intelligence is critical for managing international teams, as even seemingly small moments—like casual conversations at the start of a Zoom call—impact group cohesion. Trends like psychological safety and the collaborative economy are explored, alongside tips to anticipate cultural nuances and unspoken expectations. Chock full of vivid, real-world stories of the allures, trials, and triumphs of working abroad, this section offers leaders actionable strategies to embrace diverse perspectives in building international teams and their own global career.

For Leaders and Learners Alike

As global executives, we collaborate with a wide variety of people. As marketers, we work with all corporate departments in multiple countries and industries, as well as external agencies, influencers, and the press. As educators and writers, we work with people in academia, publishing, and public speaking. We had all of you in mind as we wrote this book.

For those of you managing international teams or building global brands, we know the weight of the challenges you face. How often is something lost in translation? Every email thread spanning multiple time zones, every product launch that must resonate from Munich to Mumbai, every campaign that must translate not just words but meanings—these are the daily puzzles you must solve. This book won't just offer solutions; it will transform how you see the puzzles themselves. For international managers with limited awareness of how culture shapes your work, you'll discover how email hides meaning otherwise conveyed in person via context and non verbal communication. You'll find practical ideas that lean into culture to build brand value, innovate goods and services, create compelling campaigns, and lead cross-cultural teams.

To our young readers—perhaps students and emerging professionals hungry to make your mark—why do my Berkeley Haas students consistently rank cultural issues as the top challenge in international business? Because they understand that in today's world, cultural intelligence is as crucial as financial acumen. Through stories of success and failure, you'll learn how to navigate cultural complexities, shift your perspective, and develop solutions for professional growth and a global career—insights that outlast a TikTok post.

And for the curious souls, the adventurous spirits who pick up this book because travel has taught you our differences make life richer: Welcome to our world. Twenty years of living out of suitcases, building brands across borders, and raising kids across continents have taught us that every cultural barrier is a path to growth. These pages contain not just business lessons, but life lessons wrapped in stories from midnight conference calls conducted in hotel bathrobes, cultural faux pas that became breakthrough moments, and friendships forged across seemingly unbridgeable divides.

Because here's the truth: As people, we grow when we open ourselves to new perspectives. Organizations thrive when they embrace diversity of thought and experience. And brands? Brands soar when they speak the universal language of human aspiration while celebrating the unique rhythms of local life.

This is more than a business book. It's an invitation to see the world through new eyes.

Let's begin that journey together.

References

1 Marketer Asia (2024) How Puma Became the Leading Sportswear Brand in India. marketerasia.com/puma-india/ (archived at https://perma.cc/N6UM-Q5YV)

2 R. Singh (2020) Inside Puma's Sprint Past Adidas in India, Forbes India. www.forbesindia.com/article/work-in-progress/inside-puma039s-sprint-past-adidas-in-india/57869/1 (archived at https://perma.cc/7W7S-LDXE)
3 D. Tighe (2024) Adidas, Nike & Puma Revenue Comparison 2006–2023, Statista. www.statista.com/statistics/269599/net-sales-of-adidas-and-puma-worldwide/ (archived at https://perma.cc/5EMC-TYRW)
4 S. Anand and R. Maheshwari (2015) Puma Is Having a Good Run in India, ET Brand Equity. brandequity.economictimes.indiatimes.com/news/business-of-brands/puma-is-having-a-good-run-in-india/47511136 (archived at https://perma.cc/6WVA-EPLZ)

PART ONE
The Foundation of Marketing and Branding

What Is Marketing—and Why Does It Matter?

1

KATHERINE MELCHIOR RAY

In the late 1990s, Asia was in crisis. Excessive borrowing, large deficits, overvalued currencies, and beleaguered banking systems created a perfect storm, rapidly spreading a financial crisis across Thailand, Indonesia, Malaysia, the Philippines, and South Korea. Businesses, including Samsung Electronics, faced significant challenges.

Samsung, a leading South Korean corporation, struggled in the crowded consumer electronics market. Lacking brand recognition and differentiation, its affordable products—TVs for watching *Friends*; microwaves for heating hot pockets; computer monitors for hulking desktop computers back when sleek laptops were still a distant dream—were trickling into Western homes but were not yet household names. Samsung's products were often white-labeled, sold by other companies under different brand names, making Samsung virtually unknown outside Asia. The financial crisis exacerbated these issues, leading to decreased demand, lower sales, and excess inventory. If you'd shaken your child's Magic 8-Ball, the answer for Samsung's future would have been clear: "Outlook not so good."

This changed when Chairman Kun-hee Lee and Executive Vice President (EVP) of Marketing Eric Kim took control. They orchestrated a remarkable turnaround, transforming Samsung into a globally recognized brand synonymous with high-end products and high profitability.

How did they do it?

The initial vision came from the top. Samsung's prior strategy of producing inexpensive products under other brand names kept it nimble but under constant competitive pressure with modest sales and profitability. The financial crisis forced Lee to recognize the need for dramatic change. He initiated a massive strategic shift to focus on innovative proprietary technology and reposition Samsung as a premium brand.

The company invested heavily in research and development in manufacturing and vertical integration, focusing on groundbreaking technologies and cutting-edge products for digital convergence. Samsung abandoned using imported components to build its own proprietary multi-layered boards, improving the quality and functionality of all its products, specifically its new powerful cameras and communication devices.[1] This emphasis on innovation enabled Samsung to differentiate itself and command premium prices.

But for that pivot to pay off, it would require an equally seismic shift in marketing. In 1999, Samsung hired Eric Kim as EVP of Marketing to lead the brand transformation.[2] Born in Korea and raised in the U.S., Kim brought a blend of tech expertise and strategic marketing acumen. He understood the importance of marketing in reshaping the company's global image.

Kim's strategy focused on innovation, branding, and customer-centricity. By establishing a market reputation for high-quality products that justified premium pricing, he elevated the brand. Internally, the task was perhaps even more daunting: Kim had to persuade skeptical managers of the value of spending money on marketing, transforming their understanding of the purpose—and power—of marketing.

Before Kim, Samsung was product-centric, with marketing teams involved only at the end of the product cycle. Budgets were controlled by product managers, focused mainly on price promotions. Little attention was given to branding or cohesive marketing strategies across different markets. Because they sold commoditized products under other brand names, the brand lacked recognition outside Korea.

Kim initiated a fundamental shift in marketing strategy to reposition Samsung as a premium brand.[3] The work began internally, educating stakeholders on the importance of marketing in driving sales and profitability. He shifted the focus upstream, making marketing an integral part of the product development process. Instead of imitating competitors, the teams leveraged consumer insights to create innovative products people wanted. This approach led to game-changers like the Samsung UpRoar, the world's first mobile phone with an MP3 player for listening to music.[4]

Kim restructured Samsung's diffuse marketing activities into three cohesive teams: a central team for global strategies and budgets, regional teams for local markets, and product-focused teams to work closely with engineers. He recruited top-tier marketers, centralized the global marketing budget, and identified high-return investment opportunities. Markets were analyzed and segmented based on consumer preferences and brand receptivity, allowing for market differentiation. Meanwhile, global advertising campaigns emphasized Samsung's commitment to quality, design, and technological advancement. This new alignment was critical, as building strong brands requires global consistency and creating local relevance requires regional focus. As you've probably deduced from the title of this book, managing that tension is essential.

But it wasn't just about the technology. Kim also humanized the brand, featuring Samsung products in pop culture phenomena like *The Matrix Reloaded* and sponsoring the 2000 Olympics in Sydney. These campaigns raised brand awareness and fostered emotional connections with consumers, driving sales and market share growth.

The results of Samsung's transformation are legendary. Sales and profitability soared, with revenue increasing from $20 billion in 1996 to over $120 billion by 2010.[5] Samsung emerged as a market leader in various consumer electronics categories, including smartphones, TVs, semiconductors, and home appliances. The Samsung brand became globally recognized and trusted.

Today, Samsung is a leading technology brand, continuing to be renowned for innovation and quality. As the largest global manufacturer of specialized memory chips for smartphones and computers, it has come a long way from those 1990s microwaves. Every year, Samsung sells millions of QLED TVs and tens of millions of Galaxy smartphones, beloved for their customizable features and powerful cameras. Samsung continues to push the boundaries of innovation to shape the future of technology. The Galaxy Watch, part of the company's wearable-tech lineup, competes at the highest level of the global smartwatch market with Apple Watch, Fitbit, and Garmin. As the world evolves, Samsung has committed to sustainability and corporate social responsibility, exemplifying a company doing its part to sustain the global ecosystem.

Samsung is an outstanding example of how marketing can lead a brand turnaround to deliver real value. Through strategically focusing its resources, listening to the consumer, and collaborating with teams across the organization and the world, Samsung was able to reposition itself as a premium brand and deliver innovative products people want.

Samsung is now a trusted brand people believe in.

In this chapter, we'll delve deeply into marketing—what it is, what it isn't, and how it came to be such a formidable force. In Chapter 2, we'll drill down into the *what*, *why*, and *how* of brands. While many people reading this book will be experienced marketers, it's always important to create shared understanding of terms and ideas, especially as we work across different languages, generations, and cultures. In fact, we focus our explanation of marketing and branding over time and across regions. Marketing and branding are not discrete entities; they are interwoven and interdependent. As we've seen with Samsung, marketing is the discipline which encompasses branding. Anything that's marketing impacts the brand, though not all branding impacts marketing. Marketing leads brand-building efforts; then brand inspires and guides marketing. And around and around they roll.

In order to brand global and adapt local, you must excel at both.

For now, let's start with the basics. Marketing is what brings a brand to life.

What Is Marketing?

In 2001, I moved with my family to Nice to lead the marketing team at Façonnable, the French fashion brand acquired by Nordstrom. Nice is on the Riviera, far from the ritzy, cosmopolitan capital of Paris, but I actually preferred it. On my way to work each day, I drove my Renault minivan away from the sparkling Mediterranean Sea and up the hill to our offices nestled amid lumbering industrial warehouses.

My team was comprised of three French women. Bénédicte had been helping the founder, Albert Goldberg, with press and promotional materials for years, helping him take photographs of their seasonal cotton shirts for the latest catalogs. She also organized press presentations in Paris. Maya managed all the customers' contact information, and Carine coordinated events throughout the Riviera, dressing everyone from the ball boys at the Monaco tennis tournament to the stars at the Cannes film festival—even printing polo shirts for the sailing teams in Saint Tropez.

Now, with a new marketing leader from the U.S., they would have to learn a new language: marketing.

"Katherine," they asked, "what does marketing actually mean? How do you translate it?"

To my surprise, I had never asked myself such a question. "Marketing" is a chameleon of a word, a term that means many things to many people, from applying discount stickers on social media to athlete marketing and strategic planning. To answer the question, I couldn't pull from a college textbook or recite a definition I'd filched from some marketing professor. The truth was that I was not a formally trained marketer. My career had started in television, leading to a high-end TV shopping show I produced out of New York for Japan. Filming short features from Detroit to San Francisco with details on where, why, and how American brands were made and popularized, I learned marketing from storytelling—which, as we'll discuss throughout this book, is an essential part of the job.

"It's really very simple," I said. "Think of what we do at Pitti Uomo, the men's fashion show in Florence. When we display our seasonal samples to the world's leading men's haberdashery buyers months ahead of the store sales period, they select the best styles and colors for their customers. We see how prices of our premium cotton shirts and cashmere sweaters compare to other brands. From this feedback, we adapt our advertising and store displays to feature the most popular outfits to appeal to our clientele.

"Marketing means addressing the market, your business market, your audience, your customer. So, to market means to understand and **deliver value** to your customer."

In the South of France, near the elegant Promenade des Anglais, we used the English word with a French accent, *marquetingue*, for I could never find an equivalent word or expression. It makes perfect sense that marketing is an English term. Americans turned the idea into an academic discipline and have been world masters at marketing since the Marlboro Man sold cigarettes on horseback, Coca-Cola offered happiness in a bottle, and Hollywood romanced the world with American entertainment. Still today, more than half of the world's most valuable brands are from the U.S.[6]

Where Did the Notion of Marketing Come From?

While the twentieth century marked the formalization of marketing as an academic and professional discipline, marketing activities began alongside the earliest forms of trade.

On the first day of my global marketing class at UC Berkeley Haas School of Business, I ask my students to imagine the earliest forms of marketing. Was it the old magazine advertising images they've seen from the middle-class growth of the 1950s, selling new color TVs or powerful laundry detergent? Or before that, they might imagine store-showroom posters illustrating new automobiles with radios and the local drugstore offering 2-for-1candy specials.

I ask them to go further, to reverse the sands of time. I urge them to think back before our modern houses and cities appeared, back hundreds of years. Occasionally a student gets it right, thinking back to the earliest trade routes for spices, teas, and precious goods exchanged between Eastern and Western civilizations.

Imagine a spice trader riding his camel on the Silk Road, dressed in flowing robes adorned with intricate patterns reflecting the exotic locales he visits. His head is covered in coarse desert cloth. His face, bronzed and creased from years of exposure to the elements, bears the signs of a life lived amidst the harsh realities of the desert.

After many weeks traveling across deserts, mountains, and seas, braving sandstorms and bandits, he arrives in a bustling marketplace and unveils his precious cargo of spices. Finding himself among other traders, he must distinguish his offerings from competitors. He unpacks the heavy wooden trunks to reveal his spices in ornate packaging, crafted from luxurious materials such as silk, velvet, or intricately woven baskets. Each package is adorned with exotic motifs and intricate designs, hinting at the mystical origins of the spices within.

To highlight the unique quality, colors, and flavors and of his spices, he gives his goods evocative names like "Green Emerald," "Cinnamon Dreams," or "Spice of Kings." As he greets visitors, he entertains them with tales of his perilous journeys to distant lands where he sourced the finest saffron from the foothills of the Himalayas or the most aromatic cinnamon from the forests of Sri Lanka. Through his banana leaf wrapping, clever naming, and captivating storytelling that connects to his customers' own world, the spice trader creates an aura of mystique and allure around his products, ensuring that they stand out in the crowded marketplace and find favor with buyers seeking a taste of the exotic.

The earliest forms of marketing probably took place along the Silk Road, the network of ancient trade routes that stretched across Eurasia, connecting the Mediterranean Sea to East Asia for 1,500 years, from when the Han dynasty of China opened trade in 130 B.C.E. until 1453 C.E., when the Ottoman Empire closed off trade with the West.[7] The Silk Road was not a single route but a complex network of trade routes that facilitated the exchange of silk, spices, and precious metals, as well as culture, ideas, and technology between civilizations.

When someone arrived from faraway lands offering items locals had never seen, the vendor would explain what it was, its benefits, and how it should be used. When others began to sell similar goods, each vendor had to work harder to explain how their tea leaves were fresher, tastier, cheaper, lasted longer, etc.

While the practice of selling goods through sensual descriptions is not new, the term "marketing" traces its origins back to the Latin word *mercatus*, denoting a marketplace, a concept deeply embedded in the fabric of Ancient Rome, and the Greek Agora before that, where commerce intertwined with community and conversation.

Fast forward to the present day, and the essence of the marketplace lives on in modern marketing practices. The mediums have evolved—transitioning from physical marketplaces to digital platforms—but the core principles remain unchanged. Marketing is about more than just transactions; it's about engaging in meaningful dialogue with customers to build relationships and value.

With the rise of globalization, many companies are once again, like the camelback trader, approaching new customers in very different worlds which requires cultural understanding for meaningful impact.

Marketing as a Competitive Sport

Though I didn't learn marketing in business school, I teach it at one. My students love my real-life stories around which I incorporate certain helpful academic frameworks. These tools—a few of which we'll review in this book—provide structure to guide our thinking as we manage abstract concepts and unknowns. A review of the evolution of marketing helps us to better anticipate new strategies for, you guessed it, ever more effective marketing. As I say to my students, to like marketing, you have to love competing.

The Industrial Revolution in the eighteenth and nineteenth centuries further transformed the practice of marketing. With the mass production of goods, companies looked for ways to stand out to broad audiences. Manufacturers and retailers began to capture people's attention by differentiating their products through function and design, packaging and logos, and then advertising their wares in mass media like newspapers, posters, and magazines.

The famous Louis Vuitton monogram was developed at this time precisely to distinguish itself from copycats. In the mid-nineteenth century, a young Louis learned the craft of "packer" and box maker (*layetier* in French) to prepare aristocrats' voluminous dresses and petticoats for travel to provincial castles or refuges by the sea. In those days, the journey from Paris to the sparkling shores of Biarritz and Deauville required long days in horse-drawn carriages on bumpy, dirty roads. Despite his best packing efforts, dust would seep through the cracks of the heavy wooden trunks onto the silks, satins, and fine lace fabrics. Working with a light poplar wood from his local Jura mountain home, Louis Vuitton designed elegant and practical rectangular trunks that could stack on the back of a carriage. Rather than cover them in the dark and smelly leather that might spoil their delicate contents, Louis developed a waterproof canvas in a light Trianon gray and lined the hinges for airtight protection. This innovation revolutionized travel luggage, and the first Louis Vuitton store opened in Paris in 1854.

As travel expanded with boats and trains, the Louis Vuitton trunks' popularity inspired manufacturers to copy their Trianon gray. Louis Vuitton responded with stripes. This cheerful approach to travel luggage delighted customers but spawned new copycats. Now working with his son George, Louis created a checkerboard design with alternating colors called Damier, the same Damier design sold today. When that too was copied, they realized they needed a more unique design than the solids, stripes and simple patterns easily duplicated by counterfeiters.

Inspired by the popular Art Nouveau movement in Paris at the time, George created a unique design intertwining the letters "LV" with decorative floral motifs. The branded monogram set the Louis Vuitton trunks apart and quickly became synonymous with luxury and craftsmanship. Adorning their trunks and leather goods with Louis Vuitton's signature allowed the company to charge a premium on its uniquely luxurious and practical luggage. Market competition led to the development of branding and not the other way around.

In the twentieth century, marketing got its name as a distinct business discipline. Experts and scholars began to systematically study consumer behavior, market trends, and advertising techniques. Two academic leaders, Philip Kotler and Theodore Levitt, played significant roles in shaping modern marketing theories and practices.

Philip Kotler is often referred to as the "the Father of Modern Marketing" as he popularized the study of marketing in the 1960s. A professor at Kellogg School of Management at Northwestern University, Kotler defined the quintessential four Ps of marketing: product, price, place, and promotion.[8] He also highlighted the importance of understanding customer needs to deliver real benefits through tailored products and services. I have no doubt Kotler would recognize the core tenet of this book about the need for global marketing to take local consumers' needs into account.

Twenty years later, Theodore Levitt expanded the marketing discipline by coining the term "globalization" as a professor at Harvard Business School. In an article titled "The Globalization of Markets," Levitt emphasized the "emergence of global markets for standardized consumer products" and encouraged companies to take advantage of "economies of simplicity."[9] He believed national and regional preferences had become a thing of the past. No longer could companies sell outdated models or inferior versions of advanced products in developing countries.

I introduce Levitt in my class as an example of how markets continue to change. In the 1980s, Levitt encouraged companies to abandon a multinational model of unique, often lesser-quality goods and services in favor of a global model offering distant consumers the same quality goods and services as their home markets. He believed national differences in tastes and business practices were disappearing as products, manufacturing, and commercial institutions became increasingly uniform to cater to common preferences across the globe. He felt that practices of industrialized nations set a global standard, with the entire world enthusiastically following suit.[10]

While Levitt's idea proved popular for several decades, it turned out consumers in most countries had trouble relating to homogenous products and communications. As market economies grow and affluence increases, consumer preferences move from what people need to survive to what they want and what they value. The debate between localization and standardization continues as companies balance competing priorities in an ever-changing world.

Levitt was prescient in recognizing technology and globalization as two trends shaping the world economy nearly two decades before the internet changed everything once again. Companies now have online access to consumers worldwide at the same time consumers are accessing new ideas, behaviors, and trends from around the world. There's been an explosion of marketing channels beyond the spice trader's market, the car dealer, and television ads. Today, marketers reach global audiences through an omnichannel mix of messages, including offline and online channels, e-commerce, social media, influencers, and more.

Marketing channels and applications are always evolving, but the core principles remain the same. As Kotler explained, marketing is much more than simply selling products; marketing seeks to create relationships with customers by understanding them in order to deliver ongoing value. Value to the customer becomes value to the company. To create this value, marketing encompasses a wide range of activities from market research to product development, pricing, distribution, communication, customer acquisition, branding, and customer relationship management (CRM).

Though we may no longer unload tantalizing spices wrapped in banana leaves from ornately carved trunks, the fundamental purpose of marketing hasn't changed: fostering relationships among people and their products and services.

How Many Marketers Are Enough?

If marketing is about human beings, it follows that they fall into one of two categories: the people you market to (your customers) and the people doing the marketing (you). There are many different people working in teams to foster the company's relationship with its customers. Coordination, collaboration, and integration among these teams is critical. They need shared goals and understanding of the intricate sequencing of their actions. Collaboration across one organization can be challenging enough. Adding in global operations multiplies the work's complexity, so let's take a look at a marketing organization's many functions and how international responsibilities might affect their activities.

Customers versus Consumers

First, we want to clarify the difference between a customer and a consumer in this book. We refer to a *consumer* as the end user of a product or service—the person who ultimately uses or benefits from it. A *customer*, on the other hand, is the entity purchasing the product, which may include retailers, wholesalers, or distribution channels. In a business-to-business (B2B) context, the customer is the business you're selling to, while the consumer remains the end user who interacts with the product.

Market Research

Market research sounds dry, but where companies do it well, this team is the source of unparalleled innovation. International growth begins with international understanding. At Nike corporate events, for instance, anticipation for the market research presentation is second only to advertising's revealing of the latest edgy campaign. Research shares videos of athletes without Olympic medals, endorsements, or fame. Those films reveal intimate portraits of athletes running, training, and eating, which offer insight into their needs. Which shoes do they prefer to run in on race day versus before? What do they worry about before a game? How might they train harder? Companies that invest in research bring the customer to life internally, so teams can create goods and services that deliver value beyond their own imaginations.

Marketing begins with broad market studies to identify a country and a target audience, and then drills down into consumer-focused research, combining quantitative and qualitative studies. Quantitative studies provide broad understanding of trends and can confirm or challenge assumptions. Qualitative research, however, offers gold mines for unique insights into consumer behavior and emotional needs. Working internationally and across diverse consumer markets, market research helps us understand real, sometimes unexpected or surprising differences of behavior. We discuss many examples in this book of how companies seize on information gleaned through consumer research to create innovative products and services for their customers in different parts of the world.

Product Marketing

Consumer insights set the stage for product marketing, which is responsible for guiding those insights into commercial goods and services. They speak for the consumer through three of Kotler's four Ps: the product, pricing, and place (or distribution). The last "P," for promotion, sits with the performance marketing, advertising, or sales teams. The product marketer defines the product strategy, its competitive positioning, features, benefits, pricing, and the go-to-market process. They work directly with the product teams, including designers, engineers, production, and sales, to deliver the goods.

In most global organizations, the global product marketing team in headquarters leads all global product development. Some companies allow more localization than others, so we'll explore that variation in later chapters. Either way, the product marketing team requires a deep understanding of each market's unique characteristics to tailor strategies such as product features, packaging, pricing, and communication campaigns. Juggling to maintain overall brand coherence while addressing market-specific requirements, these teams collaborate closely with their regional marketing and sales teams to ensure seamless execution.

Pricing is one of the most strategic aspects of marketing as it determines a product's value. Companies want to cover their costs and make some profit. But how much? Making goods affordable grows sales, but pricing goods on the higher side offers greater margin and market perception of quality, rarity, and exclusivity. Working globally, the perception of value is relative. Some companies maintain a policy of global price equalization to encourage consumers to shop locally. Others alter their prices based on market context. When I led the global marketing team at Shiseido, our products were priced differently across countries. The same product might be sold for less in the U.S. than in Europe. That's due partially to taxes and locally sourced ingredients, but also competition and positioning. (We'll talk more about positioning in the next chapter on branding.) In the world's richest country with the highest number of billionaires, U.S. consumers are very price sensitive, which creates strong downward pressure on price. With today's digital online economy, pricing differences are harder to manage as customers can easily buy directly from foreign websites, which can incur shipping and custom duties.

An important and often unrecognized part of product development is packaging. (Note it didn't make the Kotler cut as a fifth "P".) Package designers are highly trained graphic artists who love debating pantone colors and millimeter adjustments. Within one industry in one market, competition among products is fierce. But how priorities differ across markets is often surprising. For instance, Americans are relatively nonchalant about how a product is packaged. In Japan, however, packaging is extremely important. Consumers in grocery stores in Japan will not select a dented can as they imagine the product could also be damaged. The thinking goes that if a company doesn't provide an adequate can, so too the product must be inferior. Packaging represents the product.

Distribution is another strategic marketing tool and an important lever for reaching and appealing to target consumers. Global marketers need to consider not only consumer preferences and perception, but local infrastructure and regulatory issues. Not all countries offer the same economic playing fields; some have highly developed urban shopping environments, e-commerce, and home delivery systems, while others do not. Being the first to sell in a new retail environment or online marketplace can create competitive advantage but also exposes a brand to the perception of that channel. Wanting to control the brand experience, Louis Vuitton maintains a consistent global policy of selling only in its own stores and online. Other brands like Tommy Hilfiger localize their strategy and distribution to local markets. We'll dive into Tommy Hilfiger more in Chapters 4, 6, and 10.

In tech companies, a specific team called globalization or localization ensures that every aspect of a brand's digital presence—from code, to content, to user experience—is adapted to local market needs. Coordinating strategy with market research and targeting, this sub-function is generally housed in marketing or product development.

Advertising

After the product itself, advertising is the most visible aspect of marketing communication, with the largest budget. At its core, advertising communicates the product or brand to the target audience(s) by developing appropriate content and buying media for its dissemination. The options continue to proliferate, encompassing everything from broadcasting via television, radio, and outdoor posters to narrowcasting via online search engines, social media, and influencers. These two aspects of advertising, content creation and media buying, can be centralized, localized, or a combination of both.

Seeking to catch consumers' attention and spur them to action, advertising to global audiences gets complicated quickly. In a global context, meaning translates differently across cultures. People also consume information differently, so while some media channels may work in one country, they might not work as effectively in another. Today, global marketers aspire to first capture someone's attention in a 6-second TikTok video, but in Japan, television still reaches 90 per cent of the country's population. There are no right answers, only options that consider the business objectives, the budget, and the organization. Gaining an understanding and sensitivity to manage this complexity is a theme we'll explore throughout this book.

Performance Marketing

Emerging from the digital economy, performance marketing uses many strategies, such as search engine optimization (SEO), content marketing, and paid digital advertising to target and acquire new consumers through structured online media investments. This team uses complex digital analysis of customer behavior, buyer journey stages, and lifetime value to maximize conversion in the acquisition funnel. It is a results-based strategy, leveraging algorithms to process millions of online clicks the company pays for after the goal is met. The teams target like-minded customers in online channels, e.g. Google, Facebook, Instagram, and TikTok, etc. With few large partners that can access consumers all over the world, the performance marketing team is often housed globally, with regional responsibilities to optimize country-based returns on investment. China is the great exception, despite the attractiveness of its immense population. Beyond cultural barriers, marketing into China presents unique challenges due to unpredictable regulations and a distinct digital ecosystem. The Great Firewall restricts access to global platforms, necessitating new initiatives tailored to local channels like WeChat and Alibaba, which offer additional services beyond social networking and e-commerce at a rapid pace, making it hard to compete. We explore Airbnb's experience in China in Chapter 3.

Growth Marketing and Sales Enablement

In the height of venture capital funding, when raising funds was easier and valuations were at an all-time high, investors pressured senior management to prioritize fast growth over profitable growth. As a result, many tech companies tipped their marketing playbooks heavily toward generating net new revenue as fast as possible. Out of this strong tech investor focus on driving growth arose a new generation of "growth marketers" whose job was to design and execute strategies to deliver top-line revenue growth to the company as quickly as possible.

Over the last decade, this area of marketing has morphed into "revenue marketing," which serves a similar purpose. Related types of marketing common within the tech and B2B space include "demand generation," focused on generating new demand for the company to support revenue goals, and "lifecycle marketing," which ensures content is targeted for the right stage of the buyer journey via email marketing, in-app messaging, and more.

Along with this trend of tech companies' marketing teams being more revenue-focused than ever, they also work on sales enablement by providing sales teams with specific selling tools, pitch decks, collateral, competitive battle cards, and other materials to improve their win rate. In many cases, business development reps (BDRs), whose job is to generate meetings for enterprise sales reps, report directly into marketing. At some tech companies, revenue marketing and demand generation teams work closely with sales, often carrying quotas and compensation tied to performance targets like generating qualified leads or demo requests that directly impact sales results.

Retail Marketing

Stores (or hotels in that industry) provide fantastic 360-degree worlds for customers to experience the brand. From their carefully chosen locations, to all aspects of the physical space (floor size, materials, light, windows, displays), to the offerings and services, retail offers terrific opportunities for marketing. On the global level, the global team creates the overall design strategy, but managing the day-to-day aspects of retail or hotels must be done locally. (See Chapter 7.)

Retail marketing can be managed in the marketing department or the merchandising team. I've experienced both. When I was Director of Marketing for Nordstrom's French brand Façonnable, I ran our store visual marketing and worked with our architects on new store design. At Louis Vuitton, retail marketing was grouped with the merchandising team.

Website Marketing

A company's website behaves like an online retail location accessible 24/7. As a result, managing the site requires both sales and marketing skills, so website marketing might sit within the marketing team or as part of a dedicated e-commerce team. Like with physical stores, the global team sets a consistent strategy for the website content, design, and functionality. Regional or country teams with local knowledge are best at adapting content to coordinate with physical stores for speed and consistency. In many companies with digital offerings, the website also serves as an entry point into product-led growth, where the product itself generates revenue through upselling (the freemium model, where customers can access a product for free or minimal cost before paying more to access key features), cross-selling (introducing new categories and services) or refer-a-friend-type sales generation. (See Chapter 9.)

Public Relations

On the opposite end of direct impact marketing, public relations, or PR, plays an important role. When PR is done well, it is a strategic investment. Whereas advertising buys a straight-forward transaction with content to your target through a third-party channel, PR seeks to make media communicate on your behalf. As media are considered an endorsement of sorts, this can have incredible impact and return on investment if you get it right.

That's why some people say there is no bad PR; even if the media criticize you or your product, people are talking about it.

Like marketing itself, PR can be divided into smaller parts: In addition to brand PR or product PR, there's corporate PR or employer branding. The goal is to leverage all of the above to create a strong marketing strategy. Employer branding is crucial for recruiting employees in new markets. From today's consumer perspective, corporate PR is incredibly important as people are increasingly sensitive to a corporation's values on social, political, and environmental topics.

PR works globally where a centralized team sets content, objectives, and measurement goals, and local teams maximize output with a much deeper understanding of their consumer and a broader network of media and the people running them. Local PR works with both the global teams and its local product and stores teams to evaluate what aspects of a product, service, or brand will resonate with their target audience.

In digital marketing, PR plays an important role in building awareness of the brand and products to help drive traffic to a company's digital properties, such as its website, social media channels, or an online community. PR is also an important source of backlinks to a corporate website, tying into SEO strategies. We explore PR and social media across Chapters 7, 8, and 9.

Social and Influencer Marketing

The marketing teams responsible for social platforms—TikTok, Instagram, Facebook, etc.—may be independent or connected to PR. After all, PR appealed to influencers before being an influencer became a profession! Hermès' Birkin bag was created in 1984 for the British-French actress Jane Birkin, though she probably doesn't consider herself a paid influencer. Today, there are paid and unpaid influencers, reflecting how much you can control their communication. Influencers may work for brands beyond just social media, such as for events, product collaborations, etc.

Unlike television, radio, and print, social media works primarily on the same channels all over the world and therefore requires very close coordination on content with its global counterparts. A company might have multiple social channels on the same media platform, dividing them by topic, language, or country. While it may seem like there are only a handful of social media companies, there are channel preferences by audience and region, so it's important to get the channel right. Some countries have unique social media channels not used in other parts of the world, such as WeChat in China and Line in Japan.

Communication overall is often divided into "paid, owned, and earned" media. Paid content is information you pay to put in front of an audience, like advertising, performance marketing, and paid influencers. It is usually the most costly and therefore delivers the lowest return on investment. Earned refers to exposure the company gains from third parties like press and other unpaid influencers. Owned covers all the channels the company controls, like its social media, website, retail stores, and direct communication with customers.

Customer Relationship Management or Customer Marketing

One of my favorite parts of marketing is CRM. Across the organization, marketing champions a brand's consumers. The marketing teams identify them, study them, explain them, deliver value to them, and communicate with them; so, how you build that relationship is key.

If we were to adapt Esther Perel's powerful saying, "The quality of our relationships determines the quality of our lives" to marketing, we might create the following CRM anthem: *The quality of our relationships with our customers determines the value of our brand.*[11]

CRM cultivates that relationship. This team helps attract new customers and develops the loyalty of existing ones, serving their needs and managing their communication as the team works to increase purchase frequency and recency. With an in-depth understanding of the customer's spending, CRM feeds important insights back into the organization to find and deliver value to more new customers. Not just more in quantity, but the *right ones.* We'll talk more about customer service across cultures in Chapter 7.

Keeping an existing customer is cheaper than finding a new one, so loyalty is the name of the game. Think about it this way: you can have a small group of extremely loyal customers and be successful. You can also have a very large group of one-time customers, people who don't come back, so you have to keep spending money to find new customers. Door number two is very expensive. Which would you rather walk through?

In many tech and B2B settings, the area of marketing that relates to retaining and expanding customer accounts is referred to as "customer marketing" and serves as the main interface between marketing and business customers. In those settings, "customer relationship management" refers to the technology platform in which customer relationships are managed and key communication is stored. Given the complex nature of those types of products, customer relationships are managed by sales teams, which may also be responsible for account growth, renewals, professional services and consulting, customer training and onboarding, and many others.

Interestingly, you can have other departments beyond these basic ones. When I was General Manager of Women's Footwear in the U.S. for Nike, I managed the women's footwear product marketing team. When evaluating a new shoe, there were so many kinds of marketing—product marketing, brand marketing, athlete marketing, gender marketing, etc.—that we had 17 marketing people sitting around the table! It's a funny visual, but the thing about Nike is that they are masters of marketing. Everyone on their team is thinking strategically about creating demand in the marketplace, and then they go out there and—you guessed it—*just do it.*

When I (Nataly) was a Vice President (VP) of Marketing at HubSpot, a public B2B software company, I managed numerous regional marketers focused on each major language, along with local specialist marketers sitting with other core competency areas of the central marketing team. For example, when our presence in Germany was small, we had only one marketer handling everything from growing blog traffic to managing performance marketing, content marketing, and events. But as our market penetration in German-speaking countries grew, we hired many more roles to support them, including German SEO specialists, an automation marketer who designed in-app prompts for upgrades, an academy professor who created videos on specific educational content, as well as multiple German-language specialists who sat on the central localization team.

Here's one more illustrative example: As VP of Marketing in Japan for Louis Vuitton, I (Katherine) managed a team called "Patrimoine" or "Heritage." This team worked with the corporate archives team in France to develop tools to communicate the brand's rich history. The Vuitton family home in Asnières, a town on the outskirts of Paris, housed a small sample factory and museum for special guests. On display were rare, antique Louis Vuitton trunks, illustrating product innovation over time. That exhibit inspired my team to commemorate the antique trunks displayed in our Louis Vuitton Japan stores. After transporting the hulky wooden crates to a film studio and arranging them like art objects, we painstakingly photographed them in dramatic lighting with a $100,000 rented camera that burned a hole in my marketing budget. But, when Paris discovered our stunning images, they chose to enshrine the beauty of all the heirloom trunks in our stores worldwide in a larger tome. You never know where good ideas might come from. Global initiatives can be sparked anywhere in the world when there are shared values and a respectful exchange of ideas.

Brand Marketing

The work done by my Patrimoine team and by the historians in Asnières is an example of work done by a dedicated brand marketing team. That team works internally on brand fundamentals: setting brand guidelines, both looking backward to share its history and looking ahead to define the strategic annual themes for other teams to work independently, yet aligned. Ultimately everyone in the company is responsible for the brand, so we've dedicated all of Chapter 2 to the subject. All these teams work together to identify, understand, reach, serve, delight, and keep a company's customers, the human targets in the two-way relationship. How do they coordinate all these activities around the world?

The Global Marketing Organization

Global marketing organizations structure the headquarters and regional teams similarly but place accountability and budgets in one or the other. If you recall our Samsung example, Kim created three divisions: regional, corporate, and product. Depending on their objectives, the responsibilities and authority will differ. In the many organizations the authors have worked in, there is a strong corporate organization that leads global initiatives in each area, while deferring to the regional teams for local adaptation. In many tech and B2B settings, there is a central team responsible for all localization globally that works in close partnership with the local teams. (See Chapters 9 and 10.) How much to adapt is the interesting and complex challenge for writing this book.

Research may originate in the corporate or regional teams, but they work together on standards and sharing insights. You will always get better research by involving local teams. Consumers share more in their native language, and locals understand subtleties otherwise lost. (See Chapter 5.) Product marketing usually leads from a global product creation engine at headquarters, but local initiatives create new opportunities. While many organizations create one global product line or digital application, others adapt to local customer needs. (See Chapter 6.) Advertising takes advantage of economies of scale to produce content globally, though we'll see the need to adapt content locally. (See Chapter 8.) Media buying can be done centrally or regionally, but again, local teams will have deeper relationships with their media companies for better placement. Performance and digital marketing are usually managed centrally since websites and SEO tend to be global in nature, and there are only six major media companies, Google, Facebook, Instagram, X (formerly known as Twitter), LinkedIn, and TikTok. PR, like social and influencer marketing, has global metrics and relationships but content depends heavily on local networking. CRM or customer marketing teams manage their local databases, with coordination and support from global. (See Chapter 7.) As people travel more, this is a fascinating field, complicated by contrasting government rules on privacy and customer data. Why can't my U.S. Starbucks loyalty card or app work when buying a Frappuccino in Japan like my credit card or payment app does? Because my customer profile is owned by Starbucks Coffee Company, a U.S. corporation with less restrictive privacy standards than in Japan.

Each marketing team confronts unique concerns related to global consistency versus local autonomy. We will explore how they manage that balance and collaborate with their regional counterparts to service customers around the world.

The diagram in Figure 1.1 illustrates a global marketing organization with its global and regional responsibilities.

Figure 1.1 A Typical Global Marketing Organization

The Integrated Marketing Campaign

Now we've set up the marketing organization that fuels a global company. All the teams and departments are ready to run like a well-tuned performance. Imagine a full orchestra with dozens of musicians in place, the violin bows and drumsticks poised for the conductor's signal. In marketing, that jolt happens when you launch a campaign.

The best campaigns are strategically designed to build momentum before, during, and after a new product becomes available. By the time Apple launched the iPhone, we all knew it was coming. The press had already published their reviews. Early adopters could pre-order their favorite color. The integrated marketing campaign leverages all the outbound marketing departments to create a symphonic crescendo when the product first becomes available.

Think of it like building a wave that rises and curls to envelop the customer from all sides. The wave builds pre-launch, crests at the launch itself, and continues flowing through post-launch activities. PR will seed the product for expert reviews to appear in long-term media, like magazines which publish infrequently. A corporate announcement is released for maximum impact with teaser information on the website and in-store. Trade shows may be the first places for a limited audience to discover the actual product. You want to inform and may offer early access to your existing customers through CRM and/or customer marketing.

The wave curls when the product is released, along with the largest investments—advertising, PR, social, and influencers—which drive people to take action, to view and purchase online and in stores. It doesn't end there. You want to keep churning the water with ongoing advertising and online community engagement to reach the largest desired audience.

It's marketing, so naturally, we have loads of smart tricks. Sometimes you don't want everyone to know. Exclusivity creates value. You might narrow the communication channels to pass along prized insider information through word-of-mouth. Quantity can also be harnessed to company advantage. The notion of limited edition was originally a production issue, but is now cleverly used to create, and maintain, consumer demand. Couture houses can only recreate a few dozen outfits like the ones that walk the Paris and Milan fashion shows due to scarce materials, which creates demand. And hot ticket items like Travis Scott's Air Jordan are intentionally produced below market opportunity, thereby ensuring continued excitement for the next season's launch. Whatever your goals, the best campaigns leverage integrated marketing (Figure 1.2).

Figure 1.2 An Integrated Marketing Campaign

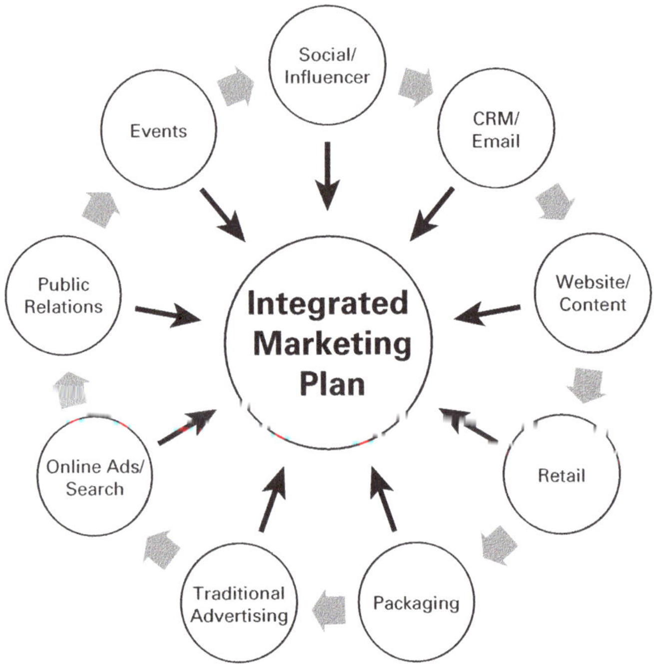

Global campaigns get complicated when considering multiple audiences and cultural sensibilities, seasonality, assortments, launch timing, advertising content, and channels. Balancing global consistency versus local relevance makes this one of the most interesting and rewarding aspects in marketing, which we explore throughout the book.

This journey through the various marketing functions illustrates their collaborative efforts to stimulate demand for the company's products and services. Marketing, through various tools and techniques, creates competitive advantage by shaping consumer perceptions and generating demand to build brand value. The brand, in turn, continuously evolves to deliver measurable value back to the business.

Marketing Technology Products

When you are marketing a tech product that sells primarily via your website, there are some unique variations to the marketing sub-category definitions discussed previously. For instance, location might not matter as much as language. Depending on the product and digital marketing, you can offer largely the same platform globally to anyone who speaks a given language, with only minor changes to maximize reach and minimize feature adaptations.

As an example, when I (Nataly) worked at HubSpot, we offered one platform for all Spanish-speaking users globally, regardless of whether they hailed from Spain, Mexico, Chile, or any other Spanish-speaking country. Certain features needed to be tailored locally, but 99 per cent of the platform required no country-specific adaptations. Many large global tech companies do not localize price or currency.

If you're in a B2B industry, marketing becomes more complex due to the numbers of people involved in the purchasing decisions and product usage. With B2B, you have two types of customers: your end user (the consumer) and your customer (the company to whom you market).

Company purchasing decisions are made not by one individual, but by an entire buyer committee, so marketing develops typologies of the most common purchasing decision-makers and influencers, known as "buyer personas." Specific communications and sales materials are designed for each persona to enable the sales teams to speak credibly and consistently to each one.

Like in other businesses, the role of marketing in technology is responsible for research, targeting new and existing customers, communication, and the customer experience. Yet in B2B tech companies, where the product is digital, it is often changing—both its own content and that of its competitors. New features can be released more easily and frequently than in hard goods and services, so updating product marketing, knowledge-base articles, training content, and customer marketing materials requires constant attention. We dedicate all of Chapter 10 to these nuances of taking a B2B company global.

Summary

- **What is marketing?** Marketing delivers company value by creating value for customers.
- **Why marketing?** Marketing creates competitive differentiation.
- **How?** Marketing is a discipline that encompasses branding, market research, product development, pricing, distribution, communication, customer acquisition, growth, and CRM.

The Global Digest

Chapter 1 Takeaways

1 **Position marketing properly in an organization:** Marketing delivers enormous value to the business when positioned properly in an organization. Bring in marketing at the beginning of the business strategy to help a company lead the market. Use market research and consumer insights to inform product development and prioritize key innovation for marketing support to take advantage of the power of marketing's interconnected functions.

2 **Leverage marketing internally:** Marketing works not only externally to engage its consumers and partners, but also internally to gain support and create momentum through education, team alignment, prioritization, and budget discipline.

3 **Leverage data for market opportunity:** Looking forward at market potential versus evaluating budgets against prior performance allows a company to invest in growth.

4 **Consider high-value product benefits:** Investing in unique high-quality products creates business advantages. The company can sell unique products at premium prices to generate high profitability for reinvesting in company growth. Companies that rely on lower-priced products must compete on slim margins and high volume.

5 **Identify your brand's "pillar products:"** Flagship offerings that embody your core values can serve as the face of the brand in marketing campaigns. Prioritize innovation by investing in research and development and creating groundbreaking, proprietary products to differentiate the brand in the marketplace.

6 **Clarify divisional responsibilities:** Effective global marketing organizations structure headquarters and regional teams with similar marketing functions, so setting clear accountability and budgets is essential.

7 **Balance global consistency versus local autonomy:** While centralization can ensure efficiency and consistency for global initiatives, product marketing, and performance marketing, localization is essential for adapting to diverse cultural nuances, consumer behaviors, and regulatory environments. Effective collaboration between global and regional teams is key to navigating this balance, ensuring that marketing efforts maintain a cohesive global strategy and resonate with local audiences.

8 **Build effective teams:** Managing people across various functions, regions, languages, time zones, and cultural backgrounds requires cross-cultural communication, collaboration, and team-building skills.

9 **Mastering the role of the CMO:** CMOs succeed more effectively with strong support from the Chief Executive. Local language skills and nationality help but are not required.

10 **Never waste a crisis:** Crises are not the time to panic. Like Samsung, leverage the energy of change to re-evaluate the company direction. Communicate the brand vision to comfort, focus, and align teams. Reinforce company values to give teams their functional and emotional road maps for decision-making. Leverage the energy unleashed in a crisis to accelerate into the future. Having lived through several crises, I coined this trifecta: vision, values, and velocity.

References

1 Samsung Newsroom (2012) History of Samsung (9): Restructuring the Company to Clarify Its Purpose: 1988–1989, June 13. news.samsung.com/global/history-of-samsung-9-restructuring-the-company-to-clarify-its-purpose-1988-1989/1000 (archived at https://perma.cc/K35A-A5YT)

2 M. Corstjens and J. Merrihue (2003) Optimal Marketing, *Harvard Business Review*, October. hbr.org/2003/10/optimal-marketing (archived at https://perma.cc/CB49-B93A)

3 T. Khanna, J. Song, and K. Lee (2011) The Globe: The Paradox of Samsung's Rise, *Harvard Business Review*, July–August. hbr.org/2011/07/the-globe-the-paradox-of-samsungs-rise (archived at https://perma.cc/M3S3-5HTA)

4 Mobile Phone Museum. Samsung SPH-M100. www.mobilephonemuseum.com/phone-detail/sgh-m100 (archived at https://perma.cc/48T2-X3BF)

5 Intel (1997) Intel to Make Investment in Samsung Advanced Memory Factory in Austin Texas, Intel News Release, February 13. www.intel.com/pressroom/archive/releases/1997/CN021397.HTM (archived at https://perma.cc/DK4M-HA4D); Reuters (2010) Samsung Eyes 2010 Profit Rise, Double-Digit Sales Gains, March 18. www.reuters.com/article/business/samsung-eyes-2010-profit-rise-double-digit-sales-gains-idUSTOE62H04T/ (archived at https://perma.cc/XU3P-CZXE)

6 R. Tucker. Value of Top 100 US Brands Tops $3.81 Trillion, Kantar. www.kantar.com/north-america/inspiration/brands/value-of-top-100-us-brands-tops-3-81-trillion-dollars (archived at https://perma.cc/BGP7-797L)

7 History.com editors (2023) Silk Road. www.history.com/topics/ancient-middle-east/silk-road#silk-road-spices (archived at https://perma.cc/7FTN-KK5S)
8 P. Kotler (2024) The Past, Present, and Future of Marketing [Philip Kotler's Insights], American Marketing Association, March 12. www.ama.org/2024/03/12/a-lifetime-in-marketing-lessons-learned-and-the-way-ahead-by-philip-kotler/ (archived at https://perma.cc/A24Y-9G75)
9 T. Levitt (1983) The Globalization of Markets, *Harvard Business Review*, May. hbr.org/1983/05/the-globalization-of-markets (archived at https://perma.cc/3NV9-C39L)
10 T. Levitt (1983) The Globalization of Markets, *Harvard Business Review*, May. hbr.org/1983/05/the-globalization-of-markets (archived at https://perma.cc/5TGB-NFBR)
11 E. Perel (2023) Esther Perel – Your Guide to Relational Intelligence. www.estherperel.com/ (archived at https://perma.cc/8YUM-TTFQ)

The What, Why, and How of Brand

2

KATHERINE MELCHIOR RAY

I was hired in hospitality without hotel experience, but I had something else. I knew how to build luxury brands, having worked for years at Louis Vuitton and Gucci in multiple marketing roles. The hotel chain was looking to grow by diversifying its umbrella brand into multiple, targeted sub-brands.

As Head of Luxury Brands, I had to unite the hotels of the same name under authentic brands positioned among their rightful competitors and distinct from the company's other brands. My job was to figure out what my brands were all about and bring them to life. I knew our ultra-luxury brand from staying in the hotels around the world, including those coveted, hard-to-get rooms during the Paris and Milan fashion shows. In my previous roles, we had orchestrated elaborate events in the hotels in multiple cities, so I felt I knew the brand.

Now I needed to define it.

I conducted a vigorous search. To create the brand map for our hotels all over the world, I scoured corporate documents looking for its history. The dry facts were all there: The company was started when a family purchased a small hotel on the U.S. West Coast. Twenty years later, they inaugurated a boutique brand under a new name. Designed by a renowned architect, the hotel set the standard for the brand with its timeless design, luxurious accommodations, and personalized service.

That was it. A history easily attainable on Google with no soul, no spirit. It was a Wikipedia page, not a story. And without a story, there can be no brand. After weeks of trying to ferret more information from my colleagues and coming up empty, I had little choice but to speak with our founders.

One day I climbed the stairs to the top floor of our building where ceiling-high windows overlooked rooftops for miles. Walking into the Chairman's office, I spotted a phenomenal piece of art on one wall and tasteful black-and-white family portraits on another.

After the introductions, I began. "I'd like to know the story behind our premier luxury brand. I can't find much in our corporate documents."

He held my gaze. With a smile and a shrug, he said that's because there is no story.

I blinked. This was a member of the founding family, and I didn't want to start our working relationship by telling him he was wrong.

All great brands have stories. Nike has running; Louis Vuitton has travel; Coca-Cola has happiness. There is always a story. It just has to be found.

"Well, then," I said smoothly, "tell me why you opened the first one."

The words began to spill out of him. The family had started building big hotels for the convention business. When their European investors came to the U.S. for meetings, they spared no effort to wine and dine them, and even occasionally hosted them at their home.

Eventually, it became too much, so they needed a place for them to stay. They wanted to surround the guests with the things they loved—like great wine, good food, and interesting art—and with people who would welcome them as friends and family. So they bought a quaint hotel downtown like the boutique hotels they were accustomed to in Europe and named it from the neighborhood.

He gave an almost imperceptible shrug and leaned back in his chair, signaling there was nothing more to tell.

Is this glass half empty or half full, I thought to myself. My pulse quickened as an idea formed in my head.

"Thank you," I said. "Actually," I continued, "I believe that *is* the story."

He sat motionless, so I explained. "Excellent food and wine, stunning art, and warmly welcoming guests like friends and family. That is the story we're going to tell."

The path was clear; better yet, it was authentic. Our hotels around the world would bring to life the brand's three pillars: exceptional food and wine, fine art, and personalized customer service.

Our hotels already excelled in fine food and wine that resonated with their setting, seasonal resources, culture, and clientele—guests enjoyed tramping for truffles in Milan and sipping savory, aged teas in Shanghai—so we branded a new umbrella food and wine program.

The foundation for the second brand pillar—art—was already laid. With the hotels' art collection and the family's philanthropic endeavors, few hotel groups matched our credibility in the fine art world. In our lobbies, we displayed world-renowned art, one of which recently had sold at Sotheby's for tens of millions of dollars. The following year, we planned to open a flagship hotel in Manhattan at the same time another favorite painter would be featured at the New York Museum of Modern Art. We sponsored the exhibit so our select guests could receive special access to art shows and *avant-première* events. The future hotel in New York stood across from a famed concert hall, so I initiated ideas there too. Hotel guests gained VIP access to performances and rehearsals, and, in the hotel, I suggested pre-concert dinners and music streaming through our lobby.

The Operations Department said no, music in the lobby would be too noisy.

Not to be thwarted, I proposed an alternative.

One of the hotel's signature features was its swimming pool, situated on a high floor overlooking our musical neighbor's beautiful architecture, so I suggested curated underwater soundtracks, imagining Brahms and Beethoven before breakfast, or peaceful Puccini and Mozart for mid-afternoon relaxation! The general manager loved these ideas and installed underwater speakers.

From hotel bathing to original bar cocktails, I was inspired by art. As our hotels were known for their understated style, we collaborated with a minimalist fashion designer to transform the typically staid hotel uniform into signature fashion.

Expanding the art pillar to our hotel guests worldwide, we partnered with a premier auction house to lure global art enthusiasts and aficionados to our hotels in major art capitals. To integrate and amplify all aspects of the art initiative, we launched our own online arts magazine covering art world happenings with interviews of major artists and collectors.

The third pillar was the most challenging and yet the most meaningful brand promise: customized customer service that hinged on treating guests like our friends and family. Connection and personalization were key to distinguishing our luxury status worldwide. Our welcome, our messaging, and our services—for better or worse—were not meant for everyone. I knew this first hand from my previous roles. The hotels had turned down high-profile multi-million-dollar events and celebrity weddings so that their VIPs could get a single-malt scotch or a poolside lounger whenever they wanted.

To gain deep insight into luxury travelers, we conducted hundreds of interviews with research teams around the world. Our findings showed that guests appreciated extra-large, beautiful rooms, fine food, and rare wines, but all the art, wine classes, and gourmet dining were more or less expected for the base-luxe price. Above all, luxury customers wanted to be seen and heard, to be recognized and understood. The concept was consistent, if expressed differently, around the world: "Presence" in Austria, "Buddhism" in Asia, "mindfulness" in the U.S. So simple to understand, so hard to ensure across millions of fleeting interactions around the world.

As it turned out, the best way to ensure our guests felt personalized attention was to double down on the thoughtful and attentive behavior among hotel staff. With our internal research and innovation teams, we developed a mindfulness training program to teach our hotel colleagues how to connect, first with one another, and in turn with each and every client; we called it "Project Namaste," after the Indian expression for "I see you." I hoped our corporate connection with the Dalai Lama might snag us a quote to inspire the initiative.

We held staff training sessions explaining the basics of neuroscience, how stress regulation would help everyone to better handle the hospitality industry's intense social interactions, and how to self-regulate for better health in general. Basic breathing techniques to remain calm and to increase awareness and focus allowed staff to read and serve guests on a more empathetic level, anticipating their individual needs. It made so much sense to me that Michael Jordan and Steve Jobs had practiced mindfulness to improve their intuition for peak performance under pressure. For the guests who arrived excited for a leisure weekend, our staff would invite them to take a seat in the lobby and offer them a drink. For the guests who arrived visibly stressed, check-in would be expedited or skipped entirely to get them into their rooms as soon as possible.

This kicked off a global brand campaign around knowing our guests' personal luxuries. We set our hotel brand apart from standard luxury hotels in a series of intimate photos of guests sitting in a hotel restaurant, bed, or poolside lounge chair, surrounded by their sometimes-quirky personal preferences, which were anticipated and offered—dark chocolate truffles, Sumo ringside seats, an oversized soaking tub, or cinnamon jellybeans.

We targeted a narrow selection of media, as our ads, like the high prices of our hotel rooms, were not meant for everyone. I had to explain to the corporate media buyers how luxury marketing was an exclusive niche.

"We don't need or want to reach *all* of our customers from our sister brands," I said. "Our brand is a luxury brand, and we want to keep the campaign exclusive."

The operations team was less diplomatic, objecting they would come to see the lobby and just soil the rug.

The campaign was a smash hit. Even the founders had to admit that the brand had a story—and the story made the brand.

Who Is Your Customer?

Our founder knew the hotel customers well since the first ones stayed with him at his home. Not all business leaders want to host their customers, but the kind of intimate insights you might gain from that are critical to understanding your audience.

The journey to identify what makes your brand unique begins by studying the market. Without a customer, there is no business. Businesses need a product–market fit. You can make something you think is fantastic, but if it doesn't appeal to others, consider keeping that a hobby. (One reason why business classes are housed in university engineering departments is because both are inventing solutions.) Narrowing from broad demographic data to a target audience, you seek to uncover deep insights about their lives, their needs, and their purchasing motivations and behaviors. Customers want different things. They place value on different features, so it's critical to understand your target audience. Some people prefer investing in quality clothing, while others want to spend as little as possible. Those same people who invest in quality clothing, however, may not want to splurge on an automobile, which they perceive as simply getting from one place to another. Some people are early adopters, wanting to be the first to try a new iPhone, whereas others want to wait.

Remember, Nike began its internal sales meeting with intimate portraits of athletes. Nike segments its audience by sport category—runner, basketball player, soccer player, cross-trainer—to understand what makes them unique to create shoes, shorts, and sweatshirts to meet specific needs. Through this holistic approach to customer understanding, you not only identify your target audience(s) but also forge deeper connections with them, laying the groundwork for a brand that speaks directly to their hearts and minds. We'll explore some of the many ways to understand an audience in Chapter 5.

Branding Starts in the Mind

What is a brand? Is it a hotel property? A product? A logo?

The short answer is yes—it's all those things—but it's more than any one of them. It's more than the sum of those parts.

A brand is an idea and a promise. That's the big secret, the special sauce. And marketing is the means by which you bring that promise to life. Though you're selling products and services, an effective marketing campaign launches an idea into consumers' minds, and the product, service, or, yes, hotel experience delivers against that promise.

A good idea has power. It nestles deep inside your mind, your thoughts, maybe even your dreams. That's what we marketers want a brand to do. We want to make a brand stand apart from others, fill your imagination, create desire for something both tangible and intangible—a tangible product or service and an intangible emotion. That idea is represented by logos, products, stores, uniforms, advertising, and social media: all ways that a brand comes to life. But the intangible promise is only as good as the brand's ability to tangibly deliver against it. So baked into that promise is the notion of trust.

Strong brands—which is to say brands that are unique and meaningful—command value through trust. In order to build trust in someone's mind, you have to be consistent; you have to be reliable; you have to deliver. Trust supports higher prices and extends customer loyalty, which increases lifetime value: the amount of money a customer typically spends on your brand over time.

Let's revisit Nike. "Just do it" is a slogan that challenges people to be their best. It suggests that Nike is a product that will help you be your best, with a sense of freedom, agency, and power, spurring you to get better, stronger, faster. Nike's marketing whets the appetite, creating this brand promise. Then it's up to the whole company to deliver on that promise. That's why marketing, which establishes the brand guardrails, is so important both externally *and* internally.

In Chapter 1, we looked at Samsung's rags-to-riches reinvention. The company shifted to a manufacturing innovation business strategy. Then marketing structured that strategy internally to shift people's behavior and align their focus on high-value products. Marketing elevated the brand from a commodity manufacturer to an innovative brand promising cutting-edge products internally first. They developed the rationale to rally the teams. With product teams delivering inventive products filled with cool features, the new brand promise became assured externally, one product and one satisfied customer at a time. Better-quality products commanded higher prices. Higher prices created larger profits. Those profits were reinvested in innovation, product development, and more marketing, driving a widening circle of growth. Company sales and the Samsung brand value soared. The business strategy was the first to change and the new brand strategy assured the business success.

Brand strategy supports the business strategy. Brands represent an idea (in the marketplace) that differentiates the company from its competition, aligns employees in that direction, and fosters trust and customer loyalty, which together build long-lasting and resilient corporate value. Over multiple years of product and service innovation, a strong brand provides both an anchor and shield that helps companies mitigate economic downturns.

Positioning a Brand Is Like Raising a Child

At the heart of branding is the question: Who are you, really? The unique way you answer that question defines your brand.

As a professional mom, I have found guiding a brand is a bit like raising a child within a family. You have existential values that are important to you. Clarifying them instills a strong sense of who you are, of what you are about. Usually your values don't radically change, but they do evolve as you grow over time. Each generation expresses those same values differently as culture evolves. Brands grow the exact same way.

Defining a brand is one of the most rewarding aspects of marketing, and one of the most challenging. You are uncovering the foundational beliefs of the company. What promises does the company make? How are they different from those of its competitors? What is its purpose?

Defining this idea is profoundly important to a company's activities and market impact, so this work must be done with top leadership's direct involvement and embraced throughout the organization. Getting management aligned can be challenging. As we've seen with our hotel example, sometimes founders don't recognize their own brand tenets.

When I was CMO at Babbel, the online language-learning company in Berlin, Germany, we needed to differentiate ourselves from the fast-growing, free competitor Duolingo. Gathering the executive team, I asked one of the founders why he created the app in the first place. The origin story often provides a clue to the company's unique offering.

"I wanted to make a better mousetrap," said the engineer.

"Better how?" I asked. "What did you want to offer?" I persisted. "Why did you feel people should learn languages?"

He didn't answer why people should learn languages; he was motivated to invent a new online tool. Babbel was the first company to offer an online SaaS (Subscription as a Service) model for learning languages on an app. Yet being the first in a market differentiates a company only until a competitor catches up. I sought to understand how learning with Babbel differed from learning with Duolingo. First, Babbel charged a fee for its service, whereas Duolingo offered its instruction for free. (Since then, Babbel launched free trial periods and Duolingo added paid subscriptions.) In 2007, long before the rise of artificial intelligence, Babbel hired teachers to develop its online instruction, which meant each lesson was developed by human hands. Headquartered in Europe, Babbel created unique dual-language learning combinations so German customers could learn English in their native German, French customers could learn Italian in their native French, and English-speaking customers could learn

Spanish from English, for example. Compared to Duolingo, which was built through crowd-sourcing its users, Babbel offered a premium learning experience. But with the rise of online translation services, would anyone still want to learn a language? After months of comparing our approach to more playful models and generic translation services, we found that learning a language with effective, teacher-crafted Babbel could transform someone's life. Translations are simply transactional, whereas Babbel offers a premium and personal transformation.

Clarifying Babbel's unique offering helped our teams double down on those same values internally in how we created our lessons and externally in how we crafted our message differently to the target markets.

While brand concepts are theoretical, there are practical tools to structure the discussion. People use many different names for these models, but the ideas are the same. The brand platform consists of several important features. You want to define what you're all about (positioning or promise), how you express yourself (adjectives that illustrate the brand character), and why people can believe in this (proof points of how you deliver that promise). The promise your brand delivers has to match a consumer's needs, so the better you know your target audience or consumer, the better you can determine how your offering will meet, or better yet exceed, their needs. As those needs change over time or from one culture to another, so too should the ways you bring these promises to life. This is the notion of brand global, adapt local. Use the structure in Figure 2.1 to develop a brand platform which defines what the brand is about, how it expresses itself, and why people can believe in it.

Figure 2.1 Brand Platform

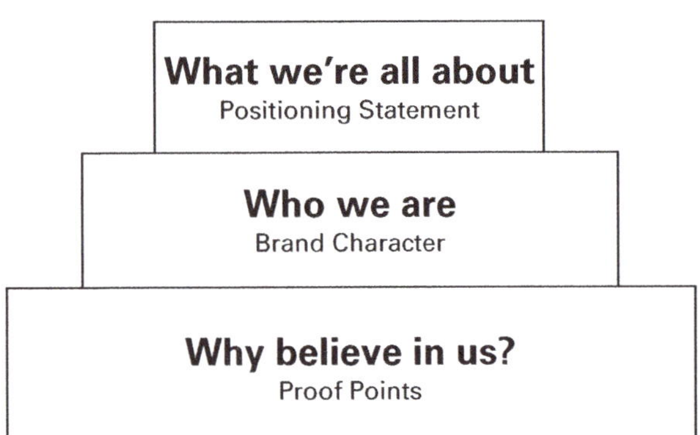

Branding is alchemy. Making a brand captivating, one that ignites passion, purchase, and loyalty requires a blend of strategy and creativity. That process begins by creating a brand platform like Figure 2.1 with your core team. The brand platform aligns all teams internally so they can each design products, features, and services inspired by and delivering against the promise. Kotler's four Ps—product, price, place, and promotion—convey a brand's positioning, also captured and communicated by the brand's identity: its name, logo, colors, and tagline. All the owned, paid, and earned marketing—website, stores, social, CRM, advertising, and PR—bring the brand to life with engaging content in compelling and cohesive narratives that resonate with the target audience. From the sleek lines of the logo to the packaging material and carefully chosen words of a salesperson, every touchpoint reflects the brand. (These terms are reviewed in Chapter 1.)

You can't define your brand in a vacuum. Your offering sits in a competitive marketplace, so you want to position your brand with intention. Create a competitive grid with meaningful x and y axes, i.e. price x organic; technical x sensual etc., by asking these types of questions:

- Who are your competitors and how are you different from them?
- Are you more or less expensive?
- Are your materials all natural and sustainably sourced?
- Is there a key person or designer who sets the artistic direction or are your top-selling items crowd-sourced through community?
- Are you a minority-owned business?

This competitive process helps clarify if where *you think* your brand sits matches where *the market perceives* it to be. If there is a gap and you intend to shift your position for market advantage, this competitive grid helps clarify this too. In this case, you need to identify where the current market perception is versus your competitors and where you seek to shift it. Figure 2.2 is an example of a brand positioned between Expensive and Innovative, while many of its competitors are Classic and Affordable.

Brand Positioning across Cultures

Competitive positioning may reveal differences across markets. Those variations might be organic due to economic or competitive differences, but

Figure 2.2 Competitive Grid

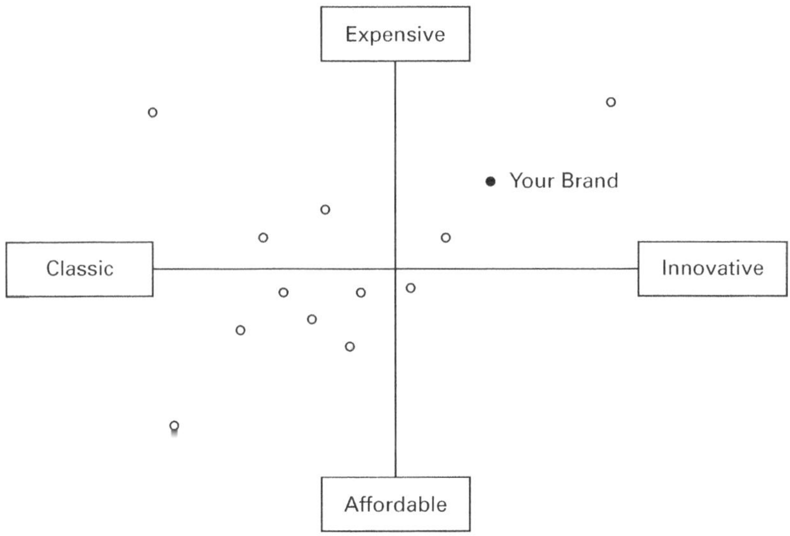

inconsistent brand positions are usually due to company decisions, either intentional or not. Brands may maintain a consistent global theme but be positioned differently across markets due to various strategies, including the business structure (joint venture, licensing etc.), distribution, consumer target, product and pricing adaptations, and communication.

Budweiser, for example, is considered a quintessential American beer, steeped in heritage around the world. In the U.S., Budweiser communicates national pride and traditions to a large middle-class consumer base, with campaigns featuring iconic American imagery, baseball, barbeques, and Clydesdale horses, around major sports events and summer celebrations. Conversely, abroad, Budweiser leverages its American image as a cultural differentiator for a more sophisticated, urban, and aspirational positioning as a premium imported beer.

In China, Pabst Blue Ribbon is also marketed as a premium, upscale beer under the name "Pabst Blue Ribbon 1844." Unlike its blue-collar image in the U.S., Pabst Blue Ribbon tapped into Chinese consumers' appreciation for status symbols by creating a high-end product tailored to their preferences. Priced at $44 per bottle, the premium beer is positioned as a luxurious spirit and marketed alongside prestigious alcoholic beverages like Scotch whisky and Bordeaux wine.

In the 1990s, the Tommy Hilfiger brand took advantage of its popularity with an urban hip-hop culture in the U.S.—but to an extreme. Flooding the market for the younger customers with cheaper designs of its iconic red, white, and blue eroded the brand's premium cachet. Hilfiger himself admitted they were "chasing trends" rather than staying true to the brand's roots and heritage. To revive its premium positioning, the company removed itself from several American department stores and expanded internationally, particularly in Europe, India, and China, where it was still perceived as a higher-end label.[1]

Hilfiger also adopted a localized strategy for different international markets. Garments were tailored to fashion trends in different regions—darker colors for Germany, lighter shades for Spain, bulkier sweaters for Ireland, and a focus on feminine designs for Italy. Hilfiger noted, "We mold and shape to the region, so we have a brand that goes all over the world." *The New York Times* highlighted in 2009 that Tommy Hilfiger was producing "two distinct collections—one for the United States, one for the rest of the world" to maintain its premium global positioning outside of America.[2] The Hilfiger story is emblematic of how companies level up or level down their brand positioning based on business dynamics and marketing decisions in each region. Levi's and Wranglers are additional examples of brands that are more premium in Europe than they are in their home country. While you can find a pair of Levi's or Wrangler jeans at a local discount store in the U.S., the denim brands are sold as fashion items in Europe.[3]

What do American beer and sportswear brands have in common that they can charge more for their products outside of their home market? Consumers often associate certain attributes or characteristics with products from specific countries which influence their attitudes and purchase decisions. We discuss this "country of origin" concept as a marketing issue in greater detail in Chapter 6. Blue jeans have always been associated with the American cowboy, and the image of jeans as a Western heritage item is sticky in the minds of consumers.[4] Levi's and Wrangler are therefore able to charge more for their jeans not in spite of their American heritage, but because of it.

Brands and Culture

Brands are born from culture, aligning with societal trends, values, and needs. They remain relevant by evolving along with them.

Babbel, like Duolingo, was founded when online learning and gaming met on powerful smartphone apps in the early twenty-first century.

Coca-Cola was created by pharmacist John Pemberton in 1886 as a non-alcoholic tonic for ailments during a temperance movement in the U.S. The soda's original formula blended cocaine from coca leaves and caffeine from kola nuts to help people overcome minor aches and pains.

Levi Strauss & Co. began by selling durable denim pants with copper rivets to miners in San Francisco during the California Gold Rush in 1853.

Nike innovated gripping but lightweight running shoes during the fitness boom of the 1970s and capitalized on the growing popularity of jogging and recreational running. As we saw in the streets of Surat in the introduction, the sportswear market in India took off only in the 1990s, with a wave of economic reforms and a growing middle class. As the government invested in urbanization and public parks, people with greater disposable income developed an interest in health and wellness and a desire for global sportswear brands.

Not only do brands arise from such economic and cultural trends, they grow alongside them. They survive by staying relevant to them. (This is the value of the market research we discussed in Chapter 1.) Nike evaluated which countries were receptive to its expansion as incomes increased along with prioritizing health and wellness around the world. Samsung grouped target markets by their economic and cultural development to guide its growth in each. Brands can be at different stages of growth in one country or another, or they might simultaneously be positioned differently in each cultural context.

It's a Small World... Except When It Isn't

There's an inherent tension in global branding that has always fascinated me. It's one of the key themes of this book—and a big reason I chose to write it. Competing in the world of global brands, you need to love the conflicting pressure of consistency versus cultural relevance.

On one hand, you have your brand, which clarifies what the company stands for and which sets global guardrails. Nike, for instance, stands for performance and irreverence. That's not going to change.

Then there's the other hand. Brands live in the minds of consumers, and consumers differ around the world, so brands must lean into the culture they target to understand not where the market is, but where it is *going*. To make a brand relevant in international markets, you have to study those other markets. You have to *respect* them. You have to *interpret* them. The connection to their culture must be forged. While the brand remains the same, its values land in foreign territory. Culture is where brands create meaning. Assuring those values echo appropriately across vastly different languages, expectations, and norms requires a unified yet flexible strategy to create brand relevance at the foremost edge of culture.

How a global marketing team manages one brand across multiple markets requires continual communication between headquarters and regional teams to balance market and commercial priorities versus global brand consistency, a strategy often referred to as glocalization. In simpler terms: it's like the most important type of juggling you've ever done.

That's why the story is so important. Whether through compelling narratives, engaging content, or immersive experiences, storytelling enables brands to create emotional connections and establish lasting bonds with their customers. While the methods and channels of marketing evolve, the fundamental essence of the marketplace—of connection, conversation, and community—remains as relevant today as it was long ago for our spice trader on the Silk Road.

Which brings us back to the luxury hotel brand. The founder's simple story about creating an intimate hotel experience to welcome travelers as his personal guests evokes timeless values that resonate across cultures. From Sydney, Australia, to Buenos Aires, Argentina, the hotels welcomed guests from varied backgrounds with a consistent warmth, understanding, and trust. Yet they offered vastly different food, wine, and cultural experiences anchored in and evoking the brand. First, they had to lean into those different cultures to understand the unique values of their local customers.

Summary

- **What is a brand?** A promise that lives in the minds of the consumer.
- **Why brand?** A brand is a company asset that engenders trust, customer loyalty, and resilience in the face of adversity to help mitigate business downsides.
- **How to brand?** Identify the main idea the brand stands for.

The Global Digest

Chapter 2 Takeaways

1 **Brands live in the minds of customers:** A brand posits an idea or makes a promise which lands in the consumer's imagination. Delivering against that promise, the brand builds trust with the consumer.

2 **Brands are assets:** Investing in the brand drives consumer demand for products, supports higher prices, and helps the company withstand market downturns.

3 **Find the origin story:** Even when you think there isn't one, there is. Dig deeper than just the factual history. The bones of a brand are in the story you craft—they give the brand authenticity, depth, character, and something ineffably human.

4 **Brand positioning is crucial:** Be strategic about how you differentiate your brand's identity from competitors. Your positioning communicates the brand's values and unique promise through marketing.

5 **Look for timeless values as brand pillars:** Identify several pillars which illustrate the brand's identity and priorities. For our hotel brand, these were exceptional food and wine, art, and personalized service. Once you've defined the pillars, bring them to life with unique programs and partnerships. Look for creative ways to leverage your brand's location and context to deliver a bespoke experience.

6 **Brand storytelling is vital:** This is how you create emotional connections with customers. While marketing tactics evolve, the fundamental role of brands in facilitating community and conversation remains constant over time.

7 **Know your consumer:** Identify and understand the correct target audience. Conduct extensive customer research to truly understand your customer's unique needs and motivations, knowing these may differ across regions and demographics. Don't fall into the trap of mass marketing a luxury brand.

8 **Culture trumps strategy:** Brands must lean into the cultural context and mindset of whom they are targeting. Customer perspectives and needs differ across geographies, so smart brands adapt localized positioning while staying true to the core brand idea.

9 **Global brands cannot take a one-size-fits-all approach:** Even iconic brands like Tommy Hilfiger, Starbucks, Budweiser, and others have localized product lines, store designs, and marketing to remain culturally relevant in diverse international markets while still delivering their essential brand experience.

10 **Relish the tension:** Global brands navigate a constant challenge of maintaining consistency while allowing flexibility for cultural relevance. Managing this balance with clear brand guardrails that allow localized strategies is key. Dive into that tension with verve and aplomb. It's where the fun begins.

References

1 Knowledge at Wharton Staff (2010) "Keep the Heritage of the Brand Intact": Tommy Hilfiger on Weathering the Ups and Downs of Retail Fashion, Knowledge at Wharton, March 17. knowledge.wharton.upenn.edu/article/keep-the-heritage-of-the-brand-intact-tommy-hilfiger-on-weathering-the-ups-and-downs-of-retail-fashion/ (archived at https://perma.cc/NLL3-M7P5)

2 O. Horton (2009) U.S. Brands' Many Routes to Europe, *The New York Times*, January 18. www.nytimes.com/2009/01/18/style/18iht-rus.1.19458976.html (archived at https://perma.cc/XY38-H22Y)

3 O. Horton (2009) U.S. Brands' Many Routes to Europe, *The New York Times*, January 18. www.nytimes.com/2009/01/18/style/18iht-rus.1.19458976.html (archived at https://perma.cc/XY38-H22Y); Walmart. Wrangler Mens Jeans in Mens Clothing, Walmart. www.walmart.com/browse/clothing/mens-jeans/wrangler/5438_133197_6127105/YnJhbmQ6V3JhbmdsZXIie (archived at https://perma.cc/VK2C-7922)

4 J. Fallon (1994) Wrangler Takes Aim at Europe Again: The American Denim Line Is Using Its History for Marketing, *Women's Wear Daily*, March 2. wwd.com/fashion-news/fashion-features/wrangler-takes-aim-at-europe-again-the-american-denim-line-is-using-its-history-for-marketing-1152638/ (archived at https://perma.cc/97HS-P2L3)

PART TWO
Culture, Consumers, and Communication

Lower the Waterline 3

Navigating Cultural Landscapes

KATHERINE MELCHIOR RAY

Amid the bustling streets of Wuhan, China, imagine 27-year-old Zhang Wei and his friend Li Ming are planning a trip to Shanghai for the Duanwu Festival (Dragon Boat Racing). They're eager to explore the fast-growing city and explore beyond the confines of traditional hotels.

"Why don't we try an Airbnb?" suggests Li Ming in a text on WeChat.

Zhang Wei replies with a thumbs-up emoji while casting his eyes down on his smartphone. He hasn't used the company before. He begins to scroll through the Airbnb app. His eyes dart across the screen, scanning through listings near the Huangpu river.

He thought it would be easy to find something unique, but the apartments look eerily similar.

"It's not that cheap," he texts back. "Hotels are only ¥100 RMB" (Chinese yuan, approximately $15).

"We have to pay in advance and then contact the apartment owners, but we don't know them. And before leaving, we have to clean it!"

"*Méi mén er!*" (No way!) "Working 996, I'm not cleaning on my weekend off!"

"Yeah. My mom is asking why we would stay with strangers. She thinks it's not safe."

"Fine, let's stay at a hotel we know will be clean. And the Wi-Fi will probably be faster."

While this is a fictional scene, Zhang Wei and Li Ming were not alone in traveling around China. In 2016, local Chinese travelers were the largest and fastest growing part of the Chinese travel market, with four billion trips each year and growing nearly 10 per cent annually.[1] No wonder Airbnb, enticed by the young, digitally savvy, and fast-growing market, was eager to expand its global footprint and capture a significant share of this burgeoning market. Yet, as we see from Zhang Wei and Li Ming's example, Airbnb faced substantial cultural gaps.

In 2016 Airbnb had already achieved significant global scale, serving over 40 million guests in more than 100 countries. But regulatory concerns in China had limited its expansion as private residences were not allowed to function as hotels. The short-term sharing economy created a shimmering gray area of opportunity. Brian Chesky, co-founder and CEO of Airbnb, spearheaded the company's foray into China, recognizing it as a strategic imperative for sustained growth. Chesky secured strategic investments from prominent Chinese investors, including Sequoia China and Hillhouse Capital, to fund its local foothold and to support their work catering to the travel needs of Chinese consumers.

Airbnb recognized both the opportunity and the challenges in adapting its offering in China. Chinese authorities imposed restrictions on the types of properties that could be listed for short-term rentals, often requiring hosts to obtain specific licenses or permits. Unlike many Western markets with established credit systems, China lacked similar financial guarantees for payment. This made it challenging to ensure users would pay for their accommodations, posing a risk to hosts and undermining trust in Airbnb's platform.

Airbnb was not the first company to offer short-term vacation rentals in China. They faced strong local companies like Tujia and Xiaozhu, whose business models were tailored to the Chinese market. Tujia partnered with real estate agents and cleaning crews to instill confidence among travelers with cleanliness standards and hotel-like amenities. Meanwhile Xiaozhu reduced uncertainties between the traveler and property owners with personalized profile pages highlighting user reviews, free insurance coverage, and dedicated customer service hotlines.

Many of the issues Airbnb faced in China were cultural. The company discovered that standards and expectations varied widely among diverse Chinese consumers, exacerbating concerns about the quality of the offering. As we saw with Li Ming and Zhang Wei (and his mother), Chinese consumers are apprehensive about staying in strangers' homes. What if something went wrong? The notions of security, privacy, and cleanliness are of great concern in Chinese culture.

To be fair, the reluctance to use someone else's belongings or share personal space were initial obstacles in the sharing economy in other cultures. But in China, with its own vast domestic range of cultural, linguistic, regional, and generational diversity, relationships are not easily initiated; they are often created from trusted third-party partners who provide certainty, rather than through an anonymous online portal.

Airbnb worked hard to adjust to the Chinese market. Co-founder Nathan Blecharczyk assumed the role of Chairman of Airbnb China as the company invested millions of dollars adjusting its business model. Airbnb partnered with Alibaba for its popular payment system. To create familiarity and communicate its emotional promise in a way the Chinese would understand, Airbnb rebranded its operations there with a Chinese name, 爱彼迎 or *Aibiying*, meaning to "Welcome each other with love."

Nonetheless, cultural barriers continued to slow Airbnb from gaining widespread acceptance and trust among Chinese consumers. Five years later, the company had not overcome travelers' concerns about renting strangers' homes, while local competitors expanded services like airport pick-ups and car rentals for travelers and professional photography and maintenance for property owners. The Covid-19 pandemic in 2020 further hindered momentum as China's extended lockdown shuttered the travel industry. Facing an uphill battle, Airbnb leadership reassessed its strategic priorities and withdrew from the Chinese market in 2022.

It's a sobering story. Despite financial and strategic resources, Airbnb, one of the more dynamic and nimble global startups, failed to adapt enough to succeed in the enormous Chinese market. We mentioned cleanliness played a key role in this cautionary tale, but Li Ming and Zhang Wei's concerns actually reflected deeper concerns. While the standards of cleanliness may be subjective—two people will clean differently, and their perception of what is clean and what isn't may differ—hotel guests rely on professional standards. When they step into their room, they expect the bed sheets to be clean and crisply folded, the bathroom sparkling, and all of the previous guests' detritus cleared away. If you walk into a hotel room to find the bed unmade, the linens dirty, and the trash bins overflowing, the hotel has failed to deliver on its promise.

The underlying issue is one of trust. Airbnb's retreat from China underscores the formidable challenges of introducing a new brand across cultures. In Chapter 2 we explained how brands represent promises which come with assumptions on both sides. Chinese consumers prioritize certainty and safety over risk-taking; they are generally uncomfortable staying in strangers' homes and prefer known platforms with which they're familiar. Without a secure credit system, all parties were concerned about payments. Airbnb could not build enough trust in their offering to satisfy a sustainable portion of China's 1.4 billion population.

In this chapter, we delve into strategies for overcoming the most common challenges associated with building a brand across cultures. As we did for marketing and brand, we must begin by defining the concept of culture itself. Then, we introduce practical tools for developing cultural intelligence, an essential asset for building trust across cultures. But before that, how can companies more effectively anticipate the complex and often unspoken challenges they may face when entering a foreign market?

The C.A.G.E. Framework

There is a simple framework I teach in my courses that helps businesses identify potential barriers to new markets by evaluating the similarities and differences in four specific aspects of distance: cultural, administrative, geographic, and economic—C.A.G.E.[2] Developed by Pankaj Ghemawat, a professor at the University of Navarra IESE Business School in Barcelona, the framework helps businesses anticipate where the biggest challenges may lie so they can prepare to adapt to local expectations and norms.

Cultural Distance

Cultural distance refers to the degree of difference between two countries' values, beliefs, languages, religions, and social norms. The greater the difference, the more likely this dimension will impact consumer choice. Businesses closely connected to culture—foods, retail, hospitality, and entertainment—may face substantial challenges in markets with significant cultural distance from the home country. For example, the cultural distance between the U.S. and Saudi Arabia is significant due to differences in language (English vs Arabic), food (fast and informal vs Halal communal traditions), religion (predominantly Christian vs Muslim), and social norms (dress, gender, family roles etc.). A Western lingerie brand selling to Saudis needs to completely rethink how they present and promote their products to align with the modesty of a Muslim country.

Administrative Distance

The "A" of C.A.G.E. refers to the legal, regulatory, and political environments that govern business operations. A company looking to launch in a new country must navigate the intricacies of local trade policies, laws, tax requirements, and intellectual property protection, which can vary significantly from their home market. Brands accustomed to operating in stable and transparent regulatory environments will face administrative distance when entering countries with opaque, frequently shifting policies and laws.

Geographic Distance

Geographic distance isn't only physical; it also encompasses disparities in infrastructure, logistical networks, climate, and topography. A good example is a company seeking to sell heavy machinery such as boats and trucks should take into concern the cost of shipping its goods a long distance. But distance also impacts a clothing brand accustomed to operating in temperate regions which may need to adapt its product lines and supply chains when expanding into markets with extreme weather conditions.

Economic Distance

Consumer spending power varies widely. What's considered affordable luxury in one market could be astronomically expensive in another. Smart brands may need to tailor their pricing, distribution channels, and value proposition to match the economic realities and income levels of each new region.

Before entering new international markets, savvy companies leverage the C.A.G.E. framework to plan ahead. Which of these differences may be most problematic? What strategies and solutions can mitigate these challenges? By analyzing and addressing each of the four categories, a company can, from the outset, proactively develop plans to overcome them.

If we apply the C.A.G.E. analysis to Airbnb in China, it might look like Table 3.1.

Table 3.1 Applying the C.A.G.E. Framework of Distance to Airbnb's Expansion into China

	C.A.G.E. Framework of Distance
Cultural Distance	Language: Airbnb created a Chinese-language platform and brand, acknowledging the significance of the local language to enhance user experience. Social norms: Chinese consumers' aversion to risk and insecurity hindered the widespread acceptance of home-sharing. Domestic rivals like Tujia and Xiaozhu adapted to these cultural nuances by providing additional services. Banking: China lacked an accepted credit system that would provide financial security for real estate owners. Eventually, Airbnb partnered with widely used payment platforms Alipay and UnionPay. Trust: Airbnb was unable to create enough familiarity and confidence in its local operations and marketing to build the trust necessary for people to rent strangers' homes for travel.
Administrative Distance	Government, legal, and administrative policies: Opaque and fluctuating regulations for private short-term rental created business uncertainty, especially for a foreign entity.

(continued)

Table 3.1 (continued)

	C.A.G.E. Framework of Distance
Geographic Distance	This did not present a challenge for Airbnb's expansion into China, as the supply and demand came from within the market.
Economic Distance	Income levels: Airbnb targeted the growing, digitally native middle class traveling locally and actively seeking distinctive opportunities worthy of Instagram.

While Airbnb faced challenges across multiple dimensions, cultural differences posed the most significant hurdles, with trust at the core. Chinese consumers didn't trust unknowns such as staying in strangers' homes, unverified credit, and vague cleanliness standards. This hindered the company's ability to gain widespread acceptance in the Chinese market. In spite of hefty financial investment and local advisers, Airbnb didn't adapt well enough. Despite its Chinese brand name and language platform, Airbnb was unable to overcome the Chinese need for familiarity: it failed to invest enough in culture.

Why Is Culture So Complicated?

Recognizing and adapting to cultural nuances pose challenges for any brand pursuing a global presence. Mastering this starts with understanding culture itself. One of the most recognized experts in cultural research, Dutch scholar Geert Hofstede referred to culture as "collective programming."[3] This elaborate web of shared values, beliefs, preferences, and behaviors of a society or group varies dramatically across countries, regions, neighborhoods, and even families.

Culture is complex and difficult to define. Why? Because *much of it is hidden.*

Imagine you're on holiday in Zanzibar, the Tanzanian island off the coast of East Africa. Vivid colors and exotic spices stimulate your senses. But you get irritated because no one sticks to a schedule. Stores don't open on time; people take long breaks in the middle of the day; meals go on forever. The third time your bus is late, you make a judgment: Tanzanians are chronically disorganized and don't respect other people's time. But you're missing the larger cultural context: if you probe deeper, you'll learn the locals have a fluid and flexible approach to time, like many cultures in Africa, and prioritize human interaction and fellowship over strict adherence to timetables.

Or let's say you visit Paris for the first time. As you walk six miles (ten kilometers) each day, you observe how many designer fashion brands line the wide boulevards and plaster their massive logos on the Louvre and Musée d'Orsay museums. The ubiquity of luxury brands leads you to believe that the French are obsessed with expensive goods and designer fashion. But you're missing the values stitched into those beautiful clothes: a cultural reverence for refinement, creativity, and craftsmanship.

One of my favorite illustrations of culture is the image of an iceberg (Figure 3.1). The image of culture as an iceberg shows how much of it is hard to see. Only a small portion is visible above the waterline. The aspects of culture we readily observe—language, dress, food, art, punctuality—are merely the tip of a vast, submerged reality. These visible aspects of culture are infused with hidden values.

Figure 3.1 Iceberg of Culture

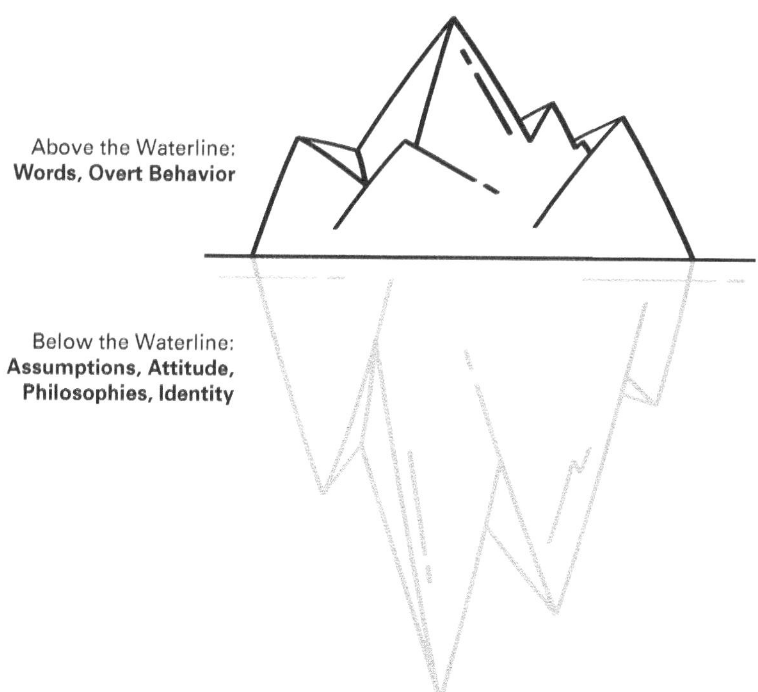

Beneath the surface lie all the things we *can't* see: assumptions about behavior, etiquette, attitudes, philosophies, gender roles, body language, and identity that have been engrained over centuries. Every culture has them, and every culture is shaped by them. These concealed gems can provide invaluable insight and opportunity, but if you aren't aware they exist, they could very well sink *you*.

How to mine the treasures of the deep? We need to *lower the waterline*. Lowering the waterline of culture helps expose hidden values and assumptions (Figure 3.2). The goal is to make the hidden values and underlying assumptions explicit. Doing so, we learn to recognize that things are often not what they seem. With an open, inquisitive mind, we can develop a keen eye for nuance. In essence, we become cultural detectives, shining light into the murky depths—observing, questioning, and investigating the subtleties of the unseen.

Let's go back to cleanliness. As we saw with Airbnb, the Chinese didn't trust the unknown, and when paying for service, they expected just that—service. The no-frills approach to cleaning yourself did not match their expectations. The local competitors solved that by adding a third-party cleaning service, or standard, thereby mitigating the unknown. Cleanliness standards vary by culture. The Japanese, a very detail-oriented culture, have famously high hygiene standards. After each train arrives at the final terminus station, a team of cleaners boards and, in a matter of minutes, vacuums and wipes down seats and floors, using lint rollers to remove debris and hair from fabric. They disinfect door handles and other high-touch areas to clean every nook and cranny of the train car. Discomfort with unknowns, or risk aversion, is one of those below-the-waterline values that change across cultures.

Figure 3.2 Lowering the Waterline

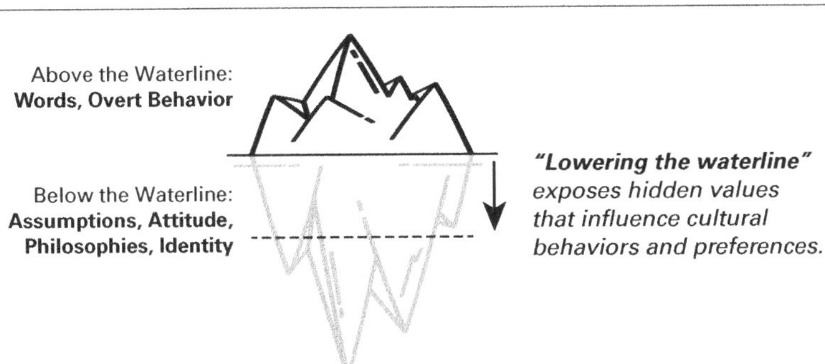

Time is another malleable concept that shifts between cultures. While many people think time is fixed, I've learned it's relative. I hate to admit it, but I'm often a few minutes late. I'm a responsible person; I keep my word. I certainly don't intend to be late; I'm usually doing lots of things (maybe too many) and simply misjudge how long it will take me to get ready or travel somewhere.

Imagine my joy when I moved to France and discovered a frequent ten-minute lag to any rendez vous. No *Mon Dieu* or exasperation shown. Once, I entered a colleague's office to discuss an event that evening just as he stood to leave for a meeting. "*Pas de problème*," he said and took five minutes to talk with me. I learned the French prioritize the person who appears or calls over those who are somewhere else. The French people value relationships over being right on time.

I've also spent years working in Japan, where people are punctual. In a country where image and impression count, I know it's important. Each time I get on a plane bound for Japan, I set my watch ahead at least five minutes, enough to assure I won't be late. I try to respect this high priority in Japan, where subtleties carry repercussions on relationships and business dealings.

On a recent trip to Tokyo, I took the subway to meet a friend for dinner. I reached the meeting spot with plenty of time, even a few minutes early. I was proud of myself. My friend was sitting at a cafe table just finishing his coffee.

"Hi there," I said. I thought we were meeting at six?"

"We were. It's fine. I always arrive about fifteen minutes early. I knew you'd be late."

It's a humorous but illustrative example. Over the years, I've learned to appreciate the cultural differences between the three countries where I work most, and I adapt my behavior accordingly. I try to remain both aware of these differences and proactive in addressing them.

Lowering the waterline is a figurative expression that recognizes things are not always what they seem, that perceptions are subjective, and we must work to interpret behavior. Face value belies hidden emotions and wonderfully complex assumptions that we must decipher. It's like reading cultural tea leaves. Think of it as a challenge—can you figure out someone's intention beyond, or despite, what they say? If you want to leverage global opportunities, think of building this capacity like an ongoing game of Clue.

Fortunately, there are specific tools and processes that help us to improve our cultural knowledge and practice this skill.

Cultivating Cultural Intelligence

In a global business landscape, you might expect a leader's intellectual quotient (IQ) and emotional intelligence (EQ) to be key indicators of success—which they are—but I like to highlight an unsung hero of the Qs, one many do not know about. In order to brand global and adapt local, cultural intelligence (CQ) is essential. CQ refers to the ability to adapt to new cultural settings and work effectively within them.[4] To be culturally intelligent, you do not have to be an expert in all cultures. Instead, you must be curious and open-minded about understanding other cultures and interpreting people's behavior in the context of their culture.[5]

CQ builds upon intellectual and emotional intelligence but goes further. Having a high IQ makes you a strong strategist and problem solver. A high EQ makes you empathetic—critical for marketing, as understanding consumers' needs and desires leads to better products and messaging responsive to those concerns. (We'll dive deeper into creating customer value in Chapter 5.) Together, IQ and EQ allow you to anticipate trends, identify challenges, and innovate for evolving markets. But operating globally adds layers of complexity. Developing strong CQ gives you knowledge and skills to adapt to the complicated interactions across cultures.

Sixty years ago, a businessperson might have been able to get by without CQ. Many still do. But we live in a world where cross-cultural nuances significantly impact business outcomes. An experienced leader in Silicon Valley may excel in a culture that values innovation and challenging authority, but struggle in Singapore, where hierarchy and adherence to established procedures are paramount. Global marketing goes beyond the skills that create success in one market. Striking the right global–local balance requires adopting a global mindset to recognize that cultures are diverse; practicing being open-minded and curious about different values, beliefs, and behaviors; and developing skills to adapt your communication and collaboration styles. This knowledge is useful whether you're marketing to consumers internationally or to diverse consumers in your domestic market.

How to develop CQ? When I teach CQ, I outline four specific skills that flow in a virtuous circle, as in Figure 3.3. The more you build each one, the more competent you become.

Figure 3.3 Developing Cultural Competence

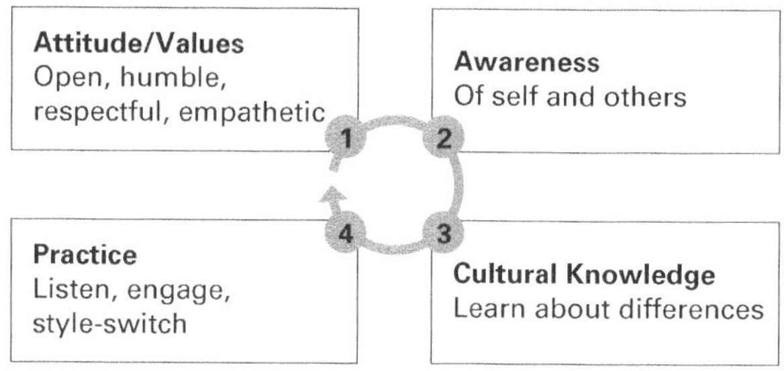

Attitude/Values

CQ requires the right attitude and motivation. Are you open-minded, humble, respectful, and empathetic toward others? Are you curious and motivated to understand different cultures and work through cross-cultural differences?

PRACTICAL TIPS:

- Approach each new market or cultural context with curiosity and a willingness to learn.
- Recognize that your existing knowledge and assumptions are subjective and may not apply. Try to understand there is always more than one perspective.
- Engage in open and respectful dialogues, asking questions to deepen your understanding without judgment.

Awareness of Self and Others

Being conscious of your own actions and aware of others are key components of EQ, on which CQ relies. Are you self-aware? Can you step outside your own subjectivity to observe how you present in other cultures and how others might perceive you?

PRACTICAL TIPS:

- You have two eyes and one mouth. Listen more than you speak. One of my favorite expressions is "Listen with your eyes." Watch what's going on around you, for you can get many clues from nonverbal communication.
- Notice your first reaction and wait a beat (or two). If you usually respond quickly, wait and think about your answer before replying. Observe the timing and pacing of communication, and be aware of your natural inclination. Some cultures wait for everyone to speak, others interrupt while people are speaking, and some cultures encourage silence.
- Observe who sits where in an office, meeting room, or social situation. Notice who enters the room first or last, who pours the wine, who pays the bill. These clues are subtle references to a culture's view of status, responsibility, and power.

On the first day of my class at Berkeley Haas, I make clear that I will not necessarily call on the first people to raise their hands. I explain that some people are not native English speakers and need more time to understand, to formulate an answer, and to commit to raise a hand. I encourage my eager native English speakers to allow space for others. Through greater awareness, cross-cultural competence helps unlock the power of diversity to improve collaboration.

Cultural Knowledge

Learning about other cultures is not only essential to CQ but offers an enriching benefit. How much do you know about the history, geography, language, food, and family rituals of other cultures? How much do you appreciate the values and behavior of the culture where you live, work, or study?

PRACTICAL TIPS:

- Explore insights into a culture's values, customs, and way of life through books, movies, videos, podcasts, music, restaurants, and cultural experts. Pay attention to the nuances in language, behavior, relationships, and societal norms.
- Learn the language, visit museums and temples, join a cooking class or wine-tasting group, etc. Follow your interests and make it fun!
- Invest in resources that explain hidden cultural values and expectations. We'll explore one called GlobeSmart®, which offers not only cultural insights, but a personalized snapshot of your behavioral preferences. Understand how your GlobeSmart® Profile reflects your own culture and then compare it to your target country.

Practice

Starting out in a foreign environment can be hard, but learning to adapt your behavior builds the skills, capability, and self-confidence to eventually culture-flex more easily. How much do you adjust your behavior to different cultures? Are you willing and able to adapt your actions and expectations to work effectively in new environments? Awkward misunderstandings can arise, but learning from them to persevere builds resilience and high CQ.

PRACTICAL TIPS:

- Observe, then mirror or adapt to other people's communication, body language, and customs.
- Proactively show that you're trying and ask for feedback. Explicitly discussing cultural observations and differences lowers the waterline for all to see.
- Be patient with yourself; believe you are capable of adapting to differences—and don't give up when feeling challenged. Remember, it's a practice. You don't develop CQ overnight; it builds over time.

I am sometimes asked how much to remain true to yourself versus adjusting to a culture. It's an excellent question. Remaining authentic to oneself while being respectful of other cultures involves a delicate balance of self-awareness, empathy, knowledge, and adaptability: the four steps of CQ. If certain cultural practices conflict with your core values, explain your perspective in a way that is considerate and seeks mutual understanding. Maintaining an open mind and a willingness to learn about how others see things differently helps avoid offense, build trust, and facilitate understanding and collaboration.

Facing cultures and perspectives that are different from our own can feel uncomfortable, pushing us toward the safety of our familiar ways. Fear not. There are valuable tools to help us see a multitude of perspectives, enabling us to navigate cultural differences with greater ease and empathy. When we challenge ourselves to understand and embrace our differences, we can create a richer, more fulfilling life—and a more vibrant and bountiful world.

Braiding Languages

Leveraging cultural differences can be a superpower, going far beyond mere adaptation. When I worked for Louis Vuitton in Japan, our marketing team of 30 was composed entirely of Japanese nationals, except for me—the lone American. In the office, we naturally spoke Japanese. However, when colleagues visited from France, conversations switched to English as our lingua franca. This trilingual setup was fantastic for me, fluent in all three. I could follow the main discussion while also picking up on the French sidebar conversations with other ideas or contextual nuances. Brief chats are common in French culture, contrasting sharply with the Japanese tendency to rarely speak out of turn.

I learned that intentionally shifting between languages could actually shape the nature of our discussions. To explain strategic objectives, I used English—its simplicity helped us focus on goals, tools, and timelines. But when ideating on creative concepts, I switched to French, leveraging its flair for vivid exploration and passionate appeal. Among my Japanese team, however, I took an entirely different approach for sensitive or personal topics. Not only did I converse in Japanese, but I also carefully employed indirect phrasing and pregnant pauses—subtle cultural cues that encouraged others to reveal underlying concerns. By consciously navigating these linguistic and cultural nuances, I could tailor my communication style to drive more effective dialogues, foster openness and intimacy, and, ultimately, stronger collaboration within our multicultural team.

GlobeSmart® Profile

One of the most effective tools I've found to help cultivate CQ is called the GlobeSmart Profile. Developed by Aperian®, this tool helps people understand their own, often unconscious, behavioral patterns and compare them to that of other countries and cultures. Countries are placed on a spectrum of low to high on each of five dimensions which correlate to multiple academic theories on cultural differences.[6] These dimensions, which make the biggest difference in reducing misunderstandings and in improving collaboration across cultures, represent aspects of culture that are hard to see—the underwater part of the iceberg. There are no "right" or "wrong" answers; they are simply different. The goal is to create shared understanding and find common ground through open discussion about different styles and preferences. Figure 3.4 illustrates five dimensions of cultural values and behavioral norms that make the biggest difference in understanding and communication. Countries are placed along a range between the two edges to reflect their relative preferences.

The GlobeSmart Profile—part of the Aperian platform with a deep well of resources, cultural guides, learning modules, and seminars—offers a personalized profile of your individual working style. Your preferences are

Figure 3.4 GlobeSmart® Dimensions of Culture[7]

Independent	**How do I derive my identity?**	Interdependent
Egalitarianism	**How should my group be structured and power distributed?**	Status
Risk	**How do I make decisions in uncertain or ambiguous situations?**	Certainty
Direct	**How do I communicate requests, tasks, and feedback?**	Indirect
Task	**How do I prefer to approach a new work project?**	Relationship

Reproduced with permission

highly influenced by the culture(s) in which you were raised or spent long periods of time. Thinking of our Chinese travelers, let's use an example to illustrate how a GlobeSmart Profile helps visually understand how preferences vary across American and Chinese cultures (Figure 3.5).

The first dimension, independence and interdependence, refers to identity and how much one prefers to work independently versus collaboratively. Said another way, it measures the importance one places on individual identity and individual action versus group agreement and cooperation. Conflicts can arise when those who prefer to work more interdependently wait to collect feedback on an action item from a group. Chinese often have more interdependent working styles, whereas Americans usually work more independently. Mr. U.S. could become impatient with Ms. China for taking the time to gather consensus from the group on a project and asking for others' input rather than taking more ownership of the project herself.[8] Likewise, someone who likes working interdependently may feel excluded by an individual worker's decision not to consult them on a project before moving ahead.[9]

The second dimension refers to where authority lies and ranges from egalitarianism to status. Someone who is very status-oriented prefers not to challenge those above them and believes that power and authority should be reserved for a few members of a group.[10] People from the U.S. tend to be more egalitarian, meaning they believe power and authority should be shared broadly among a group. They are more comfortable challenging the views of

Figure 3.5 GlobeSmart Comparison U.S. and China

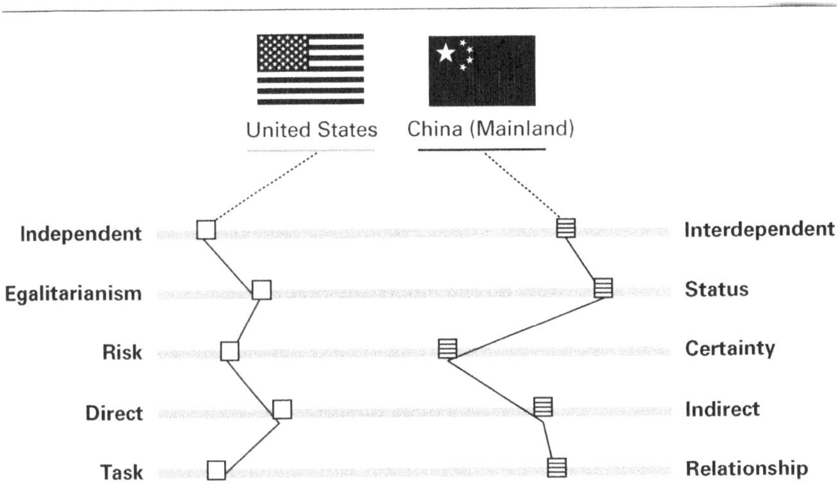

Reproduced with permission

superiors and are flexible about roles and titles.[11] Conflict can occur in this dimension when an egalitarian manager confronts a status-oriented junior employee. The junior employee will not want to embarrass their boss in front of others, but an egalitarian manager could interpret this as being dishonest or non-cooperative.[12] On the other hand, someone more status-oriented may become frustrated with an egalitarian manager's slow decision-making, finding it unnecessary for someone with decision-making authority to solicit so much feedback from other members of the group.

The third dimension covers how decisions are made across a tolerance of risk. Perhaps one of the most intuitive elements of the GlobeSmart Profile, cultures that value risk prefer rapid decision-making and quick results over thoroughness and research.[13] The U.S. culture tends to be very risk-taking, and Silicon Valley technology companies in particular have just such a reputation. Facebook founder Mark Zuckerberg coined the saying "Move fast and break things," which underscores his emphasis on speed and flexibility over procedure and precision.[14] (We explore global expansion in tech and B2B companies in Chapters 9 and 10.) As we've seen with Airbnb, Chinese culture wants certainty, seeking more information before making decisions.[15] Japan is one of the most certainty-oriented, or risk-averse, cultures. Conflict can arise when risk-takers grow impatient with people who seek certainty and want more time for additional research, data, and input. On the other hand, the certainty-oriented folks can get frustrated when speed is prioritized over thoroughness.

The fourth dimension refers to direct versus indirect communication. Those who prefer direct communication say what they mean, without much context or concern for those they're speaking with. The German workplace culture is even more direct than the U.S.; people get to their point quickly and state facts honestly. They are comfortable making requests, providing direct feedback, and openly disagreeing with others.[16] By contrast, Saudi Arabia has a more indirect working culture. Those in Saudi Arabia may give direction or express disagreement in subtle ways so as not to offend others. They may spend more time explaining context for decisions or feedback.[17] People who communicate indirectly might get offended by the blunt communication style of direct cultures. On the flip side, those who use direct communication might miss the subtle communication in indirect cultures. They may grow impatient and need more explicit information more quickly. (We'll discuss communication more specifically in Chapter 4.)

The fifth and final cultural dimension determines whether one's focus is around the task or the relationship. Those who are task-oriented tend to focus on action items and activities, and less on maintaining good relationships between colleagues. They focus more on individual achievements over who they are and their connections. Germans tend to be task-oriented—little small talk is needed before diving into project particulars. Brazilians, on the other hand, tend to have a more relationship-oriented work culture; people want to spend more time getting to know each other before diving into the specifics. Conflict can arise when task-oriented people overlook building a relationship before diving straight into work. While the task-oriented person feels that personal conversation is unnecessary, the relationship-oriented person may feel offended. Conversely, the task-oriented person may get frustrated that the relationship-oriented person doesn't want to jump into the work at hand.

I found my GlobeSmart Profile to be illuminating. While I was born and raised in the U.S., my profile didn't match that of the average American. I recognize all data points are relative, and the curve of my GlobeSmart Profile does parallel the U.S. curve until the final dimension on focus, where my preference is vastly different than my origin culture (Figure 3.6).

Figure 3.6 GlobeSmart Comparison K.M.R. and U.S.

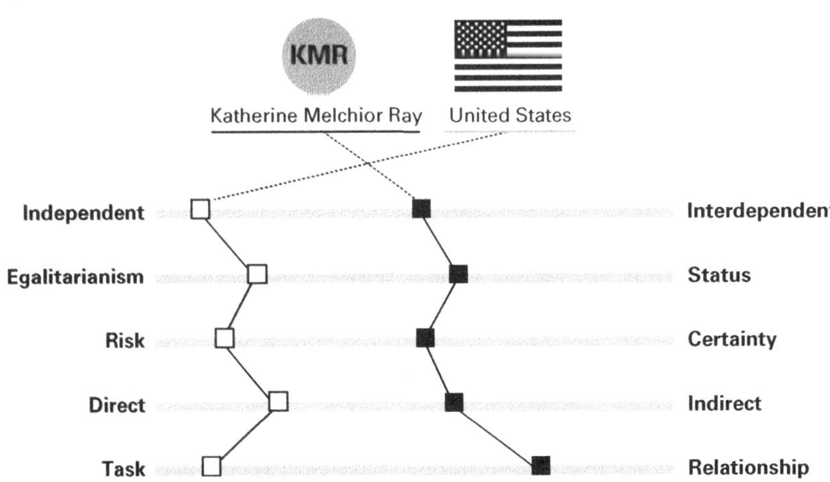

Reproduced with permission

Figure 3.7 GlobeSmart Comparison K.M.R. and Japan

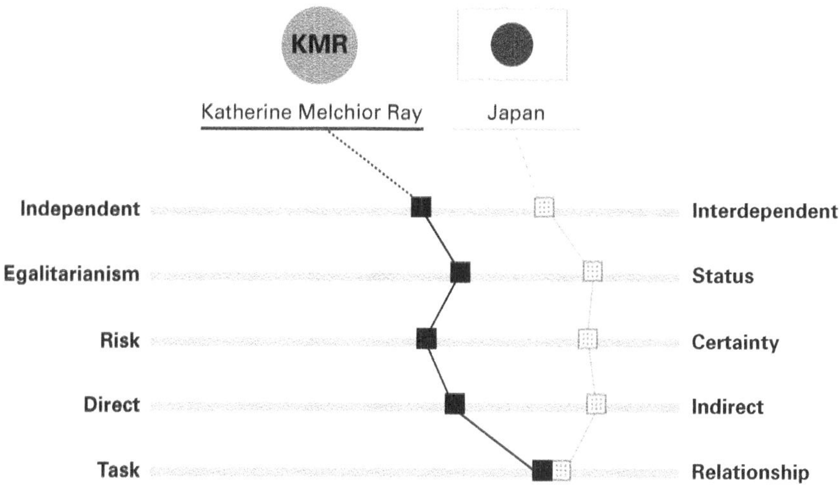

Reproduced with permission

Out of curiosity, I plotted the country in which I have lived and worked the most—Japan—and discovered my high relationship-orientation approximates the Japanese one (Figure 3.7). As I spent my early career in a Japanese company in Tokyo, the GlobeSmart Profile comparison helped confirm what I felt but lacked words to express—that I value relationships. Indeed, I recommend when people do business in Japan, they arrive the night before a meeting to have dinner with their counterparts, getting to know them before they engage in the next day's business topics. As a relationship-oriented leader who has worked in many companies and cultures, I consider myself lucky to maintain such strong bonds around the world. Many of the contributors to this book and my class guest speakers are colleagues from decades of international work.

Seeking more understanding of my own atypical preferences, I added a third culture to my profile (Figure 3.8). Raised in San Francisco, I attended from age 4 to 13 the French American Bilingual School (now called French American International School or FAIS), where I spent every day learning both French and English. The school was run by French administrators. Adding French culture to the American and Japanese comparison on my profile, I discovered I match the French culture's preferences across three of the five dimensions. Hallelujah! Not only did this make sense to me, but it has also given me a helpful tool to understand, and predict, how I will react to others' communication. It deserves repeating that our preferences are

Figure 3.8 GlobeSmart Comparison K.M.R., U.S., Japan, and France

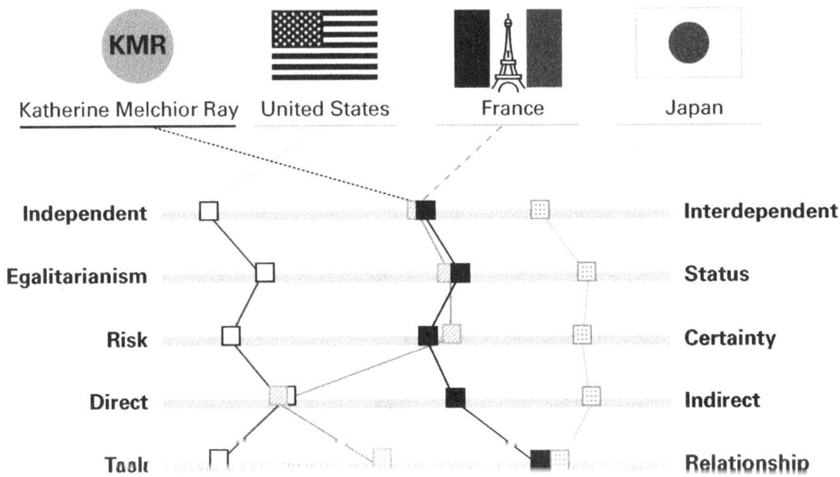

Reproduced with permission

influenced by, but do not necessarily match, where and how we were raised. We are all individuals, reflecting unique personalities with complex and hidden preferences. While GlobeSmart provides country-wide averages, individuals can vary widely within any one culture.

I recommend anyone interested in working globally take a cultural assessment to uncover their behavioral preferences. Remember, self-awareness is the second requirement for CQ. Not only do we gain a deeper understanding of our own unspoken assumptions and expectations, but learning about alternative ways of viewing these dimensions expands our aptitude and empathy to better understand others. I've found it to be an incisive tool to create shared understanding and communication, which we'll see are foundations of building trust.

A Kiss Is (Not) Just a Kiss

CQ is not built in a day. It is an ongoing, ever-evolving practice with an expanding toolkit. I've developed my own CQ in various ways over the years, some surprising, some complex, and some as satisfying as a simple kiss. The key, as always in international settings, is context.

La bise is a common French greeting, whether you are family, friends, or work associates. (It is somewhat less popular post-Covid.) It doesn't matter if it's morning or evening, at someone's home, or in the office. In France, women kiss men, men kiss men, children kiss adults, children kiss each other. When my children were small and our family lived in Nice, France, the kissing tradition would commence at the front door. Even five-year-olds are not excused; our adult friends would kiss us upon arrival, then bend down to kiss our children and expect a kiss back, and then our friends' young children would greet us, and the kisses began anew.

After learning this behavior growing up in France for four years, my children looked to kiss new friends when we moved to Japan. As my son leaned toward the cheek of a friend, the young Japanese boy backed away. He pulled his neck to the side and took a step back, creating space for a bow.

It took many months of living in Japan to observe and master the art of the bow. The formal bow of those you meet the first time descends forty-five degrees from the hip. The more you respect someone, or simply wish to convey respect regardless of your true feelings, the deeper and more thoughtfully you bend. An informal bow requires only a simple nod, but the eyes must always descend to communicate respect. To not lower the eyes carries a risk; you may be perceived as ignorant, or worse, intentionally rude.

It can be awkward with Japanese friends who have traveled a lot or have worked for foreign companies, like me. They hope to put me at ease, and I want to adapt to our surrounding culture. When meeting a local friend on the street in Tokyo, there are a few awkward seconds between us when he might open his arms for an American hug while I am keeping my distance for a respectful bow.

Working as a fashion executive in Japan, I collected cultural greetings along with different colored handbags. Walking into the office each morning, I voiced the expected "*Ohayo Gozaimasu*" (Good morning) loudly as I crossed the floor of my large marketing team, gliding in my heels among cubicles until I reached my corner office. Entering a vendor meeting late, I gave the guests a simple but satisfactory nod so as not to sway the negotiation. Meeting important journalists for the first time, I stood and bowed, but moved quickly to evoke friendly communication. The most formal bows, the ones that would go back and forth several times, I saved for senior executives of department stores, politicians, and Buddhist priests.

But when our French colleagues visited the office in Tokyo, I always fashioned my greetings for my audience. While they greeted Japanese colleagues with the international business handshake, I jumped at bringing more Latin warmth to the meeting and puckered for a double-cheeked air kiss. With that perfect peck, I stood both in Japan and firmly in France, so my comments that day would be heard without cultural suspicion.

To kiss, to shake, or to bow, and occasionally—only with those I knew well—maybe to hug, my collection of cultural greetings allowed me to play with, in, and through cultural expectations. Sometimes I chose to match, while at others, I purposely accessorized in contrast, each time fully aware of the power of impression.

Trust Begins with Shared Understanding

A brand puts a promise in the marketplace. For it to be successful—the brand, the campaign, the business—you need to deliver against that promise. When a company provides the value promised in its brand, it builds trust with its consumer. Therein lies the central tension at the heart of this chapter: Brands imply trust, which relies on subjective values, and which is exactly why it's so difficult to build a brand across cultures.

Trust is tricky because it's abstract. Necessary for good relationships, trust is critical for brands. I believe trust requires three things: shared values, open communication, and a history of promises kept (Figure 3.9). When there's a breakdown in any of these, a relationship or a brand gets derailed; if you commit to doing all of them well, you're on the right track.

Shared Values

To build trust, you need shared values. This goes for people in the same way it does for brands. Do you (or your brand) know your values and communicate them clearly? Do you (or your brand) behave in line with those values? To be successful, you (or your brand) must ensure your values connect across

Figure 3.9 What Is Trust?

Trust is comprised of three parts:
shared values, open communication, and a history of promises kept.

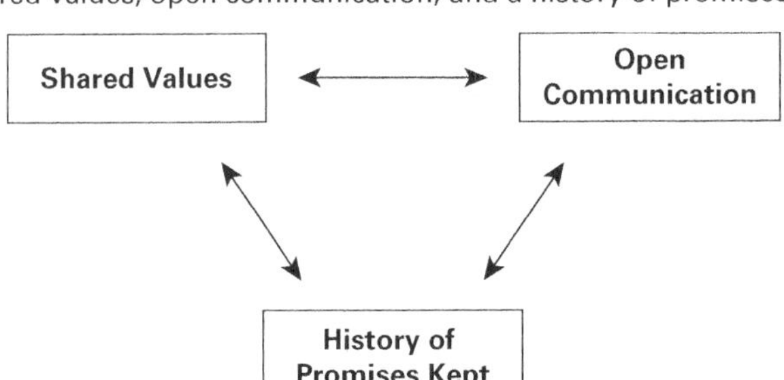

cultures. You have to expose any hidden expectations, first to understand them, and then to find common ground where values are shared.

Open Communication

Open communication is the primary means of connecting, understanding, and building intimacy in a relationship. Brands seek relationships with their customers. They want to understand them and deliver to their needs. They want their audience to engage and share their needs, desires, and aspirations. Brands communicate through all the marketing touchpoints we reviewed in Chapter 1. When customers are pleased with a product or service, they show their satisfaction by buying again; they become repeat customers, and the relationship grows. In fact, when a company successfully turns a dissatisfied customer into a newly satisfied one, when it transforms frustration into feeling heard and fulfilled, the company creates a much more loyal customer.

A History of Promises Kept

The single most important aspect of trust is keeping your promises. You've created expectations, so you need to deliver against them. To reach this ultimate test of trust, first make sure you share the same values and communicate them clearly, so the promise is understood on both sides. A brand loses its value when it doesn't deliver the experience it promises. If you set up a car service for an early morning pickup to the airport and the car doesn't show, you will find a different car company next time.

Louis Vuitton created enormous trust in Japan by keeping its word, even when that meant sacrificing sales. When I was at Louis Vuitton Japan, the brand promised standardized prices across countries, aside from duties and shipping fees. This policy discouraged customers from going abroad for discounts. Currency fluctuations meant that when the yen was low compared to the euro, we raised prices in Japan. That change generated much higher total sales and benefited the Japan business. When the yen was strong, however, we lowered our prices. We were clear about our promise and transparent about our prices. By keeping that promise, we built credibility, trust, and deep loyalty in the Louis Vuitton brand.

Trust is key to building brands across cultures, but you cannot do so without first creating shared values and open communication. The ideas and tools provided here—the C.A.G.E. framework, CQ, and GlobeSmart—offer practical strategies for identifying and overcoming cultures' hidden challenges. Values contain subjective meaning, easily distorted across cultures.

When we lower the waterline, we expose those concealed cultural treasures for all to see and understand. In Chapter 4, we'll delve into communication across cultures and the challenges it presents—as well as the delights.

Summary

- **What is culture?** The shared values or collective programming of any group.
- **Why is culture complicated?** It is like an iceberg, with much of it hidden, so lowering the waterline exposes many unspoken values.
- **How to understand culture?** Practice CQ through attitude, awareness, knowledge, and skill.

The Global Digest

Chapter 3 Takeaways

1. **Learn from Airbnb:** Cultural differences posed the most significant hurdle for Airbnb's expansion in China, particularly issues around trust, credit, cleanliness standards, and aversion to staying in strangers' homes.
2. **Culture is complex:** Many cultural misunderstandings arise because powerful values lie hidden beneath the surface in the form of assumptions, values, behaviors, and preferences that vary across groups.
3. **C.A.G.E. narrows the unknowns:** This framework offers insights across four dimensions—cultural, administrative, geographic, and economic—to help analyze potential challenges to entering new markets and plan strategies to address them.
4. **Concepts and meanings can distort across cultures:** Seemingly innocuous aspects of culture, such as greetings and perceptions of cleanliness, can carry significant meaning and impact business relationships. Keep an open mind as you learn perceptions other than your own.
5. **Lower the waterline:** Much of culture lies beneath the surface of the iceberg, invisible to the naked eye. Making hidden cultural values, assumptions, attitudes and beliefs explicit is crucial for understanding and bridging cultural divides.

6 **Cultivate cultural intelligence (CQ):** CQ combines EQ with IQ—and then takes it even further. An individual with high CQ has an open mind, self-awareness, cultural knowledge, and an ability to practice these skills, useful when marketing internationally or to diverse consumers domestically.

7 **Listen with your eyes:** When communicating across cultures, listen more than you speak. Pay attention to body language, seat locations, speaking order, silence, and other subtle, nonverbal clues which convey meaning.

8 **Leverage cultural tools for self-awareness:** Cultural assessments like GlobeSmart from Aperian provide a snapshot of your own working preferences, which will help you better adapt to the styles and behaviors of other cultures.

9 **Brands must build trust:** For a brand to succeed across cultures, it must create trust in the marketplace. But cultural differences make trust harder to establish in the face of ample opportunities for misunderstandings and miscommunication.

10 **Trust requires shared values, open communication, and a history of promises kept:** This is equally true for relationships between people and that of a brand and its consumer.

References

1 A. Blazyte (2024) China: Number of Domestic Tourist Arrivals 2023, Statista, September 19. www.statista.com/statistics/277254/number-of-domestic-trips-in-china/ (archived at https://perma.cc/67J7-PTF5)

2 P. Ghemawat and J. Siegel (2011) *Cases about Redefining Global Strategy*, Harvard Business Review Press, Brighton, MA, Chapter 2.

3 G. Hofstede (2011) Dimensionalizing Cultures: The Hofstede Model in Context, *Online Readings in Psychology and Culture*, December, 2(1). scholarworks.gvsu.edu/orpc/vol2/iss1/8/ (archived at https://perma.cc/7JHR-VC43)

4 Mindtools Content Team. Cultural Intelligence. www.mindtools.com/aisl5uv/cultural-intelligence (archived at https://perma.cc/6WUJ-FAMH)

5 B. Marr (2022) Cultural Intelligence (CQ) Is an Important Predictor of Success. Here's How to Boost Your CQ, *Forbes*, September 5. www.forbes.com/sites/bernardmarr/2022/09/05/cultural-intelligence-cq-is-an-important-predictor-of-success-heres-how-to-boost-your-cq/?sh=2cff61e2de26 (archived at https://perma.cc/GAZ8-RMS2)

6 Aperian. GlobeSmart Profile: How Culture Placements on the Profile Are Determined. aperian.zendesk.com/hc/en-us/articles/360034245273-GlobeSmart-Profile-How-Culture-Placements-on-the-Profile-are-Determined (archived at https://perma.cc/XES5-TBYR)

7 Aperian. Understanding the GlobeSmart Dimensions. gslearning.aperianglobal.com/mod/scorm/player.php?a=319&currentorg=B0&scoid=729 (archived at https://perma.cc/U28B-AGM9)

8 Aperian. *GlobeSmart Profile*. aperian.com/globesmart-profile/ (archived at https://perma.cc/N97W-8XTJ)

9 Aperian. *GlobeSmart Profile*. aperian.com/globesmart-profile/ (archived at https://perma.cc/H3DW-2X7L)

10 Aperian. *GlobeSmart Profile*. aperian.com/globesmart-profile/ (archived at https://perma.cc/4Y7Q-JKRG)

11 Aperian. *GlobeSmart Profile*. aperian.com/globesmart-profile/ (archived at https://perma.cc/1NDY-37XV)

12 Aperian. *GlobeSmart Profile*. aperian.com/globesmart-profile/ (archived at https://perma.cc/SE3A-LDV9)

13 Aperian. *GlobeSmart Profile*. aperian.com/globesmart-profile/ (archived at https://perma.cc/NUQ9-GZLZ)

14 I. A. Hamilton (2022) Meta: Mark Zuckerberg Hasn't Let Go of "Move Fast and Break Things", *Business Insider*, February 16. www.businessinsider.com/meta-mark-zuckerberg-new-values-move-fast-and-break-things-2022-2 (archived at https://perma.cc/FDP4-NFWE)

15 Aperian. *GlobeSmart Profile*. aperian.com/globesmart-profile/ (archived at https://perma.cc/A7T3-X88C)

16 Aperian. Germany: Communication. app.aperian.com/guides/de/communication (archived at https://perma.cc/SD7S-YG6V)

17 Aperian. Saudi Arabia: Communication. app.aperian.com/guides/sa/communication (archived at https://perma.cc/8B9T-TL4V)

Back to Basics 4

Cross-Cultural Communication Is Anything But!

KATHERINE MELCHIOR RAY

The 1970s was a decade of bold colors, disco beats, and revolutionary fashion. In Dallas, Texas, the headquarters of Braniff Airlines buzzed with creativity and ambition. Under the leadership of a young executive, Harding Lawrence, the airline catapulted itself into culture, revolutionizing how airlines presented themselves to the public.

Braniff hired known artists to design its planes' exteriors, interiors, and uniforms. Alexander Girard, and later mobile artist Alexander Calder, designed planes with bright, vibrant colors, transforming jet aircrafts into flying works of art. Inside, Emilio Pucci created space-age-themed couture uniforms in geometric blues and greens. Designer Halston followed suit as Braniff elevated air travel to new heights of sophistication. These initiatives were groundbreaking and captured the imagination of travelers worldwide. Flying was bold, stylish, and sexy.

Until it was a little too sexy, even for them. With newly expanded flights to international destinations, a new marketing campaign appealed to a higher level of comfort and sophisticated travel. The campaign highlighted new First Class leather seats with the tagline, "Fly in Leather," evoking images of passengers sinking into plush seats, sipping champagne, and enjoying the epitome of unparalleled airborne elegance. With disco hits blaring in the background, the campaign rolled out with fanfare. Glossy advertisements featuring stylish models draped over sleek leather seats were splashed across magazines and billboards.

Excitement soon turned to confusion and embarrassment. In Spanish, the slogan "Fly in Leather" was mistranslated as "*Vuela en Cuero*." Unbeknownst to Braniff's marketing team, "*en cuero*" is colloquial in Spanish for "naked". Instead of conjuring images of luxury and sophistication, the campaign suggested that passengers should "Fly Naked."[1]

The reaction in Mexico and Spain was immediate and not at all what Braniff had anticipated. Passengers and industry insiders alike were perplexed, amused, and dismayed, wondering how such a reputable airline could make such a blunder. The mistranslation became a topic of jokes and led to a public relations debacle that underscored the importance of cultural sensitivity in global marketing. Not only did the campaign fail, but the airline damaged its reputation and consumer confidence—a critical mistake for any airline.

Errors can also imply ignorance. Pepsodent is a 100-year-old American toothpaste brand with a social mission. Stating "Every Smile Matters," the brand seeks to unlock the power of a smile through preventative behavior and motivation.[2] The Pepsodent logo shows the brand name with a curved red line below it—smiling.

In a sleek, modern office adorned with pristine white decor to symbolize the promise of brighter smiles, the marketing team had just launched their latest global campaign with the slogan, "You'll wonder where the yellow went / when you brush your teeth with Pepsodent!"[3] The strategy was a simple yet powerful message: Using Pepsodent resulted in sparkling white teeth, a presumed universal marker of cleanliness and attractiveness. The campaign was crafted to emphasize the benefits of whiter teeth. Glossy advertisements showcased confident smiles, highlighting the motivational power of white teeth.

In certain Southeast Asian countries, the marketing message fell flat.[4] In these regions, chewing betel nuts (also known as betel quid) is a longstanding tradition. Betel nut chewing stains the teeth a reddish-black color, which is not only accepted but also considered attractive and a sign of social status. The idea of having sparkling white teeth was not universally appealing; in fact, it clashed with local beauty standards and cultural practices.

Instead of appealing to consumers, it inadvertently suggested that their cultural practices were undesirable. The marketing team at Pepsodent had not anticipated this cultural nuance, leading to a campaign that did not connect with the very people it was intended to persuade. While it worked in other regions, the misstep illustrates the critical importance of understanding and respecting cultural differences in global marketing strategies.

These examples reveal vital lessons in cross-cultural communication. What works in one cultural context may not translate to another, highlighting the complexities and challenges of international marketing. Product names, advertising slogans and campaign concepts cannot simply be translated; they need to be culturally transformed. Certainly, in the past 40 years, global marketing has come a long way, but these beloved bloopers are valuable lessons in the power and peril of words.

The ability to communicate effectively across languages and cultures is paramount for any brand looking to market its products and services on a global scale. Language stands as both a bridge and a barrier when it comes to cross-cultural communication and marketing. Open communication is the second critical link for building trust. (Remember, building trust requires shared values, open communication, and keeping your promises.) While words have utility in conveying literal meanings, they also carry immense cultural significance, nuance, and subtext that can be difficult to translate. Even seemingly straightforward marketing slogans or friendly concepts can get lost in translation, fail to resonate, or, worse, offend cultural sensibilities. From direct translations to idiomatic expressions and culturally laden concepts, the challenges of communicating authentically in different languages and cultures are vast. This chapter explores the pitfalls and best practices for avoiding language barriers, ensuring marketing messages transcend words alone to connect with the true cultural context.

Language, Signs, and Symbols

The previous examples illustrate a campaign slogan for Braniff and a strategic benefit of whiter teeth with Pepsodent. Not all communication is verbal. We communicate with words, but also with images, objects, and gestures. These are sometimes referred to as codes and conventions.[5] Codes refer to things: a network of signs that each conveys specific meanings. Language, for instance, is a code that is shared by people in a group or culture. Conventions refer to shared norms for when, where, and how those codes might be used.

For instance, the same language might be used differently in varied contexts or cultures; this is an example of the same code with different conventions. English is spoken by people in the U.S. and in England, among other countries, but they don't always use one code with the same conventions. In England, the parts of an automobile are personified, with what Americans refer to as a hood called a "bonnet" and the trunk called the "boot". For someone in fashion like me, I find this unusual and even humorous. When people do not share the same codes and conventions, misunderstandings can arise. Again, the iceberg analogy—the idea that most of culture is hidden—is helpful to understand that the same sign may have multiple meanings based on unspoken assumptions. (See Chapter 3 for a full explanation.)

While living in France, I read all the *Harry Potter* books aloud to my children. The books we bought were published in the U.K. When I read about Harry's first visit to Diagon Alley with Hagrid, I wasn't sure what the *trainers* he was wearing referred to. Our English friends helped me understand that *trainers* referred to what we in the U.S. call *sneakers*, and *jumpers* refers to our American word *sweaters*.

I learned the power of symbols the hard way when I was 21 years old. Fresh out of college, I went to work in Japan. I was interested in journalism and fascinated by Japanese culture, so when an opportunity came to combine my interests and work for Japan's largest television network, I accepted. I was hired by the parent company of Fuji Television, which also managed newspapers, radio stations, and dozens of other media businesses.

I started in the publishing field as I had been the editor-in-chief of a monthly magazine at Brown University. I joined the public relations department, where I quickly improved upon the three years of Japanese language courses I'd had in college. Our team sat in one long row of connected desks; the manager, or "Buchō," sat at a horizontally placed head table to face us and, in descending order of seniority, we fanned out from him. As the lowliest-of-low entry employee—my Ivy League diploma notwithstanding—I sat at the caboose desk, with several other young employees and my mid-level boss lined up between me and the Bucho. From there, I could complete the assigned menial tasks, like clipping newspaper articles and completing expense reports and taxi vouchers. I did what I was told and tried to fit in, but I couldn't help but stand out. At 5'11" with curly brown hair, the great advantage of my height was being able to breathe above others in the jam-packed subways on my morning commute. At the office, I struggled to fold my legs under the formica desk.

One day, I spotted a somewhat larger chair propped against the wall near me. No one was using it, so, eager to create a little more room for my over-sized body, I switched it with mine.

"*Kyasarin*!" screamed Buchō. "*Nani wo yatte'ru no*?!" (What the heck are you doing?!)

All eyes rolled down the row of desks to see me, now sheepishly sinking lower into my new chair.

"*Ahhhh, gomen nasai*," I began apologizing, though I didn't think I had done anything wrong. In Japan, one apologizes profusely and frequently for all kinds of things, even, for example, when allowing someone else to go first.

In my elementary Japanese, I tried to explain that no one was using the chair and I thought it would be easier for my large frame.

"*Kyasarin!*" Buchō continued in frustration, "that armchair is fifteen years too senior for you!"

Those seemingly innocuous arm rests that I'd hoped would help me slide my legs under the table every day had to be earned over years of loyal service. In moving to Japan, I had known I would learn a lot about its culture, but I had no idea I would discover symbols of power in a simple desk chair.

Know Your Audiences, All of Them

Communication is a fundamental building block of marketing and, beyond that, of our social interactions. We communicate with our audience—the customer—and we communicate with our colleagues. Whether branding, naming products, developing marketing campaigns, negotiating budgets, working in teams, or simply chatting among friends, we communicate. I like to draw the distinction between our external communication with our audience and our internal communication among teams. More often than not, our teams are composed of individuals from diverse backgrounds. Working across international markets, teamwork requires cross-cultural communication to be explicit, to prevent such misunderstandings. We can leverage this internal communication to improve our external communication.

I was hired by Uniqlo's parent company, Fast Retailing, to help them grow two French brands they had acquired: Comptoir des Cotonniers and Princesse Tam Tam. Comptoir des Cotonniers is a mid-level women's fashion brand and Princesse Tam Tam is known for its lingerie and swimwear. After conducting a brand analysis and visiting stores, I presented plans for how to grow the business and improve the working relationships between Paris and Tokyo. We needed to align the strategies between the French merchandisers and Japanese managers on assignment from Uniqlo.

"We want the French team to make more basics," repeated the Japanese merchants in the Parisian showroom.

"We already have many basics," repeated the French designer, growing frustrated at repeating herself. "Our clientele wants more fashionable designs, more frills."

Comptoir sold its products to 30–50-year-old women, competing against other trendy fashion brands which updated their offering frequently. Without a strong point of view adjusting fashionable elements of material, color, cut, and adornments like fringe, buttons, and accessories, the French designer knew they could not charge the same prices and would lose market share to their competitors. Simple designs from more affordable brands, like Uniqlo itself, were already stealing their entry-point products. Both sides were arguing about whether the products were or were not basic enough.

It was only when we conducted our ethnographic research that I found the solution.

We talked with our customers about their fashion tastes, brand preferences, and product choices. One woman explained what she did and didn't like about the Comptoir brand and its competitors. She had been a loyal

Comptoir customer and was eager to show us her wardrobe. We followed her into her bedroom. From the armoire, she pulled out various tops.

"This is a Comptoir basic I love," she explained as she held up a white short-sleeved top in white lace fabric.

In that split second, I realized that for the French, a basic top includes one made of lace. For the Japanese team from Uniqlo, a brand which specializes in affordable high-quality cotton T-shirts and pants, lace would never be considered basic. Our business challenge began with a communication breakdown. How would we agree on a growth strategy if we couldn't even agree on the meaning of one word? Both sides were using a word not from their own language, but from what they believed to be a neutral language. The reality is that there is no neutral language. Each side interpreted the same word silently but subjectively, reflecting their respective perspectives, values, and contexts.

This example illustrates not only how we may inadvertently stumble in communicating, but how we can gain in understanding. The fact that French women perceive lace as a basic reveals so much about French culture. Since the sixteenth century, French royals and aristocrats have prized the delicate fabric as a symbol of their wealth and sophistication, embodying the values of elegance, craftsmanship, and a love for the finer things in life. Small indulgences bring beauty and pleasure to everyday experiences in France, like buying freshly baked baguettes, enjoying an omelet with a glass of wine, or taking time for a luxurious skincare regime. From our communication barrier, we created a bridge of cultural understanding.

To share insights on both cultures, I asked the French team a simple, but provocative question, "When might you expect to wear wool and cashmere?"

"*Bien sûr*, Katherine, those are fabrics for winter," replied a French merchant.

"Ever heard of summer cashmere?" I continued. France and Japan share four annual seasons, but Japan's winter and summer months have a much wider range of dry and humid weather.

"With Japan's extreme humidity, companies have perfected different weights of cashmere for all seasons, including an extremely lightweight version that allows the skin to breathe in a hot, humid climate."

Each culture gained a new appreciation of the other's perspectives, formed from the context of their lives. Before we expanded working on the rest of the collection, we created a glossary of terms to improve our communication, collaboration, and mutual confidence. Even the same word can have multiple meanings across different cultures, proving that communication is anything but basic!

Finding Common Ground

Our "basic" communication breakdown led to a positive turning point for teamwork. When working with internal teams, communication is critical. We need to learn to pause our own unconscious recognition of meaning to listen openly and objectively unpack what someone is trying to communicate (words, symbols, or otherwise.) Curiosity builds empathy, understanding, and collaboration. I find internal cross-cultural communication can act as a laboratory for the external, consumer-facing kind. With the various cultures in your team, you can explicitly explain unconscious codes and conventions to create shared understanding and, together, "lower the waterline." That, in turn, helps orient how to create meaningful communication externally. And you can't afford to fail with your customers, as we saw with Braniff. Additionally, global marketers need to empower local teams to manage customer communication for the most powerful impact. In return, when they explain what and why they made changes, you continue to improve your cultural intelligence.

Tommy Hilfiger is an iconic American fashion brand that epitomizes a classic, preppy style with a cool, modern twist. Founded in 1985 by designer Tommy Hilfiger, the brand is recognized globally for its all-American, East Coast varsity-inspired aesthetic.[6] The signature look features patriotic red, white, and blue color schemes with lots of crisp stripes, nautical themes, and the iconic flag logo. Quintessential preppy items like polo shirts, chinos, blazers, and boat shoes make up the brand's bread and butter.

When I was working as a consultant and temporary head of marketing for Tommy Hilfiger Japan, the Japanese head merchant, Taka Yamada, wanted to complete the upcoming fall collection by rebranding a boat shoe from another brand. As it was an unusual request, I sought approval from headquarters and reached out to the CMO, Avery Baker, who had hired me.

"Is he kidding? No way," is a paraphrasing of Baker's less-than-diplomatic reply. She began to worry if he understood the brand and whether she could trust his judgment.

I could understand both sides. Japan was a growing market where the merchandisers had wide freedom to produce their own styles. But as a key window for other Asian markets, the global team needed to assure the Hilfiger look and feel represented the best of its global collection. This would prevent selling lookalike styles from competitors.

We were not making progress through phone calls and video conferences. Searching for a solution, I suggested we continue the discussion when we were all together in person.

We met at the new collection presentation in Europe.

Yamada explained that to highlight the iconic, American navy-blue blazer as the signature piece for fall, they needed a head-to-toe preppy look. So, in addition to the Hilfiger button-down oxford shirts with the signature Hilfiger flag logo and autumnal-colored khakis, shoes would help grow the business. Colorful slip-on loafers were very popular in Japan for their preppy look and easy removal for sitting on tatami mats. He had found a shoe from another American brand and hoped to add the Hilfiger logo to complete the look. From his perspective on the sales opportunity, it made good business sense.

Baker was having none of it. "Absolutely not. We don't do knockoffs here," she stated firmly.

Both perspectives had merits, but we needed a solution.

"*Yamada-san*," I began, switching to Japanese. "What specifically appeals to you about those shoes?"

Our Japanese-style maven described how the retro American look was so popular even young suburban girls were wearing classic penny loafers with their high school uniforms.

"Penny loafers?" Baker chimed in. "Hilfiger made iconic penny loafer styles back in the day. If we've done it before, we can do it again."

Yamada insisted on various colors in order to sell customers more than one pair.

"I am happy to do that," Baker smiled. "Why don't we include a set of gumball-colored American pennies to mix and match with their outfits?"

Tommy Hilfiger Japan's fall collection around the classic yet cool navy-blue blazer was a huge success. More importantly, in the critical relationship between marketing and merchandising, between headquarters and a fast-growing region, we found common ground. By clarifying a misunderstanding through explicit and contextual dialogue, we solved the business challenge. Additionally, we built trust through shared understanding and open communication. (See more on the management of the Tommy Hilfiger brand in Chapter 6.)

I have found it's best to talk it out, especially across cultures. We have to learn to live with abstraction to some degree, to expect and accept a lack of closure. But too many unknowns transform subjective perception into false realities. By reaching out and communicating, we learn context. Challenging people and organizations to look beyond the familiar, to get uncomfortable and curious enough to step into one another's shoes, helps align on common ground. As we will see in the next chapter, this approach helps to better understand the person who really matters—your customer. Bringing people together across differences is one of the joys and benefits of working globally, but it requires openness, honesty, and care.

Communication Tools and Techniques

Effective cross-cultural communication requires a nuanced approach to account for the rich complexities and unspoken cultural undercurrents underlying how messages get decoded. Best practices help avoid those potential barriers and instead create bridges for connection across cultures and markets.

On the first day of my global marketing class at Berkeley, I show students an image of a bright red muscle car immensely popular between the 1960s and 1990s.

"Do you know what this is?" I ask.

Occasionally, one of the several car fans recognizes the angular shape and asks, "Is it a Chevy?"

"Yes. What is important about this car?"

The compact car offered style at a great price and became a hit with American consumers. Indeed, the car sold 350,000 units in its first year alone, and nearly five million over its 25-year lifecycle.[7]

When the students look puzzled, I continue. "To convey innovation with the literal translation of 'new' from Latin, the car was called 'Nova.' But don't try selling this great-looking and affordable car across the border in Mexico or any Spanish-speaking country for that matter. The name in Spanish translates phonetically to 'No va,' which means 'Doesn't go.'"

In fact, this vehicle sold okay in Latin America, but the point is one that students can easily remember: You must think through product names from a global perspective, long before you take those products across borders.

Start Global

The best place to start is to think globally from the beginning. When a company is naming its brand, products, or services for the external marketplace, consider how the words or expressions translate into different languages. As seen with Chevrolet's "Nova" nomenclature issue in Spanish-speaking countries, even a product name cleverly conceived from Latin—the father of many languages—can create steep hurdles or unintended offense when translated verbatim into other languages. To avoid such costly and reputationally risky mistakes, companies must implement rigorous linguistic screening protocols that analyze potential brand names and taglines across major markets and dialects before locking them in. There are naming experts who specialize in exactly this. Failing to catch these nuances in naming during development can lead to disastrous and embarrassing product launches down the line.

Admit a Rose Is Not a Rose

Literal word-for-word translations rarely suffice for brands seeking to connect in authentic, culturally resonant ways. Braniff got more sex appeal than intended when its "Fly in Leather" slogan revealed more than desired from a literal translation. Rather than accepting direct translations, brands must localize their messaging by creatively rewording idiomatic content to convey meaning in a locally relevant way.

Avoid Idioms

Idiomatic expressions and slang present translation trauma. Ideas and phrases that make sense in one language or culture can become incomprehensible or, worse, insensitive, when translated into another tongue. This is where the artistry of "transcreation"—a process of adaptive recontextualization—becomes essential. Transcreation goes beyond literalism to thoughtfully translate the underlying meaning, tone, and emotional context into a different cultural framework.

Pepsodent's communication blunder makes us cringe precisely because the approach was culturally insensitive. Eventually, Pepsodent's whiter teeth campaign was reframed for Southeast Asia as promoting brighter, more youthful smiles—achieving the desired aesthetic while sidestepping negative connotations. More than ever, brands are expected to respect diverse cultural backgrounds, both globally and domestically. Demonstrating cultural relevance not only avoids costly missteps, but helps businesses foster trust and inclusivity, expand their customer base, and enhance their brand reputation.

The diverse cultures represented within your own teams present an invaluable laboratory for honing cross-cultural communication. Fostering an environment of open dialogue can enable team members to explicitly unpack unconscious cultural codes and conventions. The process of bridging internal cultural gaps orients the mindset needed to meaningfully connect with external audiences. Internal diversity links to external relevance. Embrace cross-cultural discourse within your own talent base, then amplify that externally via empowered local partners. Communication relies on verbal and visual codes, which are embedded with unspoken conventions, so the best global brands know how to adapt those signifiers across cultural contexts to convey meaning and create new value.

Caught in the Web: When Things Go Wrong

Communication is increasingly sensitive in the twenty-first century as the world has grown smaller and consumers more demanding about corporate, political, and cultural issues. Let's look at how geopolitical issues can rapidly escalate into brand nightmares, and what to do about it.

In 2018, Dolce & Gabbana (D&G) planned its largest fashion show ever in Shanghai, China.[8] A team of over 1,000 models, stylists, beauty professionals, and show producers had prepared a giant collection of hundreds of new silhouettes. The brand was targeting a broad array of fashionable, well-traveled young customers who exhibited a cross-cultural, multigenerational, geographical East–West attitude as a stepping stone to expand opportunities in the vibrant China market. I remember this well, as one of those initiatives was the launch of the D&G perfume, licensed by the European offices of Shiseido, of which I was CMO for luxury brands.

To promote the event, D&G released a video campaign featuring a Chinese model in a luxurious D&G dress and dangling earrings struggling to eat Italian food—pizza and pasta—with chopsticks. Reeking of cultural insensitivity, the scene sparked a storm of criticism on social media. Within 24 hours, the video was removed from Weibo, China's largest video platform.[9]

That would have been bad enough, but the situation got worse when Stefano Gabbana, one of the two co-founders, dismissed the reaction on Instagram with derogatory comments that further inflamed public outrage. Sitting in Tokyo, we were highly aware of China's increasing sensitivity to geopolitical topics, learning, for example, to triple check how we referred to Taiwan. We were surprised how global brand leaders could be so misinformed, caustic, and culturally insensitive.

Despite claiming their accounts were hacked and issuing apologies, D&G faced severe backlash that began with the cancellation of the fashion show. Major Chinese e-commerce platforms and luxury retailers removed D&G products and customers returned D&G goods to department stores. Planned campaigns, promotions, and window displays were all abandoned. Chinese celebrities and influencers publicly expressed their solidarity and withdrew support for D&G. Our new perfume launch was postponed indefinitely.

Several days later, D&G released an official apology video featuring the co-founders expressing respect for both China and the Chinese people. That was too little, too late.

Only a few weeks earlier, we had overcome another global cultural communication crisis. One of our other licensed brands managed out of New York had hired the Middle Eastern beauty influencer, Sondos Al Qattan, to promote its products to her online base of millions. Fans followed her discerning beauty regime, make-up tutorials, and luxury international lifestyle—until, in a dismissive post, she criticized the new Kuwaiti law governing household employees.

Al Qattan expressed shock about allowing home servants to keep their own passports and granting them one day off every week, sparking outrage across the Middle East.[10] Her comments appeared to dehumanize domestic workers and she seemed out of touch with the country's efforts to raise the region's living standards. Our beauty brand quickly found itself in a heated cross-cultural firestorm and looked to us for advice.

This is how we began an overdue global initiative in the prevention and response to any communication crisis, which I believe is essential for today's marketers. In the era of influencers and social media, brands no longer fully control their own communication, but they remain responsible for vetting all associated messaging. The responsibility has expanded along with the number of marketing channels. These cases show how brands today must thoroughly understand not just the cultural context, but the geopolitical climate surrounding any message, and be prepared for a reaction that can arise at any time, from any place.

A robust crisis management protocol can help prevent blunders from occurring in the first place and rapidly mitigate any crisis if it does. The brand will be held responsible, no matter from whom the comments came. The first step is to maintain an always-on social listening service to gauge potentially viral issues before they combust. When an offensive slur slips through, the response plan should involve swift escalation to the brand team for situational assessment and informing concerned teams. Today, teams are working on 24-hour time zones from all over the globe, so a rapid-response ladder of communication can save valuable time while others sleep. What, how, and from whom to respond is also a cultural issue, so once again, know your audiences. Americans prefer fast and full apologies that usually beget audience forgiveness. The French prefer to explain how a crisis occurred but avoid admitting mistakes. Working in Japan, it is important to explain that taking responsibility does not mean corporate suicide. Offensive material should be removed and appropriate cross-cultural apologies offered. We delve more into customer service topics in Chapter 7.

In our interconnected age, marketing missteps can amplify exponentially into multi-market brand crises. Since building trust is so hard to begin with, it is emotionally and financially worthwhile to prevent damaging brand value. Steering clear of these hazards demands investing early in CQ, empathetic teams, approval processes, and agile crisis management. The penalties for tone deaf cross-cultural messaging have never been higher.

Summary

- **What is communication?** Shared codes and conventions that convey meaning.
- **Why is communication complicated?** The same words, gestures and images can convey vastly different meanings across cultures.
- **How to improve communication?** Replace judgment with curiosity to find common ground.

The Global Digest

Chapter 4 Takeaways

1. **A rose is not a rose:** Recognize that the same words, images, or symbols can carry vastly different meanings and associations across cultures—what seems innocuous in one context may be offensive in another.
2. **Direct translations are not your friend:** Direct translation of product names, slogans, or campaigns may not effectively convey the intended meaning across cultures—and can sometimes cause huge, unintended problems. Rigorous linguistic and cultural screening is essential.
3. **Embrace "transcreation:"** This is the process of adapting and recontextualizing messaging to convey the underlying meaning, tone, and emotional context in a culturally resonant way. Working with culturally fluent and native speakers is a must.
4. **Leverage the diversity within your own teams:** Think of it as a laboratory for unpacking cultural codes, conventions, and nuances to better understand your customers. Even the word "basic" is anything but.

5 **There is no neutral:** Our interpretations of every word, action, and object are subjective and reflect underlying values, perspectives, and contexts. Create a shared glossary for mutual clarity.

6 **Foster open dialogue:** Create a space where team members can explicitly discuss and bridge cultural gaps or disagreements to find common ground internally, ultimately leading to more meaningful consumer connections.

7 **Anticipate crisis response strategies before needed:** Create an internal global communication system that identifies and escalates potential cross-cultural missteps before they go viral. Align apologies, explanations, and accountability with cultural norms and expectations.

8 **Brands no longer fully control their own communication:** But they absolutely can't "check out." In an era of social media and influencer marketing, brands must monitor and remain vigilant about cultural and geopolitical sensitivities.

9 **Invest in developing deep cultural intelligence and empathy:** This helps teams avoid tone-deaf marketing mistakes that can severely damage brand reputation.

10 **Embrace cross-cultural dialogue:** See this as an opportunity for shared understanding; bringing people together across differences drives innovation and meaningful connections.

References

1 G. James (2014) 20 Epic Fails in Global Branding, *Inc Magazine*, October 29. www.inc.com/geoffrey-james/the-20-worst-brand-translations-of-all-time.html (archived at https://perma.cc/9KT7-Q24R); S. Schooley (2023) Lost in Translation: 13 International Marketing Fails, *Business News Daily*, October 23. www.businessnewsdaily.com/5241-international-marketing-fails.html (archived at https://perma.cc/4KVS-CLLN)

2 Pepsodent. www.pepsodent.in/home.html (archived at https://perma.cc/HL9S-MLQY)

3 I. Venegas (2014) Pepsodent Brushes People the Wrong Way, September 15. ivenegas12.wordpress.com/2014/09/15/pepsodent-brushes-people-the-wrong-way/ (archived at https://perma.cc/ZZS8-V6B4)

4 D. Grahovac and B. Rađenović-Kozić (2021) 6th International Scientific-Business Conference, July 28, Belgrade. doi.org/10.31410/LIMEN.2020.301 (archived at https://perma.cc/2Z7A-23ND)

5 D. Thomas and K. Inkson (2003) *Cultural Intelligence: People Skills for Global Business*, Berrett-Koehler Publishers, Inc., San Francisco.

6 Tommy Hilfiger Newsroom (2017) Designer Bio: Tommy Hilfiger Biography. newsroom.tommy.com/rockcircus-tommynow-2017-02-designer-bio/ (archived at https://perma.cc/ZZJ5-6GVG)

7 A. Gold (2022) The Chevrolet Nova: History, Generations, Specifications, MotorTrend, September 10. www.motortrend.com/features/chevrolet-nova-history-generations-specifications-photos/ (archived at https://perma.cc/3UA3-KGLE)

8 Vogue Staff (2018) Dolce & Gabbana Cancels Its Shanghai Great Show amid Controversy, *Vogue*, November 21. www.vogue.com/article/dolce-gabbana-cancels-shanghai-great-show (archived at https://perma.cc/3P78-9Y4F)

9 Y. Xu (2018) Dolce & Gabbana Ad (with Chopsticks) Provokes Public Outrage in China, NPR, December 1. www.npr.org/sections/goatsandsoda/2018/12/01/671891818/dolce-gabbana-ad-with-chopsticks-provokes-public-outrage-in-china (archived at https://perma.cc/7M7H-MGH6)

10 R. Michaelson (2018) Kuwaiti Star Faces Backlash over Filipino Worker Comments, *The Guardian*, July 23. www.theguardian.com/world/2018/jul/23/who-will-refund-me-kuwaiti-star-ignites-row-over-filipinos-days-off (archived at https://perma.cc/8LJJ-GDWU)

The Twenty-Seconds Rule 5

Understanding the Local Consumer

KATHERINE MELCHIOR RAY

Louis Vuitton in Japan

Commuters in shades of gray and black jackets buzz in all directions in the vast belly of Shinjuku station during the morning rush hour. Three million people pass through this single subway station every workday in Tokyo. The green Yamanote line circles around the perimeter while the orange Ginza line and the red Marunouchi line cut through the heart of the city to deliver hundreds of salarymen and -women—employed workers—to their offices every 4–5 minutes. One such salaryman, Tanaka-san, clutches his briefcase tightly as he is jostled by the crowd transferring between lines from the suburbs to central Tokyo.

Tanaka's rumpled charcoal suit is a mix of Western cut and Eastern usage. His knit tie is loosely wrapped, the knot disappearing into the stiff white collar of his shirt like a soldier vanishing into ranks. His slip-on shoes gleam, freshly polished that morning before he ran out the door. He is rushing to get to work before the 9 am bell rings at the software company where he works in sales. Last night was another long night with clients, so he feels a little groggy from the *nijikai* or after-party. The cacophony of announcements, advertisements, and human shuffling wash over him in waves as he struggles through the tide.

Moving up the stairs amid a hoard of workers, he sees the train pull into the station. He can't move any faster than the wave of humanity surrounding him. He manages to board the train before the white-gloved pushers help another dozen people shuffle in behind him. As the train lurches forward, he is supported by the crowd around him.

Just then, he hears his phone buzz insistently in his briefcase. Unable to move his arms, Tanaka rolls his eyes and furrows his brow. He can't possibly reach down into his briefcase in the dense crowd. Is it his manager calling about last month's sales results? Or, more urgent, the client following up from last night? His blood pressure rises as he knows he will miss the call.

Such is the daily routine for millions of salaried workers all across Japan, the men and women who make up the bulk of the country's business for the luxury brands designing their crisp white shirts, black suits, knit ties, leather loafers, bags—and briefcases.

In this chapter, we explore the importance of understanding the customer, a challenge for global marketers as the audience is usually far away, lives in different environments, speaks a foreign language, and has unfamiliar assumptions and expectations. Having explored in earlier chapters how to understand culture and how to communicate thoughtfully, we have tools to begin to unlock the ultimate goal: understanding a foreign customer's needs, aspirations, and desires. Since their lives are so different from our own, various forms of research help to identify the right target and understand their needs. But tools and reports only expose the broad landscape. You need to learn to ask the right questions and listen—again, not only with your ears, but with your eyes. There is no better feeling than reading between the lines to discover a juicy consumer insight you can transform into corporate value. The effort pays off professionally and personally. Learning to understand different customers internationally improves our ability to do the same thing in our domestic market, where we might inadvertently make assumptions and overlook opportunities.

In 2005, I was hired to find my way into the world and the mindset of these Japanese consumers when Yves Carcelle, the longtime CEO of Louis Vuitton, hired me to move to Japan as Vice President (VP) of Marketing. Japan had long been one of Louis Vuitton's largest and most profitable markets, accounting for nearly 40 per cent of its global sales, as the brand consistently outperformed its closest competitors.[1] But there were signs of change, sending financial ripples through the weekly business reports and, along with them, *frissons* of anxiety among the executives in the corridors of the Paris global headquarters. New market research suggested a shift in consumer values. As Japan trudged through an economic slump, the generation that once indulged in unprecedented levels of luxury was no longer chasing the same dreams. Luxury had become so pervasive that the reliable luxury consumers were suddenly indicating they were done blending in with the fashionable crowd.

How to understand these consumers, whose lives were so different from my own? Japanese consumers are quietly, but consistently, demanding—caring greatly about craftsmanship, production, packaging, and service. If you can please Japanese consumers, the refrain goes, you can please consumers anywhere. But consumer preferences were shifting from external brand validation to internal gratification and meaning. Personally, I understood their evolving perspective and recognized the implications. We needed to not only find more customers, a marketing imperative, but also understand the evolving desires of notoriously reserved consumers to adapt our offerings to their evolving needs.

We gathered small groups of our target audience for discussion. To begin, the questions focused on our most popular products for men and women: leather goods of all sizes and shapes. In such circumstances, I find theoretical discussions don't get you very far. Instead, showing examples of your products as well as your competitors' helps elicit actionable insights. From the broad to narrow, get specific and try to understand not only when, why, and how they use your goods, but where they buy the products and how those bags, wallets, and keychains fit into their lives.

- What do you use on a daily basis? For work? For pleasure?
- What do you like about one bag versus another?
- What do you think about the color, the material, the shape?
- What's good? What's missing?

In our Tokyo focus groups, several topics mentioned in passing created opportunities for deeper study and observation. Japanese women would leave their homes early in the morning and return often after dinner late at night, so bag weight was a real concern. As the vast majority of consumers use public transportation and walk long distances, they wanted large but light bags to carry all their needs and accessories for a full day.

For men like Tanaka-san, the most important concern provided us with great insight—they had to be able to access and answer their phone within twenty seconds or less, or risk losing face, or worse, a client. The message was clear: beyond brand, style, and price, briefcase functionality was of paramount importance to middle-class office workers.

Market research, demographics, and psychographics (data showing cultural and behavioral changes) provide broad data for an overall snapshot of an audience, but you need to zoom in for actionable insights. This is where understanding culture plays a role. The better we understand a consumer's lifestyle, daily routine, and personal and professional pressures and values, the better we understand the cultural context. We can begin to interpret a consumer's spoken and unspoken needs through verbal and nonverbal communication.

Often, I find the small and unsuspecting nuggets of ideas turn into big opportunities. That's where the magic happens. Consumers rarely tell you exactly what or how to make something, but if you ask the right questions, they'll share their pain points which reveal their needs. Interpreting consumer insights is much like lowering the waterline, honing your senses to discern explicit and implicit meaning.

As the line often attributed to Henry Ford goes, "If I listened to my customers, I'd have made a faster horse."

Who Is Your Audience? The Role of Research

So, how do you know who the audience is in the first place?

The C.A.G.E. framework of distance helps to anticipate challenges of doing business between two markets. Then, it is important to target the appropriate audience.

Research provides data on markets' size, demographics, behaviors, and trends to define a desired target. The first goal is to identify a specific market for its size and receptivity to a product or service and its likelihood to convert into a paying customer. The second goal seeks to determine what drives that audience to consume, what factors are most important to them. For instance, are they motivated by price, convenience, quality, or status, to name a few? Culture plays a pivotal role in consumer behavior. From deep-rooted traditions and societal norms to personal values and aspirations, culture influences how consumers perceive and respond to products, services, and brands. Understanding the cultural dimensions that underpin consumer motivations, preferences, and purchasing patterns, marketers gain invaluable insights into the emotional and rational drivers that shape consumer choices.

Research is split into two broad categories. "Secondary research" refers to industry reports, market databases, and governmental statistics which are conducted and compiled by others.[2] These reports provide essential, broad data for honing your target. "Primary research" refers to unique studies you commission or do yourself and includes quantitative studies and qualitative projects such as interviews with customers and competitors. Through visiting your stores and your competitors, observing consumers in their environments, and talking to salespeople, hands-on research provides invaluable information. (The different interpretations of the word "basic" discussed in Chapter 4 on communication were gained from qualitative studies.)

I knew my research on the daily commute habits of Japanese would be valued, not only by my local teams and the product designers in Paris, but all the way up the corporate ladder. Even Bernard Arnault, Chairman of Louis Vuitton Moet Henessey, considered one of the world's richest men according to *Forbes*, with a net wealth of $195 million, visits stores regularly on weekends.[3] I know firsthand, having accompanied him myself on many store visits in Tokyo.

When reviewing all this information, I find it especially helpful to study trends and their *pace* of acceleration. Spotting an emerging behavior creates competitive advantage. Keep an eye on those nascent behavioral buds to determine if they are a passing fad or an emerging shift in values. If you wait until the trend accelerates and becomes widely accepted, it may be too late to influence the long lead time necessary for developing products and services at the forefront of cultural change. Remember the Blackberry? In 2002, Blackberry created a first-mover advantage in the smartphone market, enabling people to do email on the go.[4] As smartphones innovated with touchscreen displays, powerful cameras, and third-party apps, Blackberry lost its top spot in market share. In 2013, hemorrhaging money, Blackberry was sold. In 2020, my 95-year-old father was one of the rare holdouts. When he wanted to order an Uber, Blackberry had nothing to offer him.

While product innovation takes time, marketing communication strategies can be adjusted much more quickly. Consumer insights offer rich information for all marketing and product teams. The purpose of research is not to follow customers' needs; instead, strong brands use research to get inspired, service their customers' needs, and push cultural boundaries.

Revlon in Africa: Blankets as Display Cases

As the marketing director for Revlon in the Europe, Middle East, and Africa (EMEA) region, Jennifer Anton had to ensure the brand ethos came to life consistently across countries from France and Germany to Saudi Arabia and South Africa. Preparing for market visits involved reviewing financial reports and local market research. On the plane, she read the Euromonitor report for cosmetics in the region to focus on consumer trends, distributors, and category performance before meeting with the local teams. But prereads only tell you so much.

Anton knew post-apartheid South Africa was unique and planned to visit both luxury malls and everyday townships to see how the local teams brought the brand to life. She was accompanied by the company's local head of marketing, Ndungu Wanjohi, an experienced marketer who lived in South Africa. They visited a mall where the usually mass-market Revlon brand was professionally sold by beauty experts like luxury brands are in Europe and the U.S. The staff's passion and product knowledge were impressive and inspirational, a new take on selling the brand by engaging South Africa's upper middle class with the product. In the same mall there was the more common option for customers to self-serve at Clicks, a pharmacy similar to Boots or CVS.

Later in the day, Anton and Wanjohi drove through sparse and more industrial terrain to a cash-and-carry-type sales outlet. Outside, along the dusty roads and cluttered street corners, men and women stood outside small metal kiosks or sat behind blankets, displaying products for sale.

This type of distribution was unusual to Anton, and seeing it from her Western point of view as evidence of deep poverty, Anton felt sad.

"Do you see how entrepreneurial our people are?" Wanjohi proudly explained. He helped her to understand that, although informal, these shops played a significant role in what South Africans call "*kasi*-nomics" or township economics, bridging the gap for ordinary people who seek convenience for specific everyday items without having to visit malls or shopping centers.

Anton looked again, and this time, she saw the commercial aspect from his perspective. She focused on understanding the variety of ways business was done, instead of on a way of living she was not used to. This was where business transactions took place in South Africa, not just in the indoor malls and pharmacies she was used to in Europe and North America. If she had only read about it instead of seeing it, she would have never understood.

Anton learned that South Africans of all races had come to new ways of living together post-apartheid in a confluence of living standards, embracing the concept of a "Rainbow Nation," living together under the "ubuntu" belief, which emphasized their interconnectedness. Nelson Mandela's impact, commemorated all around Johannesburg, was a constant reminder of the struggle the country had gone through to get to the place it was then.

On other occasions, Anton met Wanjohi in New York to work with the global brand president on building a new brand identity at global, regional, and country levels. Wanjohi's time in the New York headquarters helped him to experience the heart of the global brand he brought back to South Africa. They enjoyed meals and socializing together in Manhattan and Johannesburg and spoke several times per month by phone when Anton was in the London regional offices.

Back in the South African office for a business review, Anton worked to balance her mission: seeing through the eyes of the locals and achieving the global brand objective. She spent time one-on-one with Wanjohi's team members, reviewing key elements of the brand principles. Together, they toured the manufacturing plant.

Anton and Wanjohi worked collaboratively to develop local marketing plans for the *Live Boldly* global brand campaign, allowing his team to create some unique assets with local talent which still respected global identity rules and aesthetics. They selected a locally recognized model and DJ, Bonang, as the Revlon brand ambassador. A force of nature as an entrepreneur and mother, the celebrity spoke her mind while remaining kind and graceful, someone all of South Africa respected as boldly beautiful. Highlighting Bonang as a Revlon ambassador helped ensure the team maintained the brand's global identity with local influence. They also approved additional multicultural influencers to complement Bonang, showcasing the diversity and breadth of South African society.

Anton feels the strong results from South Africa is largely due to the trusting relationship that she and Wanjohi built together, walking in the streets of Johannesburg and the avenues of New York City: "We were both open to listening and seeing things differently to bring a global brand to life authentically. Local customers felt the brand was theirs, while at the same time part of something bigger."[5]

Anton's experience managing Revlon in Africa highlights the importance of embracing a global mindset for meaningful and actionable consumer insights. Cultivating an open, empathetic and receptive attitude is paramount when trying to understand a foreign audience. Marketers must shed preconceived biases and, instead, immerse themselves in the local cultural fabric. Only through this lens of curiosity and empathy can they unravel the intricate tapestry of values, beliefs, and behaviors that shape consumer decisions. By seeing through the eyes of their target markets, brands can forge deep connections and create lasting relevance at the forefront of cultural trends.

There is another, very important reason to embrace seemingly strange, confusing, or unknown aspects of someone else. Cultivating this quality allows us to effectively market to people different from us. If we could only understand people who behave and speak like we do and who share our values and preferences, we would only be able to market to ourselves. I have built my career marketing to different people across countries and industries while using the same cultural intelligence and marketing tools. Not only have I helped businesses to grow, but I, too, have gained appreciation and understanding, learning to see the prism of meaning—in handbags, sneakers and hotels—in cultures all over the world. (These stories and more infuse my upcoming memoir.)

What Are Consumers' Needs?

> *Listening is not just what happens to the person who listens. The listening is what shapes what the person will tell. The listener creates the speaker. The openness, what you divulge, how you connect, how vulnerable you are.*[6]
>
> Esther Perel

Hanna Andersson in Japan: Communication Design

In the 1990s, Japanese housewives discovered the children's clothing brand Hanna Andersson from friends living in the U.S. Considered specialty items in North America, Hanna Andersson cotton clothing was of equal quality to the expensive and pristine children's clothing available in Japanese department stores, but much less expensive. The brand was sold through direct mail in U.S. dollars, avoiding the middlemen that increased costs in Japan.

But buying directly meant these women had to choose carefully, consider sizing and currency exchanges, complete their orders in English, and send them by fax. Once they overcame the challenges of ordering, these innovative housewives not only found great quality at reasonable prices, but dressed their children in colorful, relaxed styles appearing more modern and international than their peers. Japanese customers ordered the more expensive styles in large quantities, frequently, and never returned anything from overseas.

As Hanna Andersson's VP of International, I was eager to expand this profitable and low-maintenance market. I planned a trip to Japan with the president and founder of the family-run company for us to learn more about our customers and for our customers to learn more about us—half research and half public relations.

One day, about 45 minutes after leaving our Western hotel, a taxi dropped us off at a small concrete building in a suburban park outside Tokyo. We climbed cement stairs into an old wooden room with tatami mats and a low table. We wanted to meet our customers where they lived, but didn't expect this level of intimacy.

"You need to remove your shoes," I whispered to the company founder, Gun Denhart. "And turn them to face the exit."

We entered in our stockings as four Japanese women greeted us. After a few awkward silent moments, one woman bowed.

"*Tokyo ni irrashaimase*," she welcomed us.

I introduced ourselves in Japanese, and the ladies whispered about the foreigner speaking their language. It took a few minutes for them to absorb this rarity.

"We thank you for coming," I said, nodding to underline our gratitude. "We're here to tell you about the Hanna Andersson brand and hear about your experiences."

Denhart explained the company she had founded to offer other families the high-quality cotton clothing she remembered from her native Sweden. She named the company Hanna Andersson after her own grandmother. Then Denhart shifted to her real goal: asking questions to learn from them.

"Why do you order in such quantities? How can we improve your experience?"

The Mama-san began with apologies, uncomfortable sharing negative feedback.

"*Nihongo de doozo*," I offered, welcoming her to speak in Japanese.

We waited patiently. I smiled and nodded, coaxing the truth.

We learned they very much liked the product, which offered a rare alternative in both style and value to the formal, traditional, and expensive children's wear in Japan. However, they faced challenges we had not imagined.

"The clothes are too big," Mama-san admitted. The catalog suggested our customers size up, anticipating shrinkage from American washing. But in 1990s Japan, few people had dryers; they used cool settings or hung clothes outside to dry. Shrinkage was perceived as a product defect. We hadn't realized the foresighted approach to our home market might penalize customers in another culture.

The women were also concerned about styles pulled on over their children's heads, like T-shirts, sweatshirts, and long johns. Japanese are hyper-conscious of their cultural and physical "uniqueness." This is often said in Japan as a point of pride, or as a barrier to protect local industries like rice and beef, highlighting supposed anatomical differences to require specially tailored products. These worldly women were parroting the same refrain as negotiators on big trade topics to say they think they have large heads! They wanted to know the neck diameters, as they thought the way American kids pulled on their pajamas and messed up their hair was uncivilized.

We returned to the U.S. with invaluable insights and proceeded to tailor our catalogs—not our clothes—with Japanese product descriptions, sizing instructions, body measurements, and care instructions. By connecting personally, putting customers at ease, and listening closely, we learned good lessons. It didn't require big budgets or global research firms, just determination to reach out to our customers and listen with empathy to understand their concerns.

Successful global marketing hinges on your ability to connect with diverse audiences. Leveraging a global mindset helps to shed preconceived notions and embrace curiosity to understand foreign customers' needs. Research reports are a helpful place to start as they provide useful consumer behavior analyses. Next, I find meeting, talking with, and yes, observing a target audience the most valuable way to surface personal, social, and cultural factors affecting their brand experience. This works equally well in a foreign country and in your domestic market.

Nike in the U.S.: Seeing Differently, Even at Home

When I was General Manager of U.S. Women's Footwear at Nike in 1998, Mia Hamm was the face of women's soccer in the U.S. (called football in other countries) and the U.S. women's team dominated the global World Cup.[7] A women's national professional basketball league, the WNBA, had been formed two years earlier.[8] But at the Nike headquarters in Beaverton, the approach to designing women's shoes was mired in the commonly used expression, "Shrink it and pink it." (Unbelievable, but true.)

As a former college varsity and junior Olympic volleyball player, I was eager to build the market and help women and young girls expand their own opportunities. I managed a team of product line marketers dedicated to individual women's sport categories where we did business, and a team of salespeople dedicated to selling only women's shoes to expand distribution. Like many female athletes, I too had undergone knee surgery. Women have two to eight times as many ACL surgeries as men.[9] What was the reason for this? Was there a way for us to transform this problem into an opportunity? It turns out women's wider hips put greater stress on the external side of their knees. This reality even had a name: the Q angle.[10] Neither women's shoes nor the traditional jump training for sports were designed with female athletes in mind. Women's shoes used men's lasts, meaning the shoes were designed around men's foot shapes, rather than taking into consideration the anatomical needs of women. Our team designed a new insole specifically to address a woman's different weight pressure on her foot.

Eager to test the shoe, I set up a focus group one afternoon with a high school basketball team after practice.

"Tell me about the shoes you like to wear, on and off the court," I said.

"Nike is the best for basketball, so we always wear them on the court," one player responded.

"On the court?" I probed.

"Yeah," she continued. "Nike doesn't have good colors, so we wear Adidas during the day."

Adidas, the enemy, I thought. The shoe designer who accompanied me slumped in his seat.

I pulled out our new shoe, designed from the inside out with women in mind. I showed it to them the same way we looked at shoes at Nike headquarters: horizontally. Like the shoe walls in athletic shoe stores. Like the fast car posters adorning the offices of many shoe designers, who were mostly men.

"May I see it?" asked an athlete, wishing to hold it herself.

She stood up and placed the shoe on the floor next to her foot, looking at the design from the top down, not from the side.

At that moment, I realized we were looking at shoe designs all wrong. These women looked at shoes like they were shopping in department stores, top down, with shoes placed on round tables, often in pairs. I would have never thought to ask, "How do you look at shoes, from the side or from the top?" We have to work twice as hard to remain open to things we don't know and things we don't know we don't know. Familiarity can blind us from recognizing our own assumptions.

Once you identify your target audience and understand their concerns, it's up to you to decide how to provide value in a new market. This is where marketers thrive. You get to design new ways of creating value that meet or exceed your customer's needs.

Back behind the berm on the Nike campus, we created a retail marketing campaign integrating our brand's athletic performance with our audience's needs, with the slogan "Engineered for Female Athletes."

How to Provide Customer Value? The Three-Form Model

The notion of competitive differentiation is to create unique value versus competitors, either by finding a new customer or offering something new.

Expanding globally provides access to new markets. You determine if your offerings meet their needs or consider how to adjust them.

- Will you keep your product or service the same or adapt it?
- How will you sell your products and services, through the same channels or new distribution?
- How does your price compare with new competition in a different market?
- How will you reach your audience and communicate value to them?
- Does the customer require additional information?

All of these questions offer value-creation playrooms for global marketers. Throughout this book, we explore how companies in various industries in different countries answer these very questions.

I find it useful to focus customer value on three different forms of needs: functional value, emotional value, and monetary value. You need at least one to create unique customer value, but you can deliver on more than one. See Figure 5.1 for a model of these three forms of customer value.

The Louis Vuitton cell phone pocket offered functional value to accompany the emotional value of the luxury brand. Revlon offered its South African customers functional value through multiple points of distribution and emotional value from localized marketing campaigns. Hanna Andersson provided its customers with monetary value by offering quality children's clothing at a lower price than domestic brands. Nike's women's basketball shoes were finally designed to add emotional value to the functional value of the shoe's components.

Figure 5.1 Customer Value Model

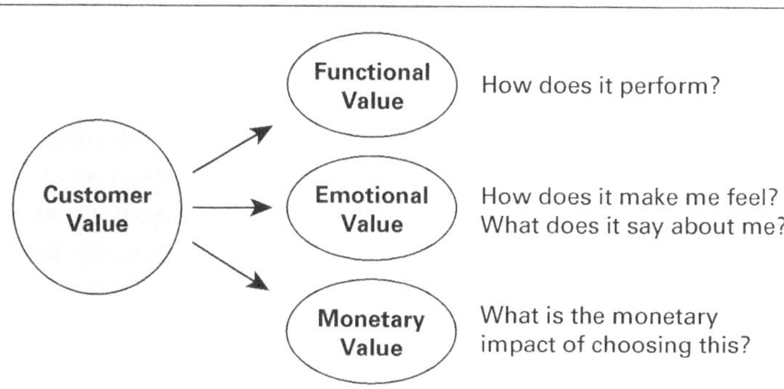

Goldman Sachs in Japan: Turning Challenges into Opportunities

The Tokyo skyline glimmered in the fading light as Lisa Shalett gazed out of her new office window. In 2000, she had just arrived in Japan with an important task: to take the Goldman Sachs' Japanese Shares business to the next level. She was responsible for overseeing sales and trading related to the Japanese market across all regions as the co-head of the global business. But there was a significant challenge—these clients didn't know her, and in a relationship and trust-based business, it was very important that they did. Another point of note: She was the first woman to lead this business, and a foreign woman at that. All the clients were Japanese men. How would she build and lead the key relationships necessary for the business to grow?

Outside of the markets, many people in Japan had never heard of Goldman Sachs. That was unusual for such a powerful global firm. When calling to make appointments for clients wanting to meet with the management of the companies they invested in, the reception desk would ask, "Goldman Fax? We don't need a fax machine." Or worse, "Goldman Sex?" That was an amusing reminder that despite its global stature, Goldman Sachs was not as well-known as the local household names: Nomura, Daiwa, and others.

She thought back to the rich history of Goldman Sachs, founded by German immigrant Marcus Goldman in a Manhattan basement office in 1869. Over a century of providing invaluable financial tools and resources had led the company to expand into over sixty cities worldwide. But here in Japan, that legacy meant little in the face of established domestic giants like Nomura Securities. Goldman had its work cut out for it in a country of relationships when potential corporate clients might not know the name.

Shalett had to figure out how to brand herself, in addition to the firm. As she strategized, a realization dawned on her—for these Japanese clients, she, as a foreigner, represented this foreign brand. Moreover, as a woman in a traditionally male-dominated industry, the hurdle was particularly high.

"I had to work hard to develop relationships and build trust with my clients, as well as with my own team," Shalett reflected. "Fortunately, I arrived with a lot of good relationships with Goldman colleagues in Tokyo. We had worked together across time zones when I had been in New York. Yet, it was very much a drinking culture, and as a foreign woman, I was not invited along for the late-night drinking that creates strong bonds."[11]

Undeterred, she leveraged the very aspect that created distance: curiosity—her interest in them and theirs in her. She dubbed it, "the talking dog effect." It was unusual to meet with a Japanese-speaking foreign woman—and that made getting the first meeting pretty easy. What really mattered, she realized, was if she could get a second meeting! She and the team worked hard to prepare and impress, and focused on that second meeting, when the real relationship-building could start. The driving question in Shalett's mind was: "What could Goldman Sachs uniquely bring that would enable me and my team to differentiate ourselves, and help our clients do their job well?" She needed to understand not just the portfolio managers, analysts and traders, but also how their firms competed versus their peers, and their specific operational needs.

She developed a set of probing questions and listened carefully to their responses:

- What is important to my customers?
- What defines success for them?
- How do I make resources available to them when they need them?
- Are there any unique resources I can bring?

As she delved deeper, Shalett realized that clients sometimes didn't know what they needed or how she might provide new value. She had to think about needs they were not even asking for.

Shalett says, "I realized I needed to identify the things they don't even know we can do for them that could be very, very helpful."

This insight led her to expand her inquiry:

- What are my customers already getting that we could do better, and how?
- What might they still need that they don't have?

"By virtue of having so many discussions with many clients, you start to 'hear' the needs they're not articulating," she explained. "And those can be the source of great ideas!"

As she engaged with clients, Shalett had an epiphany: As part of Goldman Sachs, she was sitting on a treasure trove of global resources and information that the Japanese clients were not able to access. This became Goldman's competitive advantage.

"We differentiated ourselves by tapping into Goldman's global insights, which the domestic brokers did not have," Shalett said. "We followed trends in other markets to create a uniquely global perspective." She leveraged the interconnected global aspects of her role—and the valuable differentiated ideas and insights to which she could give clients access—to transform challenges into opportunities. In addition, Goldman, as a global powerhouse, could provide access to markets, capital, and talent in ways that other firms could not. Her team became more valuable, and Goldman Sachs increased its presence, impact, and market share.

Understanding customers for any product or service means understanding their needs. Sometimes, people may not even know what those are. Putting yourself in their shoes helps to understand their needs, spoken and unspoken, and to imagine how your company can provide a unique and differentiated service that delivers against them.

Now, more than ever, the customer is global. Understanding a customer doesn't only mean your local customer down the street; a customer is aware of the global stage, and brands can leverage their access to global data and knowledge for their customers.

To be different, one must think different. Shalett turned a seeming deficit into her competitive advantage. Her clients came to rely on her team's unique access, information, and reliability. As Shalett built strong relationships with her clients, they developed trust in the Goldman Sachs brand.

Understanding customers creates the opportunity to differentiate your brand. Every customer interaction creates opportunities to understand their needs and create relevance. Relevance leads to increased trust. And as we've discussed in previous chapters, brands are about trust.

By 2010, Lisa Shalett had become the Global Head of Brand Marketing and Digital Strategy at Goldman Sachs. Early in her tenure in this role, the company found itself in a brand crisis. There may have been no one better suited to recreate corporate trust than someone who, as a young associate working in a challenging market, built trust one customer need, and one relationship, at a time.

Interview Insight: Starwood

Thinking Different in China

In the 1980s, 80 per cent of China's population lived in the countryside. Local managers visiting Beijing could choose between the Beijing Jianguo Hotel or the China World Hotel, but major international hotel brands were absent.[12] It wasn't until 1985 that the Great Wall Sheraton Hotel Beijing, one of the first major Western hotels in China, opened.[13]

Economic reforms initiated by Deng Xiaoping in 1978 spurred an influx of foreign investment and international tourism. Over the next decade and a half, China developed high-speed rail networks connecting small towns, which quickly became burgeoning urban centers. By 2011, over half of China's population resided in cities, driving substantial investments in infrastructure, including airports, housing, and hotels.[14]

Starwood Hotels, Sheraton's parent company (now owned by Marriott International), saw China's wealth creation as a major growth opportunity. Sheraton was among the first Western brands to manage reservations directly in China. By 2010, Starwood was investing 35–40 per cent of its global growth in China, opening more hotels there than its competitors Hyatt, Marriott, and Hilton combined.

The enormity of the opportunity in China was not lost on Frits van Paasschen, Starwood's President and CEO, as he sat in a company boardroom in Connecticut. Having first visited China in the 1980s, he witnessed firsthand the country's rapid transformation. He knew that the region was an important part of the company's growth, and yet he also knew that no one in that boardroom with him spoke Chinese; most had not even visited China. The volume of internal and outbound travel in China was growing. Why couldn't China be the largest market for Starwood? Why stop at only 40 per cent?

Van Paasschen had met the Sheraton executives who had worked so diligently to grow the Chinese business. The company had a head start over its competitors on introducing Chinese customers to the Starwood brand, making it uniquely positioned to transform those local customers into loyal travelers building its business in other regions. The upside was huge—but so was the challenge for Van Paasschen's American-based team.

He was no stranger to working with international teams. He had spent much of his career at Nike as the general manager of the Europe, Middle East, and Africa regions. He had seen the conflict and skepticism that can arise when Americans from corporate headquarters try to manage an important region without cultural context. He knew that it was difficult for someone in Beaverton to know how a shoe would sell in Milan.

Van Paasschen felt that in order to really understand a country, you have to live there long enough to buy groceries. He thought they might need to spend a full year in China. Recognizing that impossibility, van Paasschen proposed an alternative solution: relocate the entire executive team to China for a month.

He knew the idea wouldn't be popular with the team, but he felt it was very important to their success in the region. The team eventually embraced the idea, recognizing its potential to enhance their market understanding and business success.

Starwood Loyalty Program: Support Local Teams

One of van Paasschen's early initiatives was to revitalize the Starwood Preferred Guest (SPG) loyalty program in China, which had only 100,000 members compared to 5 million globally. Upon asking why the enrollment was so low, his Asian team explained that to be successful, they needed the rewards program translated into Chinese. They also wanted to train their Chinese associates how to market a loyalty program, a novel concept in the market.

"Why don't you have that already?" van Paasschen asked.

"It's never been approved," came the response, "because they (at headquarters) couldn't oversee the brand consistency of the materials in Chinese."

Van Paasschen quickly approved the translation and set a goal to grow the SPG program from 100,000 to 1 million.

"It completely changed the dynamic with the regional team," van Paasschen says. "For the first time, the regional team recognized they could make requests and corporate would listen." After agreeing to their requests, he added, it became much easier to get the regional team to support corporate key performance indicators (KPIs).

"I did not go to China to oversee what the regional team was doing," said van Paasschen. "My goal was to make sure that they were getting the support from corporate they needed in order to grow the business."[15]

Lobby Design: Balance Local and Global Taste

During their stay, van Paasschen and his team also discovered a significant gap in Chinese and Western hotel lobby design preferences. Designs that appeared outdated from their Connecticut headquarters resonated well with Chinese guests.

"We had to ask ourselves, what's the deeper context in North America?" said van Paasschen. "In the West, the big lobby is reminiscent of these massive internal terrarium hotels from the 1970s and 80s and hadn't aged well." But in China, luxury hotels were a relatively new concept—the market was new and young and impressed by grandeur. Nothing was old enough to be outdated.

When van Paasschen took his board of directors to tour dozens of properties—both Starwood and competitive brands—they realized hotel design was a crucial differentiator, despite being capital-intensive and the challenge of creating relevant and lasting style. Walking together through properties inspired innovative design solutions combining local signifiers of grandeur with European elegance. This experience underscored the importance of hands-on knowledge to balance local preferences with global trends.

"As our Head of China explained to me, 'If I was a chef moving to Fiji, I have to consider how best to fillet a fish. The cheek of the fish might be the best part for my Chinese guests, but Western travelers want nothing to do with a fish head.' Global brands must balance conflicting preferences."

Mobile Booking: Globalize Local Learnings

As early as 2010, the Starwood executives noticed China's faster pace of digitalization as Chinese travelers began booking hotel rooms from their phones.

"We didn't see that anywhere else yet," he said. "This was a great opportunity to be a step or two ahead of our competitors." To accelerate this trend, Starwood invested in the infrastructure needed to enable mobile booking worldwide.

"Lo and behold, 18 months later, mobile booking became a global phenomenon. By helping our Chinese team stay a step ahead locally, we were ahead of the game globally. We looked like geniuses." Leveraging the local initiative positioned Starwood ahead of its competitors worldwide.

For Frits, this was a lesson in how learning from one global market can create global relevance. In a horizontal learning organization, ideas from one market can benefit global execution. With the increasing pace of innovation across industries, traditional top-down management is less effective to stay ahead of market changes.

Customer Service: Local versus Global Standards

Starwood's approach to standardizing the guest check-in process illustrates the challenge of balancing local feedback with enforcing global standards.

Starwood's executive team felt global standard operating procedures were necessary. The check-in process is an important first impression for a hotel brand, and repeated millions of times all over the world. The process can have 18 steps, so building standards and guidelines ensures consistency and efficiency. Allowing varied customer check-in protocol at each Starwood hotel weakens the global Starwood brand experience. At the same time, treating every guest exactly the same regardless of cultural norms ignores customer service needs, which also hurts the brand experience.

Should a guest be addressed by their first name or a more formal "Mr." or "Mrs." title? Many languages other than English have a formal and informal version of "you." In Germany, a formal "you" is the convention, so

German guests would tend to expect that level of formality. In Northern Europe a formal "you" is rarely used, so Northern European guests may find it odd if addressed that way. When should one be used over another, and how should this differ by Starwood's many individual hotel brands? An avant-garde brand like the W hotels may want to address guests less formally than a brand like St. Regis, a more traditional luxury brand.

These decisions required a careful balance between a hotel brand's essence, global traveler expectations, and local customs. Starwood developed a hybrid solution in China—one script and set of protocols associated with checking in a Western traveler and another for checking in a guest with a Chinese name.

"There are many clever solutions," said van Paasschen. "But they only emerge when you solve the problem sitting on the same side of the table as your local team.

As seen with examples from Nike, Louis Vuitton, Revlon, and others, delivering global brand value begins with delivering local customer value. Over three chapters, this section revealed how cultural intelligence helps navigate and comprehend the many layers of culture and communication. Whether it's understanding the needs of luxury consumers in Japan, the purchasing patterns of South Africans, or the traveler preferences in China, success stems from connecting with your customers. Research provides a foundation, but the magic lies in listening deeply to observe and uncover insights. This doesn't require massive funds, just the curiosity and humility to see through their eyes and discover what may be hiding in plain sight. Next, we turn to a new section that explores how businesses manage the complexity of honoring global brand standards while adapting their marketing across cultures.

Summary

- **Who is your audience?** Use research to identify the size and receptivity of a group of consumers most likely to buy your product or service.
- **What are consumers' needs?** Understand consumer behaviors and values by observing and talking with consumers and salespeople and visiting stores. Magic happens when you identify unmet needs, which are often cultural in nature.
- **How to provide value?** Customer value can be broken into three categories: functional value, emotional value, and monetary value.

The Global Digest

Chapter 5 Takeaways

1. **Don't just shrink it and pink it:** Assumptions about consumer preferences can blind you to their actual needs. Leverage a global mindset to challenge preconceptions and let consumers guide your understanding, even in your home market.
2. **The power of personal insights:** Quantitative data provides a broad picture, but qualitative insights from personal interactions reveal the nuances that drive consumer preference.
3. **The power of presence from Beaverton to Beijing:** To truly understand a market, especially a foreign one, you need to immerse yourself in it. Even a short, focused visit can yield transformative insights.
4. **Shift your perspective:** How consumers use your product can be vastly different from how you design or display it. Observe their natural behaviors to gain insights.
5. **Listening creates the speaker:** The way you listen shapes what consumers will say. Cultivate openness, empathy, and vulnerability to uncover deep insights.
6. **Shrinkage, shirts, and cultural sensitivity:** Cultural nuances, like laundry practices or perceptions of anatomy, can significantly impact product acceptance. Tailor your approach, not just your product.
7. **The blanket perspective:** Train yourself to see opportunities and resilience even in challenging environments. It's not just what you see, but how you interpret it.
8. **The Q-angle of innovation:** Understanding unique consumer needs (like women athletes' knee issues) can lead to innovative product designs and market differentiation.
9. **The horizontal learning organization:** Local innovations, like mobile booking in China, can foreshadow global trends. Foster a culture where insights flow freely across markets.
10. **The balancing act:** Effective global branding balances consistent global standards with cultural sensitivity. Collaborate with local teams to find hybrid solutions that respect both.

References

1 WWD Staff (2023) Japanese Louis Vuitton Sales Soar, *Women's Wear Daily*, January 22. wwd.com/feature/japanese-louis-vuitton-sales-soar-758160-1881007/ (archived at https://perma.cc/7SRJ-NB24)

2 Entrepreneur Staff. Market Research. Entrepreneur. www.entrepreneur.com/encyclopedia/market-research (archived at https://perma.cc/PQA3-V7XM)

3 L. Alderman and V. Friedman (2023) Bernard Arnault Built a Luxury Empire on 'Desirability.' Who Will Inherit It?, *The New York Times*, September 14. www.nytimes.com/2023/09/14/business/bernard-arnault-lvmh-family-succession.html?smid=url-share (archived at https://perma.cc/66R7-A2XE)

4 C. McEvoy (2023) BlackBerry: The Rise and Fall of the Famous Smartphone and Its Inventors, Biography, May 9. www.biography.com/movies-tv/a43840015/true-story-of-blackberry-ceos-mike-lazaridis-and-jim-balsillie (archived at https://perma.cc/GM9V-E4XA)

5 J. Anton (2024) Interviewed by Katherine Melchior Ray, October 18, email

6 E. Perel (2024) Email, December 13

7 L. M. Purtell and L. Olszowy (2020) The 1999 U.S. Women's National Team: Instant Icons, Lasting Legends, ESPN, July 4. www.espn.com/soccer/story/_/id/37573533/instant-icons-lasting-legends (archived at https://perma.cc/S4SB-YX3D)

8 WNBA Staff (2024) History, WNBA. www.wnba.com/history (archived at https://perma.cc/S4SB-zzzz)

9 Northwestern Medicine Staff (2023) Why Women Have More ACL Injuries Than Men: Gender Disparity in ACL Injuries, Northwestern Medicine, November. www.nm.org/healthbeat/healthy-tips/Why-Women-Have-More-ACL-Injuries-Than-Men (archived at https://perma.cc/SQW2-WB24)

10 R. Sharma, V. Vaibhav, R. Meshram, B. Singh, and G. Khorwal (2023) A Systematic Review on Quadriceps Angle in Relation to Knee Abnormalities, *Cureus*, January 29, 15(1), e34355. www.cureus.com/articles/128069-a-systematic-review-on-quadriceps-angle-in-relation-to-knee-abnormalities#!/ (archived at https://perma.cc/RS63-TEKE)

11 L. Shalett (2024) Interviewed by Katherine Melchior Ray, May 28, Zoom

12 CGTN Travel Staff (2018) Reform and Opening Up: A Brief History of China's Hospitality Industry, *CGTN*, December 15. news.cgtn.com/news/3d3d514d35497a4d31457a6333566d54/share_p.html (archived at https://perma.cc/9QE6-JYRS)

13 CGTN Travel Staff (2018) Reform and Opening Up: A Brief History of China's Hospitality Industry, *CGTN*, December 15. news.cgtn.com/news/3d3d514d35497a4d31457a6333566d54/share_p.html (archived at https://perma.cc/L62N-9PAY); F. van Paasschen (2024) Interviewed by Katherine Melchior Ray, April 10, GoogleMeet

14 CGTN Travel Staff (2018) Reform and Opening Up: A Brief History of China's Hospitality Industry, *CGTN*, December 15. news.cgtn.com/news/3d3d514d35497a4d31457a6333566d54/share_p.html (archived at https://perma.cc/ZC9N-K63M); F. van Paasschen (2024) Interviewed by Katherine Melchior Ray, April 10, GoogleMeet; United Nations Population Division (2018) Urban Population (% of total population): China, World Bank Group. data.worldbank.org/indicator/SP.URB.TOTL.IN.ZS?locations=CN (archived at https://perma.cc/T4H3-KRBU); S. Horwitz (1985) Sheraton to Run Hotel in Beijing, *The Washington Post*, March 18. www.washingtonpost.com/archive/business/1985/03/19/sheraton-to-run-hotel-in-beijing/8d353460-2ea0-4da5-80aa-739becf0b9d9/ (archived at https://perma.cc/6ZDS-VJPR)

15 F. van Paasschen (2024) Interviewed by Katherine Melchior Ray, April 10, GoogleMeet

PART THREE
Creating Value across Cultures

Brand Global, Adapt Local: Freedom within a Framework

This key concept crystalizes the discipline and creativity required to create value across cultures. The idea goes beyond the strict guardrails protecting brand values. For instance, brands like Hermès which pride themselves on craftsmanship will not offer something of poor quality, and brands that stand for happiness, like Coca-Cola, don't want to sell products that make people sad.

At KitKat, for example, the global team sets worldwide standards for the shape of the chocolate, the balance between chocolate and cookie wafer, and KitKat's iconography on the packaging. Beyond that, local country teams are encouraged to meet the market's needs by playing with flavor, color, and format.

"The two- or four-finger bar is KitKat's iconic shape. You can't touch that!" explains Carlota Casellas, KitKat's Business Executive Officer Confectionery, Malaysia and Singapore.[2] In contrast, she mentions OREO, which is found in various forms such as bits, chunks, and liquids worldwide. Casellas has a point: In addition to the classic cookie, OREOs are chopped into ice cream, blended into cheesecakes, and even made into coffee products with wild abandon.

Companies have their own standards for what is sacred and what is customizable. This differs greatly across industries. Think of cars. Any tourist who has tried to cross a street in London has learned to look left versus right, as cars move along the left side of the streets. Cars are sold with steering wheels on the right side of cars in the U.K., unlike in most other countries.

Fashion, hospitality, finance, and technology all work hard to maintain brand standards globally while adapting their products and services to meet customers' cultural needs. Food is one of the best examples of localization.

Taste Is King, but Brand Is Bloodline

"Food is local," explains Casellas. "You can't apply the same rules for everyone."

Asian customers, accustomed to a diet with coconut milk, like sweeter milk chocolate with 50–60 per cent cocoa, whereas Western Europeans prefer the bitter, darker chocolate with approximately 75–90 per cent cocoa. The French, in particular, appreciate the taste and explanations of premium ingredients and buy more blocks and tablets for baking desserts at home. The English, like North Americans, prefer lighter and sweeter chocolate. In Asia, Japanese consumers are interested in the ingredients' functional benefits and want a minimum of 72 per cent cocoa. As preferences differ around the world, KitKat seeks to adapt its products.

"Taste is King," Casellas insists. "You need to create the best recipe for your local market. Nobody buys chocolate because it's cheap. They buy it because they love it." She would know, having been the KitKat brand manager at Nestlé's Swiss headquarters for four years before moving to Southeast Asia. As marketers, their goal is to recognize those regional desires and create chocolate offerings to satisfy them.

The team scours market reports every year, looking for first-mover advantage for growing trends. After reviewing a general report, they often commission tailored research on a topic or key region with different agencies like Mintel and Flavor House.

Since the Covid-19 pandemic, people are more concerned about what they're eating and how food contributes to their well-being physically and emotionally, so the local KitKat team tested less sugar to create darker and healthier chocolate options.

"Dark chocolate itself plays a role," Casellas explains. "The higher per cent of cocoa, the richer in antioxidants." (Some consumers may not want the cocoa content too high, so they call it "Dark Milk.")

Wellness was not only a market trend but an important brand value. KitKat's parent company, Nestlé, believes strongly in its mission to enhance quality of life and contribute to a healthier future through foods and drinks[3] among its 200 different brands around the world.[4] There is great market growth opportunity when a trend moves squarely in the direction of a brand's values, so brands work to leverage the momentum of that customer demand.

While its parent brand promotes health and wellbeing, the KitKat brand itself is playful, seeking to create uplifting moments like its brand tagline, "Have a break, have a KitKat."

"KitKat is a brand with heart," says Casellas. "We want to bring a smile to your break." The light-hearted brand looks for new, innovative ways to create small, uplifting moments. Because the brand originated in the U.K., its dry English humor does not always translate globally, so it encourages local teams to adapt both product and marketing.

Casellas concludes: "As a brand, we have enormous opportunity to localize our products, as long as we maintain global brand standards."

Sourcing Opportunity: From Global Shortage to Local Asset

While the taste for chocolate is local, its sourcing is global. Seventy-five per cent of KitKat's cocoa comes from farmers in Ghana. During the Covid-19 pandemic, chocolate became an even more important comfort food and demand grew exponentially.[5] The category growth put more pressure on an already fragile supply chain dealing with climate-change-related droughts in Africa. Limited resources and unfavorable conditions resulted in many farmers being unable to replant, causing cocoa production to decline just as global demand was rising. As a result, cocoa has become a scarce commodity.

In light of the global cocoa shortage, the KitKat Malaysia team recognized the need to explore alternative sourcing options and sought ways to diversify and localize their ingredients supply chain. What other sourcing options were available? Within Malaysia itself, the island of Borneo offered fertile, volcanic soil, but farmers had shifted much of their crop to palm oil years ago. Cocoa farming, however, increases a forest's biodiversity and allows more farmers to earn income with small plots. To support better and more sustainable farming practices, the beans are sourced through the Nestlé Borneo Cocoa Initiative (NBCI), launched in September 2023. NBCI is a strategic partnership between Nestlé Malaysia and the Malaysian Cocoa Board (MCB) to expand the company's Farmer Connect program to East Malaysia.

"Malaysian chocolate has a really good taste," assures Casellas. "The volcanic soil makes it rich and fruity. To highlight the flavor and country of origin, we decided to use a higher percentage of cocoa in dark chocolate. So the two trends came together—the desire for healthier chocolate and the newly sourced Borneo dark chocolate."

They leveraged the package design to promote the two themes: Two bright, iconic rainforest figures peek out from either side of the must-have red KitKat logo—a large, yellow-feathered hornbill bird and a red rafflesia flower—a vivid image sure to bring a smile to your face. Eighteen months later, with a strong, fruity flavor made exclusively from local cocoa beans, KitKat Dark Borneo 52% was born, calling attention to the exact percentage of cocoa inside—just enough dark chocolate taste and health benefits for the sweet-loving Malaysian market.

The chocolate was a hit in numerous ways, positively impacting many key performance indicators (KPIs). Within four weeks of its launch, Dark Borneo sold out at many retailers and elevated KitKat's market share, the most important data point for Casellas.

The chocolate not only tasted great, but grew sales with local ingredients and domestic production. The Malaysian rainforest chocolate elevated the corporate profile of KitKat and Nestlé, which, in turn, attracted new opinion leaders and influencers for collaborations. The Nestlé Malaysia team adeptly combined new taste preferences with sourcing concerns into a great-tasting and sustainably consumable chocolate.

Seasonal Opportunity: Good Luck with Dragon Scales

It was not the first time that the team spun cocoa dust into gold. Earlier the same year, Nestlé Malaysia released the limited-edition KitKat® Golden Dragon to coincide with the Chinese New Year. The colorful package with a dramatic dragon in red and gold stood out on store shelves. The year of the dragon is the most auspicious year in the Chinese lunar calendar, as the mystical animal is revered as a symbol of power, strength, and good luck in Chinese mythology. The KitKat fingers featured patterns of dragon scales with the world's first blending of chocolate marbling and fading technology, or "farbling." The visually striking aesthetics of KitKat Golden Dragon captured the spirit of the dragon, a symbol associated with power, luck, and prosperity in Chinese culture, making it the perfect treat for the festive season. The colorful gold and red chocolate bar sold out within three weeks, compared to the regular ten-week sales cycle.

"You can elevate your brand with the right product at the right time," says Casellas.

Chinese New Year is an important holiday that lands in January or February, when people travel and socialize among family, and chocolate plays a role in that seasonal excitement. With the socializing and gift-giving every Chinese New Year, chocolate sales soar, so Casellas hosts an ideation session with her team specifically on seasonal opportunities. Each year they invent a new, limited-edition flavor designed to create excitement at retail. To celebrate the majesty and power of the year of the dragon, they toyed with creating something really innovative.

"It needed to be special, eye-catching, so people would buy it as a status gift to express, 'You're special to me.'"

Could they blend two flavors and colors to appear like dragon skin? They shared the bold idea with their research and development team, wondering if it might be too technical. After weeks of trial and error, the new "farbling" method was born.

The packaging featured a dancing dragon in powerful and auspicious gold and red—two colors symbolizing good luck, good fortune, happiness, and prosperity in Chinese culture—creating a compelling narrative of a candy bar offering a prosperous new year. Certainly, this was the case for the Nestlé team that year.

According to the Chinese proverb, as the dragon soars high, may your dreams and aspirations reach new heights.

Gong Xi Fa Cai! Xīn Nián Kuài Lè! (Happy New Year!)

What Is Innovation? Lessons from a Chocolate Bar

The KitKat stories offer excellent illustrations of how a brand creates localized value which, in turn, builds the brand's global value. Local teams had to first understand what the brand was about—a joyful break in the day that makes people smile—and honor the brand's framework: the brand logo, the chocolate bar shape, and its chocolate-to-wafer ratio. Beyond that, local teams were encouraged to innovate product and marketing ideas for local relevance, recognition, and value.

How did the teams identify creative ideas and transform them into concrete value?

How do you foster innovation?

At its core, innovation creates new value, which, as explained in Chapter 5, can be divided into three types: functional, emotional, and monetary. In global marketing, value creation includes improving existing offerings, developing new products or services, and adapting pricing, distribution, and ways of communicating value with diverse audiences. For global brands, this requires a delicate balance between maintaining a consistent brand image and adapting to local markets. The art of managing this equilibrium is sometimes referred to as "glocalization."

Innovation requires inspiring creativity and accepting failure. If teams are afraid to fail, they will fear taking risks, so leaders need to nurture a culture of experimentation. Strong and effective global brands manage that freedom through encouragement and restraint. They drive their teams to think outside the box, push the envelope, and invent the future, but their first and most sacred duty is to protect the brand by honoring its codes. Companies foster innovation by actively pursuing knowledge and then acting upon it. They share market trends and corporate information across divisions, which is how Nestlé solved the global sourcing challenge locally. They drive their teams to immerse themselves in local culture, looking for opportunities to leverage changing tastes, customs, and seasonal celebrations. Innovation sessions on culturally relevant themes encourage out-of-the-box creativity.

Innovation speaks louder than ads. Product-led innovation refers to creating or refining new products, including adapting the form, features, and functions. Louis Vuitton was built around the trunk, 501® Jeans put Levi's on the map, the Moon Shoe launched Nike, the iPod relaunched Apple. Iconic products rose to fame through game-changing innovation: monogrammed air-tight cases, copper rivets, waffle soles, mobile music. Their superior quality and unique solutions became their best marketing tools. Product-led marketing sells the use, the function, the fit, the experience, and the style for different people from diverse cultures over time. The more the brands reincorporate their product innovation stories, the richer the brand narratives become.

Another way companies innovate is by leveraging best practices across industries. High-volume fashion retailers like Uniqlo adapted the self-serve checkout from grocery stores to improve efficiency and customer satisfaction. Apple learned from luxury retailers to transform the purchase experience of technology into a beautiful, sensorial, and emotionally rewarding experience with vast, airy retail showrooms and highly trained staff, increasing sales and brand perception. Tesla took that idea further by placing car showrooms in high-end shopping malls. Sephora's Beauty Insider program was inspired by the loyalty programs of airlines and credit card companies, offering tiered rewards and exclusive perks, increasing average spend and customer retention. In the next chapter, we explore how companies adapt services across cultures.

The best kind of innovation creates ongoing value. For instance, being first to enter a market allows a company to establish its brand as the pioneer and leader in its industry. Such first-mover advantage means the brand can set industry standards and capture a large market share, creating barriers to entry for its competitors.

Some of the world's best brands have learned the secret to balancing their global brand standards while adapting products locally. They've learned that what succeeds in one country may not work somewhere else, and therefore adapt their products, and how they sell them, more than people realize. Let's take a look.

Lessons from Top Brands

Coca-Cola: It's the Real Thing

In 2023, the Coca-Cola brand value eclipsed $100 billion,[6] nearly 140 years since pharmacist John Pemberton created a soda in Atlanta, Georgia,[7] combining extracts from the coca plant and the cola nut.[8] Today, all over the world people recognize Coke's iconic red-and-white logo as they enjoy the refreshing carbonated drink from cans, bottles, and soda fountains. They think they're drinking the same thing, but that's not always the case.

I prefer Mexican Coke to American Coke, if I can find it. In many parts of California, I can. I'm not alone. The popularity of Coke *hecho en México* has risen in recent years and can now be found beyond Mexican restaurants and bodegas, even in certain Costco mass-market stores in the U.S.[9] People who prefer Mexican Coke say it tastes better, which we know is subjective. Is there really a difference? Mexican Coke uses local cane sugar while the Coke sold across the northern border uses high-fructose corn syrup. They're both made from the same crop, but high-fructose corn syrup is, as its name suggests, higher in fructose and therefore sweeter. Also, Mexican Coke is sold in the old-fashioned glass bottles, which people feel improves the taste and carbonation.[10] I agree.

Coca-Cola is ranked the world's 10th most valuable brand due to its consistent brand execution and adaptation to culture.[11] Think about that classic red-and-white logo—wherever you find it, you know what you'll get, sugar content aside. Coca-Cola's core product, the classic Coca-Cola drink, maintains a relatively consistent taste and branding worldwide, ensuring that consumers recognize and trust the brand no matter where they are. The brand promotes universal themes such as happiness, sharing, and togetherness in its marketing campaigns to resonate across cultures.

Coke also creates new products to meet local customers' needs. Recent highlights include Cappy juices in Europe, Africa, and the Middle East, and the Authentic Tea House lineup of unsweetened, cold-brewed teas in China.[12] But no other innovation at Coca-Cola has been as successful as canned coffee in Japan.

Takako sighed as she stretched her arms above her head, grateful for a brief respite from her computer screen. Knowing what she needed to power through the rest of her workday, she gathered a few coins from her desk drawer and walked over to the office vending machines.

Scanning the rows of colorful cans and bottles, she zeroed in on the Georgia Coffee options. Takako usually choses the standard milk coffee blend, but today she hesitated. The company had recently introduced new varieties with different sweetness levels.

"Hmm, should I do the black coffee option for its deliciously strong flavor?" she mused, tapping her chin. "Or maybe I need that extra sweetness kick today..."

Takako decided to try the new reduced-sugar blend—a compromise between her usual choice and a healthier option. Cracking open the can, Takako sipped the familiar coffee taste, followed by a smooth, slightly sweet flavor that was just right—not too sugary, but with enough sweetness to take the edge off the afternoon slump.

Once again, Japan offers rich inspiration for innovation. Canned coffee is one of the many unique concoctions invented by Coca-Cola's Japanese division, like fiber-fortified Coke and water that helps you sleep. Coca-Cola's Georgia Coffee, named after the company's home state, has become an integral part of not only Takako's work routine, but that of millions of other Japanese office workers, becoming the world's highest-grossing ready-to-drink (RTD) coffee product since its launch in 1975.[13]

Though Japan is traditionally associated with tea, canned coffee is a notable Japanese innovation. It was first created by UCC Ueshima Coffee Company in Japan in 1969; not long after, Coca-Cola recognized the growing demand for convenient, on-the-go coffee among Japan's busy workforce. They tailored their product to meet this need, offering a quick caffeine boost in an easily accessible format. With nearly a million vending machines already placed across Japan, Coca-Cola leveraged its ready-made distribution to get its RTD product into consumers' hands quickly and efficiently. While sweet, milky coffee blends were initially popular, Coca-Cola has consistently innovated by adjusting sugar content to match changing consumer preferences and exploring alternative production methods like cold brewing to maintain the fresh flavor. The company capitalized on its extensive distribution network and invested in local innovation to grow from a soft drink giant into a coffee powerhouse in one of the world's most competitive beverage markets.

BOX 6.1 CASE STUDIES

1. Apple

If you buy an iPhone in Japan, you cannot silence your phone camera. Why? Because of some cases of creepy men on the subway who take photos up girls' skirts. That's right: In Japan there is an epidemic of men on crowded subways who hold their phones low to photograph underneath women's skirts. And back when phone cameras could be silenced, they got away with it.

So, Apple adapted the product. They removed the feature on the iPhone that enabled you to silence the camera. Today, you cannot buy an Apple product in Japan that allows you to turn off the sound of that telltale click.

2. Starbucks

With its own origin story of bringing the Italian-quality coffee culture to Seattle's Pike's Place market, Starbucks offers a global masterclass in cultural adaptation. Before opening its first store in Tokyo's luxurious Ginza in 1996, Starbucks' market research revealed an opportunity to target trendy 30-year-old women by offering designated non-smoking sections. So it did.

Since then, Starbucks has grown to over 1,700 locations across Japan by leaning into culture through its architecturally unique store environments and menus featuring its classic cappuccinos alongside unique seasonal drinks and food items tailored to local tastes. (See Chapter 8.) In the fall of 2023, Starbucks Japan launched a costume-inspired "Booooo Frappuccino" for Halloween, out-Americanizing the American holiday with ghoulish black, bitter caramel layered over sweet orange pumpkin. While staying true to its premium coffee culture, such thoughtful localization has made Starbucks a popular destination in Japan.

3. 7-Eleven

Moving from coffee to Slurpees: In the U.S., 7-Eleven is known for its basic convenience stores peddling tired taquitos and rotating hot dogs. But in Japan, it has expanded the idea of convenience into a lifestyle. With 21,488 immaculately stocked locations across Japan, 7-Eleven is omnipresent and vital to modern Japanese life and its fast-paced workforce.

What sets Japanese 7-Elevens apart is the shockingly high quality of fresh food offerings like sushi, noodles, and now craft beer in select, premium locations for satisfying and quick meals on the go. Beyond food, 7-Eleven offers convenience and quality Japanese style. 7-Eleven remains true to its global values while expanding its offerings to become an essential part of day-to-day life in Japan.

Brands answer the questions of whether or not to localize, how, and how much to do so in many different ways. While brands may adapt their products for specific markets, they work hard to maintain global brand consistency. Occasionally, that doesn't work. Sometimes, brands seek to leverage a country's design and manufacturing expertise to create products adapted to a specific market, which may shift the brand's position too.

Interview Insight: Tommy Hilfiger

Multi-positioning Brand Management

The early 1990s were a vibrant, transformative era for sports, music, and fashion. The summer of 1992 was especially iconic, as Magic Johnson, Michael Jordan, and Larry Bird dazzled with the basketball "Dream Team" at the Barcelona Olympics and 16-year-old Jennifer Capriati won tennis gold. The Cold War had ended, the Mall of America had opened, and the internet was in its infancy with just 25 websites. Fashion trends were bold and diverse, featuring crop tops, animal prints, velvet, and platform shoes, but that was about to wash away in a coming cultural wave.

After Grand Puba collaborated with up-and-coming singer Mary J. Blige, her debut album didn't just top the charts, it propelled R&B and hip-hop into mainstream pop culture, and along with it, a new popularity for bandanas, rayon striped tees, and bucket hats. Grand Puba's mention of Tommy Hilfiger in the album's title track "What's the 411" transformed Hilfiger from a classic, preppy staple to a cultural icon embraced by both hip-hop stars and mainstream America. Explicit lyrics that called out baggy fashion and a Tommy Hilfiger top became the first cultural crossover. When Snoop Dogg wore a Hilfiger striped rugby shirt on *Saturday Night Live*, the item sold out in stores across the country. Hilfiger embraced the industry and invited rappers like Coolio to its runway shows.

Initially seen as traditional American prep sportswear since its launch in 1985, Tommy Hilfiger gained unexpected street cred from rappers like Grand Puba. The endorsement attracted Destiny's Child and hip-hop artists like Tupac and Biggie Smalls and their fans, making the brand trendy not just for the urban community, but for youth all over the U.S. Tommy Jeans emerged as a favorite among younger, streetwear-influenced consumers, while Hilfiger's sportswear retained its classic preppy appeal. The brand appealed to a wide spectrum of consumers—the hip-hop artists on one end and preppy golf-club types on the other—fueling Tommy Hilfiger's rapid ascent in American fashion.

Over the next 10 years, Tommy Hilfiger grew rapidly in Europe as well. Its two distinct customer bases followed, seeking both the preppy brand-classic styles and the urban, streetwear-inspired looks. But in its U.S. home market, the opportunistic and rapid dual audience growth was confusing customers and retail partners and diluting the brand. As the company considered wider global expansion, executives faced a brand management challenge to be more strategic and intentional about positioning the brand for long-term growth.

Avery Baker joined Tommy Hilfiger as a co-op marketing manager in New York in 1997 in the midst of the brand's skyrocketing growth from the embrace of hip-hop culture. She worked, watched, and learned over the next five years as the brand surged in global popularity and, not long after, lost its way and slid down the other steep side of that curve in North America. She would eventually become President and Chief Brand Officer of Tommy Hilfiger.

"One of the greatest lessons I've learned," says Baker, reflecting on that time, "was being with the company not just in moments of success, but during challenges or failures. You learn what to do and you learn what not to do. That time provided a great lesson in brand management."[14]

Matrix Organization Supports Regional Flexibility

As Tommy Hilfiger's European business surged in the early 2000s, cracks appeared in the company's global operations. The European team, feeling like forgotten cousins across the Atlantic, had been scraping by without proper marketing materials, product lines, or brand imagery from headquarters. Frustrated and resourceful, they'd started charting their own course.

Baker was sent to mend this transatlantic rift in 2002. Her mission was to bridge this gap, ensuring the European group received the support needed to grow the business in line with the brand's core preppy vision. She initiated a six-day photo shoot featuring stars like Naomi Campbell and Paris Hilton, creating premium content to resonate with European customers while aligning with Hilfiger's global story.

The European organization, led by CEO Fred Gehring, embraced a matrix model, a structure that requires frequent dialogue and idea exchange between headquarters and regional offices. Rather than a traditional top-down corporate hierarchy, they created a living, breathing network of shared responsibility, encouraging local initiatives to flex and adapt the brand across diverse markets.

The key to their expansion, to building a global brand, required finding the right balance between maintaining the brand's core identity and values, while adapting the execution and positioning for relevance to the local European market.

Baker explains: "One of the reasons the brand has grown and remained on the global scene for so long is that there is an element of opportunistic malleability without leaving the DNA of the brand behind. Tommy Jeans really put the brand on the map culturally and, frankly, globally, as urban culture became dominant. But ultimately, leaning only into this hype was short-term thinking."

Leadership made a conscious decision to position the brand abroad in line with the origins of the brand—affordable, premium American sportswear, "an accessible Ralph Lauren"—rather than chasing hype and streetwear trends. They would position the brand at a more premium level in Europe than in North America, which required producing products of better quality at higher prices.

Growth Creates Complexity

As Tommy Hilfiger ventured into the Far East, where consumers crave cultural aspiration and luxury, the company strategically introduced both the main Hilfiger brand and the Tommy Jeans sub-brand. Tommy Jeans played a crucial role in connecting with younger consumers, ensuring the brand remained relevant in pop culture. However, they were careful to position Tommy Hilfiger's high-end, classic American sportswear as the flagship, creating an aspirational umbrella for all the product offerings. This approach balanced trendy appeal with timeless style, capturing a wide audience while maintaining brand prestige.

As a public company, the number of licensees and joint ventures expanded dramatically, particularly in Asia. Additional revenue streams and partners helped grow the business but made it much more complicated to manage. A joint venture in China gave those involved a stake in the results and more influence in decision-making. As the headquarters lost some control over the business, Baker learned that during periods of rapid growth, it's crucial to manage opportunities for the long term.

"How do you leverage wildfire growth, but make sure it's sustainable?" Avery asks rhetorically.

A brand needs to manage supply and demand very carefully to avoid saturating the market. Balancing retailer feedback is essential. Retail partners provide valuable insights and data, but relying too heavily on them can block brands from seeing clearly at critical moments.

"You need to listen to your retail partners," Baker said, "but they're at the tail end of what consumers want. Brands are brands because they're out in the forefront, anticipating and creating desire, not just reacting to the present or the past."

"A brand must set the vision, anticipating and generating demand for what people want. Without this foresight, success is elusive."

Consumers differ around the world, so brands must lean into the culture they're targeting to understand not where the market is, but where it is going.

Brand Alignment and Adaptation

Managing a global brand across diverse markets involves balancing a cohesive identity with local adaptations. The key is maintaining alignment at the highest level to ensure a unified brand image worldwide while accommodating regional nuances.

Baker connects organizational flexibility to the concept of freedom within a frame. "The framework—our values, concept, story—is our North Star. It's non-negotiable for orchestrating massive, culturally-relevant global campaigns across teams with wildly different backgrounds and expertise levels."

"It needs to feel like the same brand, so we require aligning the visual language that tells the story. As you get closer to execution at a consumer level in different countries, we allow for more adaptation," says Baker.

The brand communicates Hilfiger's universal core values for global appeal. American values translated through pop culture, such as youthful optimism, energy, and inclusivity, keep the brand young and vibrant. The brand's commitment to inclusivity from the start celebrates diverse perspectives and expressions, and organically encourages regional teams to suggest local initiatives.

"When you get to the democratic aspect of the brand DNA or its entrepreneurial spirit, these values may or may not translate, depending on the market," Baker explains. It's important to understand local nuances, especially as social media and technology make cultural exchanges more immediate and impactful.

"We're living in a global, creator-content-led society, where you need to adapt for local relevance," notes Baker.

Baker likens Hilfiger's brand strategy to a Venn diagram, where three key elements overlap: core brand values and DNA, local cultural values, and anticipated consumer trends (Figure 6.1). When these elements overlap, when societal and local trends converge along the brand's core values, the result is a harmonious blend that resonates globally without compromising the brand's essence.

"You don't make up something new," Baker explains. "But it means that you can lean much more into one value that resonates in a particular region, such as positivity and optimism in the face of challenge."

Figure 6.1 Brand Strategy across Cultures

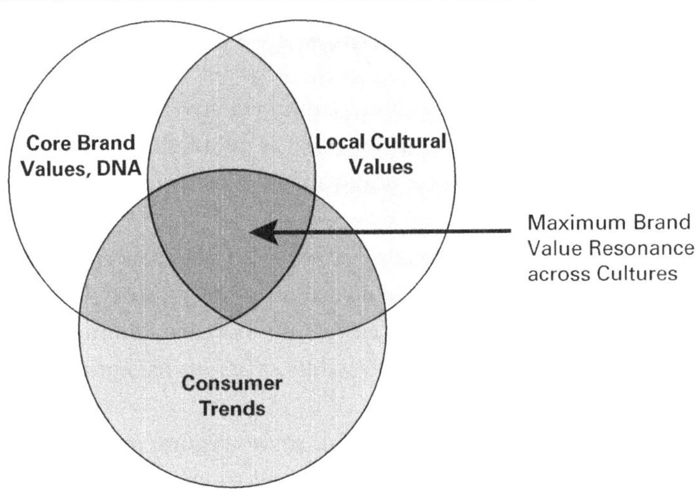

Clear boundaries set the stage for creativity to flourish, communication builds bridges of trust, and homegrown talent fuels the engine of innovation. Baker insists the key to global expansion is having knowledgeable representatives who understand and can convey the brand's essence to build a strong local foundation in each region.

I helped Avery Baker manage this brand tightrope in Japan. For the "Global Prep" campaign, the iconic preppy aesthetic was being reimagined around the world. In Tokyo, this meant transforming the concept of "prep camp" into something uniquely Japanese, with a scavenger hunt using New York City taxis transported to Japan's bustling streets, a preppy American pop-up bar, and original blazer collaborations with Vogue that sold for charity. The campaign's crowning jewel was a video cocktail—equal parts serious, sassy, and sexy—that blended high and low culture: a perfect fit for Japan's fluid social landscape. It followed one long-day's night of a classic navy-blue blazer transforming from preppy staple to hipster punk icon, then back again—a visual metaphor for the brand's adaptability across cultures.

Another pivotal initiative illustrating the power of unified yet flexible global teamwork was the breakthrough "See Now, Buy Now" extravaganza, led by Baker, that transformed the traditional fashion show into a branded media platform with immediate gratification. These events merged content, media, talent, live experiences, and online sales into a cohesive and powerful brand statement, brought to life differently in various cities around the world.

Tommy Hilfiger's approach to global brand management offers valuable lessons in balancing brand consistency with adaptability. By maintaining a strong core identity and respecting local cultural needs, the brand navigates the complexities of a global market.

The rise of e-commerce in the 2000s is forcing brands to become more transparent about products, sourcing, and brand identity. With one click online, consumers can compare products and prices around the world. Previously, companies could adapt their collections to market needs through physical stores, but with online shopping, a brand's entire range has become visible to consumers, forcing brands to align their product and pricing structures on a global scale. Companies balance short-term opportunities locally while building the long-term value of a strong and consistent global brand. The brand, in turn, communicates the promise of a certain value and quality consistently around the world.

Another way brands deliver on that promise is through direct interactions with their customers. How companies bring their brands to life across cultures through customer service and events builds the customer relationship and loyalty. Whether you're creating bespoke rituals, services, and events around selling your products and services, or responding to thorny situations, the goal is to meet both the brand's values and the customers'. Sometimes you craft those opportunities carefully in advance; sometimes you respond to disasters. What do faulty ceilings, hand-me-downs, and a pair of tires have in common? As you'll see in Chapter 7, they all provide valuable lessons on how to create branded customer experiences.

Summary

- **What is innovation?** Innovation creates new value through novel ideas and solutions with functional, emotional, or monetary benefits.
- **Why adapt?** Brands can create new value by meeting the unique preferences and cultural needs of local consumers while maintaining global relevance.
- **How to adapt products?** Allow structured flexibility that encourages local teams to respond to their market's unique cultural needs, expectations, taste, and seasonal customs.

The Global Digest

Chapter 6 Takeaways

1. **Marketing's global tightrope:** Often referred to as "glocalization," every company chooses how to balance global values while adapting to local market needs.
2. **Freedom within a frame:** This helpful approach sets consistent brand guardrails while encouraging local market innovation.
3. **Cultural chameleon:** Strong brands increase value by adapting products and marketing to align with local cultural norms and celebrations.
4. **Trend surfing:** Following global and local trends spurs ideas and opportunities to create relevant products.
5. **Flavor of the nation:** Taste is local.
6. **Seasonal sensations:** Capitalize on local holidays and seasons to create limited-edition products.

7 **Innovation incubator:** Organizations seeking to foster a culture of creativity and risk-taking need to inspire creativity, communicate openly, and accept and learn from failure.

8 **Cross-pollination:** Leverage ideas from other industries to disrupt and innovate in your own sector.

9 **Glocal goldmine:** Local successes can enhance global brand value and vice versa.

10 **Pioneer's prize:** Being first to enter a market allows a company to establish its brand as the pioneer and leader in its industry, creating brand advantages by setting industry standards, capturing a large market share, and creating competitive barriers to entry.

References

1 Nestlé Staff (2024) KitKat History: Our Story, Nestlé KitKat. www.kitkat.co.za/kitkat-history (archived at https://perma.cc/Q32N-XZX6)

2 C. Casellas (2024) Interviewed by Katherine Melchior Ray, June 13, GoogleMeet; October 9, email

3 Nestlé Staff (2024) Nestlé HealthScience. www.nestlehealthscience.com/ (archived at https://perma.cc/FQ67-8QTT)

4 Nestlé Staff (2023) 150 Years of Nestlé, Nestlé Jobs. www.nestlejobs.com/nestle-purina/blog/150-years-of-nestle (archived at https://perma.cc/A622-GSWV)

5 D. Wiener-Bronner (2022) Chocolate Is Having a Moment, CNN Business, November 9. www.cnn.com/2022/11/09/business/chocolate-sales-ctrp/index.html (archived at https://perma.cc/462Y-SGCM)

6 J. Faria (2024) Coca-Cola's Brand Value 2006 to 2024, Statista, July 4. www.statista.com/statistics/326065/coca-cola-brand-value/ (archived at https://perma.cc/ML54-5922)

7 Coca-Cola Staff (2024) The Birth of a Refreshing Idea, The Coca-Cola Company. www.coca-colacompany.com/about-us/history/the-birth-of-a-refreshing-idea (archived at https://perma.cc/2VB2-PVP6)

8 NIDA Blog Team (2025) Did Coca-Cola Ever Contain Cocaine? Just Think Twice, February 12. www.justthinktwice.gov/article/did-coca-cola-ever-contain-cocaine (archived at https://perma.cc/N6YB-F83X)

9 C. Nannestad (2023) Here's Why Mexican Coke Tastes Better than American Coke, *Reader's Digest*, May 23. www.rd.com/article/mexican-coke/ (archived at https://perma.cc/4LYC-BZ2Q)

10 E. O'Brien (2022) Mexican Coke vs. American Coke: Is There Really Any Difference?', *KSBY*, August 11. www.ksby.com/mexican-coke-vs-american-coke (archived at https://perma.cc/G3CR-UX2A)
11 G. Staplehurst (2023) How Coca-Cola Stays Refreshed, Kantar, December 7. www.kantar.com/inspiration/agile-market-research/how-coca-cola-stays-refreshed (archived at https://perma.cc/P5ND-XRQR)
12 Coca-Cola Media Team (2024) The Coca-Cola Company Is Always Innovating and Exploring the Future of Best-in-Class Brands and Experiences, The Coca-Cola Company, May 9. www.coca-colacompany.com/media-center/the-coca-cola-company-is-always-innovating-and-exploring-the-future-of-best-in-class-brands-and-experiences (archived at https://perma.cc/F7EX-Z995)
13 Coca-Cola Media Team (2017) How Coca-Cola Sparked the Surging Ready-to-Drink Coffee Business in Japan, The Coca-Cola Company, June 14. investors.coca-colacompany.com/news-events/press-releases/detail/51/coca-cola-celebrates-50-years-of-innovation-in-japan (archived at https://perma.cc/JGZ6-3NV6)
14 A. Baker (2024) Interviewed by Katherine Melchior Ray, April 23, GoogleMeet

Give the Customer a Melon

7

Service Brings Culture to Life

KATHERINE MELCHIOR RAY

Japan's Ceremonial Melon

With its serene and majestic setting, Tokyo's Meiji Shrine attracts millions of visitors every January wishing to start the year with a sense of spiritual renewal and positive aspirations. Kyo Hata, the renowned CEO of Louis Vuitton Japan who had founded the Japanese subsidiary decades prior, insisted on honoring cultural traditions. So, top executives would commence each year with a group pilgrimage to the sacred site, offering 500-yen coins for health, happiness, and good fortune. As Vice President of Marketing, I knew our business strategies were the real engine to growth, though with the intense pressure on us to deliver sales, I welcomed even spiritual support from my fellow local executives.

One year, those Monday morning plans were replaced with emergency meetings at our handsome headquarters to mitigate an accident in a flagship store over the holiday weekend. Among the New Year's holiday shoppers was Yuki Tanaka, a refined Japanese woman in her mid-thirties, accompanied by her husband Kenji and their five-year-old daughter Mika. (This story is based on real events, with customer names changed for privacy. Other scenes in this chapter are inspired by cultural behaviors.)

Mrs. Tanaka had gone into a fitting room to try on a silk dress from the latest collection. As she adjusted the garment's collar, a sudden crack shattered the tranquil atmosphere, and a ceiling panel crashed down, missing her by centimeters. Mr. Tanaka rushed to the fitting room where he found his wife trembling but physically unharmed. Young Mika trailed her father, eyes wide with confusion and fear, reflecting everyone's concern.

The store staff, more accustomed to donning velvet gloves to highlight special features of expensive monogram bags, raced to her aid with a chorus of apologies, "*Moshi wake gozaimasen*." The store manager bowed deeply, his face flushed with embarrassment.

Mr. Tanaka's anger boiled over. "This is unacceptable!" he snapped, standing protectively in front of his shaken wife. "How could this happen in a Louis Vuitton store?"

The store manager called an ambulance and followed them to the hospital, where Mrs. Tanaka was found dazed but, luckily, not injured. He then sent them home in a regular green cab—scoring no points for customer service—planning later to gift her a prized melon from the reputed department store Nihonbashi Takashimaya to make amends.

With our traditional New Year's visit to Meiji Shrine indefinitely postponed, we planned to gather and discuss what to do next. As the daughter of an American trial lawyer, I imagined the worst—a big, expensive lawsuit, bad press in the *Asahi Shimbun* newspaper, and lost customers.

"We're sending them a melon?!" I protested.

Until I questioned the melon idea, no one had recognized how our consolation fruit failed to mitigate the potential legal and emotional damage.

The following Monday morning, 10 men from the Shimizu Construction Company, all wearing dark suits, filed into our elegant conference room. Designed by Kengo Kuma, the large space is cantilevered over fashionable Omotesando Avenue. The space had frequently been used by executives to gather on the soft leather chairs around the broad wooden table, hashing out sales strategies or arm-twisting *Vogue* and *GQ* to give Louis Vuitton better editorial coverage in exchange for more ads.

Today was different. The setting and the beverages emphasized the seriousness of the discussion about to unfold. We were served Japanese tea in fine ceramic cups. This was a modern-day business tea ceremony requiring many of the prescribed gestures of a traditional one. The team from Shimizu stood facing our seated executive committee members. In unison, with their hands on the table, the construction executives bowed an unusually long time, seeking forgiveness. Not one of the guys in the room had held a hammer for decades, but they took responsibility as if they were the carpenters who had made a poor decision months ago. They would, of course, replace the damaged tile, but this formal and staged apology allowed us to continue our business relationship.

On the customer side, we agreed that no less than our respected CEO, who had built Louis Vuitton Japan into a powerhouse over 20 years, would apologize in person. In no other country would a CEO dedicate so much time, but in Japan this reflects a brand's obligation to the customer, who is considered sacred. After driving more than an hour outside Tokyo to a two-story home, he rang the Tanakas' bell. Mrs. Tanaka answered but turned him away since her husband was at work. Our CEO returned the following day, bowed deeply and offered her and her daughter a trip to Paris, including an exclusive tour of the Louis Vuitton family home and workshop in Asnières, to help ease her pain and suffering. He carried with him the large Takashimaya melon from the store manager.

The Louis Vuitton story illustrates how profoundly cultural norms and expectations influence customer relationships in international business. While offering a melon may seem mundane to some, in Japan they are very expensive and prized for their sweetness, texture, and aesthetic perfection, symbolizing luxury and prestige. Small triangular wedges are served as elegant desserts at upscale restaurants. They are laden with symbolism, much like the formal corporate apology and the executive pilgrimage to the shrine. The ceremonial components foster good luck in business and smooth relationships when something goes wrong. The thought, time, and effort invested in this example illustrates the Japanese cultural emphasis on status, formality, and relationships, as described in the culture section of Chapter 3.

In Chapter 1, we outlined the various aspects of marketing, which includes customer relationship management (CRM) or customer marketing. Since marketing seeks to find and cultivate customers, the way companies activate relationship marketing has enormous potential to develop strong, loyal, and financially rewarding customers. Leveraging culture artfully can transform an angry customer into an even more loyal and profitable one. Careful, though—if you don't understand the culture of your customers, a wrong move might offend or upset them and prompt them to post a one-star review. In this chapter, we'll explore how customer service, which touches your customer personally, may be the most important marketing function to adapt to local culture. We dive into both the cultural and legal aspects of the customer relationship. How do brands tailor the experiences along the customer's journey from special events, selling rituals, customer communication, and after-service? Beneath these proactive and engaging activities, the business is also responsible for protecting its customer information according to the privacy laws of each respective country. Those laws are different, so companies must adapt or risk legal and reputational damage. Having managed

CRM for brands on three different continents, I know this challenge well. These are the strict customer data laws that prevent me from using my U.S. Starbucks loyalty card when getting a frappuccino abroad, for example.

The Buying Experience: In-store Selling Ceremonies

Cartier in Dubai and Paris

Amina Hassan steps out of her sleek, black Mercedes, the sun reflecting off her oversized tortoiseshell sunglasses. Her tailored abaya, by a local designer, flows elegantly as she enters Dubai Mall. The deep emerald embroidery on her abaya perfectly matches her silk blouse. Her Manolo Blahnik heels distinctively click on the marble floor as she crosses the grand atrium.

The mall's expansive space and the scents of coffee and luxury perfume excite her. After a productive afternoon finalizing plans for her charity gala to raise money for a pediatric clinic, she's ready for some personal time. She checks her Rolex Datejust and sees it's already half past seven. Her mother and sisters will be waiting for her. She hastens to Cartier, barely glancing at the high-end boutiques as she makes her way.

Amina's mother is waiting, looking resplendent in a pearl-colored abaya and matching silk hijab. Amina's two sisters flank her, and Amina greets each of them with a touch on the cheek before they enter the luxury boutique together.[1]

The mosaic floor, part of a two-year renovation, features three colors of glass tile inspired by a Cartier bracelet and surrounded by gold marquetry details. This intricate technique, dating back to the eighteenth century, was handmade in Paris over six months.[2] A bas-relief at the entrance tells the boutique's story, depicting the Cartier Panthère meeting camels in a Dubai oasis. The design draws from local heritage featuring desert fauna and flora, with birds perched amidst palm tree columns.[3] Amina and her family pass under the crystal chandelier, enjoying the luxury evoked by French architect Laura Gonzalez.[4]

Amina's eyes are drawn to a showcase of diamond necklaces, each a masterpiece of craftsmanship. The sales associate greets them with a familiar smile and welcomes them to a private viewing area for more space. The women make themselves comfortable on the plush velvet chairs, relieving their shoulders of the day's shopping bags. They look forward to the sales associate bringing the customary mint tea along with Cartier's latest jewelry, selected to their tastes. Amina smiles as she relaxes into her evening—she's been looking forward to this moment all week.

Over three thousand miles away, Éléonore Chauvet strolls down the bustling streets of Paris, her classic CHANEL ballet flats padding along the cobblestone streets. Tonight, she's celebrating. The Christmas season is approaching, and she's had a great year. Years ago on vacation, a Cartier watch had caught her eye while strolling the streets in Milan. She's considered this purchase for some time and diligently researched other options, but she finds herself drawn to the piece she fell in love with on a hot June evening in Italy. What once seemed like an unrealistic indulgence now feels like an attainable luxury.

Her pulse quickens with anticipation as she heads to the iconic Rue de la Paix, where the legendary flagship Cartier store awaits. She has an appointment and is eager to sip a glass of Champagne, try on the watch, and feel the weight of the silver against her wrist, a tangible symbol of her professional achievement.[5] She hopes to display it that night at dinner with friends.

A Meta View on Luxury

Women all over the world are buying luxury jewelry at increasing rates, and for myriad reasons.[6] The luxury jewelry market is poised to grow at a compound annual growth rate of 7.85 per cent between 2023 and 2031, from 61 billion to 96 billion dollars.[7] Some purchase to celebrate a special occasion, others to reward accomplishments or commemorate travel experiences.[8] Just as the reasons for buying are varied, so too are shoppers' desired buying experiences. While a Parisian woman may duck into a store solo, a Middle Eastern woman typically wants an immersive and social in-store experience.[9]

Brands that seek to take advantage of this global growth and delight their customers must be aware of and adapt to these critical cultural differences in shopping preferences. A brand like Cartier cannot simply close its store in Dubai, as they do in Paris, at 7 pm—that's when the United Arab Emirates city is starting to come alive.

Morin Oluwole knows this well. As the former Global Director of Luxury at Meta, she managed global luxury client partnerships across platforms like Facebook, Instagram, and WhatsApp for nearly 20 years. Oluwole has spent much of her career in the tech sector, helping luxury brands adapt their digital strategies all over the world.[10] She knows the importance of keeping the brand universal and timeless while adapting customer service to the local markets' needs.

Oluwole highlights the differences between European and Middle Eastern shopping habits. "In the Middle East, you often have groups of women visit jewelry stores together. It may be a group of eight women, often family or close friends, so it becomes a shared, communal buying experience," she explains.[11] This is vastly different from an individual customer who is motivated to accomplish the task; she wants to walk in, buy one predetermined piece, and go about her way.

"Middle Eastern women want an outing. They want to sit down, they want an experience, they want to try on multiple pieces," she says. "The approach to welcoming the customers is not the same, the approach to staffing is not the same." The whole customer service experience should adapt to the manners in which people want to shop.

Women in the Middle East often have a dizzying social calendar, consisting of 15 to 20 weddings and dozens of private parties each year.[12] Brands like Cartier, Bulgari, and Van Cleef & Arpels cater to their shopping needs by offering private salons where groups of women can "buy in bulk," so to speak. These salons are separate rooms just off the central store area with a door for security that creates a place of privacy and intimacy.[13]

Providing a customized buying experience also means selecting products best suited to regional taste from the brand's global collection. In the Middle East, diamond pieces sell more than gold or silver, so shoppers will see more diamond "*Juste un Clou*" and "LOVE" bracelets in a Cartier store in Doha than they would in Athens.[14] This is different from producing unique products specifically for one region, as we explained in Chapter 6. When brands become big enough to have a truly global clientele, they maintain a large worldwide range of products, providing flexibility to modify assortments in-store and online as travel patterns and customer profiles change.

For staff, serving and interacting with diverse customers in stores and online when there is a language barrier can be a major challenge.

"It's important to have skilled representatives that speak the language of the consumer," says Oluwole. "They can share the history of the house, the story behind the product, and describe the elements of craftsmanship. This puts a customer at ease and elevates the perceived value, especially when they are investing significant sums."[15]

During my time at Louis Vuitton Japan, store staff were rewarded on their third-year work anniversary with a one-week all-expense-paid trip to

Paris. They visited the Eiffel Tower and ate rose macarons from Ladurée. Additionally, to deepen their understanding of the brand's embodiment of French history and artistic mastery, the group toured the Musée d'Orsay and the Vuitton family home in Asnières. Once back in Japan, employees were then able to describe iconic features on small, monogrammed wallets or elaborate steamer trunks, romancing the brand with details learned from their time in Paris. The brand knows investing in educating and building loyalty with staff amplifies the passion with which they will describe not only the monogram, but the tan leather borders with yellow stitching; the tumbler lock designed by Louis and his son, George, in 1886; and countless other iconic brand features.[16]

Events

As the sun dipped below the horizon, casting a golden hue over the sprawling Dubai desert, an air of anticipation buzzed around a luxurious Bedouin-style tent. Intricate lanterns glowed softly, illuminating lavish carpets and silk drapes. Wooden Mashrabiya panels carved with CHANEL's iconic interlocking C's framed the night's opulent runway spectacle. As a light show dazzled the crowd to traditional Arabic music, models emerged showcasing CHANEL's latest Cruise collection. These designs, which had debuted in Marseille, France, were now tailored to resonate with the Middle Eastern market, featuring flowing abayas with CHANEL's signature tweed, embellished kaftans, and modest yet chic evening gowns. Dubai's elite, including influential fashion bloggers and members of the royal family, filled the front row.[17]

Brands frequently aim to strengthen customer relationships through locally tailored events. These events, usually held in one location unless broadcasted globally, like the seasonal fashion shows in Paris and Milan, are especially vital for luxury brands. Customers of these brands seek to invest in a lifestyle and social prestige in addition to quality craftsmanship.[18] Ranging from intimate product previews and dinners with VIP clients and key opinion leaders to elaborate performances featuring artists or musicians, these exclusive events vividly bring the brand's allure to life.[19]

"For fashion brands, whose biggest moments are the Paris fashion show and the Milan fashion show," Oluwole explained, "they've started doing repeat editions of said fashion shows in other markets. In the post-Covid context when the consumer was not coming to Europe, this became especially relevant in China, Hong Kong, and Japan."

For the smaller, more commercial seasons, this makes good business sense, like CHANEL's Cruise collection of 2024, described previously. Eight weeks after the clothes were shown in Marseille, Dubai's top clients were treated to their own exclusive showing.

Brands are increasingly producing adapted versions of their global fashion shows in Asian markets. This innovation was developed specifically for China after the Covid-19 pandemic, as brands sought to maintain their relationship with Chinese customers unable to travel to the Paris launch.[20] These localized shows may feature Chinese models and new items produced and sold only to the Asian market.[21] Dior has been a pioneer in this area, having brought its spring collection to Shanghai in 2019.[22] After Covid, in July 2023, Dior extended its fall ready-to-wear show to the smaller city of Shenzhen, while the same year Bottega Veneta hosted its first physical show in China.[23]

"That's huge for adaptation," says Oluwole; it is indicative of innovation in the luxury space to better serve regional markets.

Customer Relationship Marketing across Cultures

Beneath the glamor and excitement of in-store experiences and on-site events, small interactions with the people who represent the brand touch customers most personally. Cultural expectations for how service is communicated—responsiveness, demeanor, even which media channel—vary around the world, requiring global brands to adapt their CRM strategies accordingly.[24]

European and Middle Eastern customers prefer to communicate with store staff via WhatsApp, whereas most Americans like text or email, and Chinese customers use Weibo or WeChat.[25] Many brands have found success by incorporating WeChat into their customer experience.[26]

Oluwole sums this up: "I see a lot of investment being made by luxury brands in the purchase and customer service experience, which is a huge factor for increasing repeat purchases and brand loyalty."

Brands in the luxury industry, with expensive goods and services, may have the most to gain or lose, yet all brands can learn from the luxury playbook to build deeper loyalty by creating emotional value through connection.

Leveraging Service to Build Loyalty

In the U.S., innovative brands like Patagonia and Hanna Andersson foster loyalty and build brand value by pioneering services that align with their consumers' shared values of sustainable, ethical consumption of quality products.

Patagonia, long known for its commitment to environmental causes, launched its "Worn Wear" program as a natural extension of its brand ethos. This service allows customers to return used Patagonia items in good condition for store credit, breathing new life into well-loved gear.[27] The company then cleans, repairs, and resells these items online and in select stores at reduced prices. But Patagonia doesn't stop there; they also offer repair services for damaged gear and provide educational resources on product care, effectively extending the lifespan of their products. Through "Worn Wear," Patagonia has transformed sustainability from an abstract concept into a tangible, community-building experience.

Similarly, Hanna Andersson, the children's clothing brand discussed in Chapter 5, introduced its "Hand-Me-Down" program, recognizing their end users literally grow out of their clothes before the high-quality products wear out. Originally called "Hannadowns" when the company donated gently used products customers returned in exchange for discounts on future purchases, the initiative has grown into a branded resale marketplace where customers shop and sell pre-loved, secondhand Hannas.[28] The initiative incentivizes existing customers to return products for cash or credit and expands its audience to a wider range of customers.

Such programs create multiple benefits that ripple through the entire brand ecosystem, creating a virtuous cycle of brand engagement, loyalty, and growth. They prove the durability and long-lasting value of the products, encouraging initial purchases as consumers feel more confident investing in items that retain value. They also enlarge the range of available products with previous years' styles. The resale platforms foster a sense of community and loyalty as customers engage with the brand repeatedly as both sellers and buyers. Moreover, by extending product lifecycles, these companies appeal to environmentally conscious consumers, enhancing their brand image and attracting like-minded customers. Patagonia and Hanna Andersson have created a win-win-win situation: customers get more value and options, the brands build stronger relationships and gather valuable data, and the environment benefits from reduced waste. In today's market, where consumers increasingly vote with their wallets for brands that share their values, such innovative services can be the difference between a one-time purchase and a lifelong customer.

Some brands invest so much in service it becomes their single most powerful feature for creating brand loyalty and value. American department store Nordstrom's legendary reputation for outstanding customer service serves as its strongest marketing message, conveying to customers that they are truly valued. This ethos was passed down through the family business, with generations of Nordstroms preaching the importance of treating customers right.

Pete Nordstrom recounts perhaps the most famous illustration of Nordstrom's customer-first philosophy from 50 years ago.[29] At a store in Fairbanks, Alaska, a customer had driven over 50 miles to return a pair of tires—items Nordstrom never sold. Instead of turning the customer away, associate Craig Trounce embodied the "Nordstrom spirit" by finding a way to accommodate the request. He researched the tires' fair market value and refunded the customer that sum. While the exact refund amount has been lost over time, the story's impact on Nordstrom's culture and reputation has been invaluable. It's become so integral to their character that some Nordstrom stores display tires as a reminder of their unwavering commitment to customer satisfaction.

Nordstrom's approach to service empowers its frontline sales staff with the autonomy to make decisions in the best interest of the customer. This "use your best judgment" policy fosters a sense of responsibility and adaptability among employees, enabling them to react quickly and effectively to customer needs.

During my time at Nordstrom, we observed that while our return rates were higher than our competitors', we viewed this as a marketing expense. The goodwill generated by our exceptional service and lenient return policy created loyal customers and positive word-of-mouth that far outweighed the costs. But while the policy worked well in the U.S., translating this cultural approach into new markets proved challenging. Japanese retail partners requested a translation of Nordstrom's reputed service manual—expecting dozens of pages covering every situation—but I had to explain that the philosophy came down to just four little words: "Use your best judgment." Implementing this subjective philosophy in different cultural contexts would require a fundamental shift in thinking to foster the same level of individual responsibility and flexibility found in the American workforce. In the end, we created a thick manual detailing dozens of real-life and imagined cases. We did not include an example of a customer returning tires.

Nordstrom's approach demonstrates that exceptional service can be a powerful differentiator. By prioritizing customer satisfaction above all else and empowering employees to make decisions, Nordstrom has created a loyal customer base and a brand reputation that serves as its own best marketing tool. This customer-centric approach, much like the innovative resale programs of Patagonia and Hanna Andersson, shows how brands can align their services with cultural expectations to create lasting value.

The Global Mosaic of Expectations

In each country, service expectations differ. In the U.S., customer service reflects a culture that values speed, efficiency, and personalization. American consumers expect quick resolution of issues, often coupled with monetary incentives like discounts or cash refunds. Notice that the Patagonia and Hanna Andersson second-use systems described earlier leverage a monetary value incentive.

Another hallmark of U.S. service is a friendly, approachable demeanor, exemplified by the common practice of restaurant servers introducing themselves by name and engaging in casual conversation. This personalized approach extends to other service interactions, with loyal customers expecting to be recognized and greeted by name. The demand for constant availability has led to the widespread adoption of 24/7 customer support, often facilitated by live chat and AI-based systems. These adaptations collectively cater to American consumers' expectations of convenience, friendliness, and customer-centric service experiences.

Unfortunately, the friendliness of American servers can sometimes make consumers from other cultures, like the British, feel uneasy, as they often perceive this manner as insincere or overbearing.[30] In the U.K., customers typically prefer service workers not to approach them unless they specifically request assistance. Being immediately available to help is more important than offering to help in the first place. If they need to raise an issue, British customers, known for their indirect communication style, will do so subtly and apologetically or be perceived as extremely rude. Brands must know and understand their customers' expectations to adapt their services accordingly.

In contrast with the English, Brazilian consumers are the world's most impatient about service expectations.[31] They are actively shopping, sharing, and interacting across all channels and expect extensive communication. As we saw in Chapter 3 on culture, Brazilians put a high value on relationships, so expressing empathy, warmth, and respect helps establish a harmonious and genuine rapport.[32] Many brands integrate WhatsApp into their CRM systems to send personal communications, which may start with "*Querido*" (Darling). They create online communities that emphasize customer testimonials in forums where users can connect with others and share experiences, thereby boosting customer engagement.

Like Brazilians, Chinese consumers are highly engaged online and respect peer opinions, being twice as likely as Americans to make purchases based on online reviews.[33] Airbnb's challenges in China (see Chapter 3) highlight the cultural importance of familiarity and trust. More than in other markets, Chinese consumers interact omnichannel—using online sites, voice, and physical stores—and expect fast, consistent after-sale services across all platforms. If they receive poor service, 63 per cent say they would immediately switch brands, making them the least satisfied and least forgiving consumers in Asia.[34] Omnichannel service requires integrated databases, as Chinese consumers expect seamless interactions, such as purchasing online and returning in-store without re-providing information.[35] This integration is easier within China but challenging across countries with different privacy laws.

While the Chinese consumer may abandon a brand that fails to adapt quickly, the Japanese consumer expects to build a long-term relationship. Customer service in Japan provides care that goes above and beyond meeting expectations, where formal greetings, gratitude, and apologies display important rituals of etiquette. Often referred to as "after-care," helping a customer after a transaction in Japan is seen as a crucial aspect of building prized relationships. The high level of respect, formality, and meticulous attention to ceremonial details reflects the cultural concept "Omotenashi," a form of selfless hospitality rooted in the country's traditional tea ceremony.[36] We saw this illustrated in the formal apology from the Shimizu Construction Company and the symbolic melon hand delivered to the customer's home by the CEO of Louis Vuitton Japan.

Once, while working in Japan, I left my briefcase in the lobby of my hotel before leaving for a meeting several blocks away. When I called to ask the hotel to hold onto it, they offered to bring it to me themselves, so within 20 minutes, I was reunited with my bag. I have seen women leave their wallets alongside their hot lattes on the table at Starbucks while they go to the bathroom. Over many years of living in Japan, I have forgotten documents and eyeglasses on the Tokyo subway, but got them all back in the end!

American service aims for quick, friendly resolution; Japanese service emphasizes formality and ongoing care; Brazilian service prioritizes personal warmth and social connection; Chinese service focuses on building trust through peer influence and omnichannel engagement. Each approach caters to the unique preferences and values of its cultural context.

BOX 7.1 PRIVACY IS CULTURAL

A Word on Data Protection

As brands enter new markets, they must understand not only the cultural preferences for services and how to communicate them, but the expectations and legal restrictions regarding customer data. In today's digital age, customer data is one of the most valuable assets a business can possess. It not only captures the source of revenue, but reveals individual preferences, fuels personalization, helps to optimize operations, and informs strategic decisions.

However, with great value comes great responsibility. Sensitivity about personal information, privacy, and consumers' legal protection are not small matters. The American concept "Buyer Beware" should be replaced internationally with "Brand Beware!" Each region has distinct legal and cultural expectations regarding data privacy that brands must honor and follow to build trust and global value.

The U.S. has traditionally had the most laissez-faire approach, where personal data is collected and shared unless the user "opts out" to request confidentiality. This system prioritizes business, but consumer pressure is growing. In contrast, the European Union (E.U.) has long considered customer data protection a fundamental right. Since the European Data Protection Directive passed in 1995,[37] customer information stays private unless users actively "opt in" and consent to its collection. In 2016, the E.U. elevated its own regulations to a new gold standard in the General Data Protection Regulation (GDPR), giving users more control of their personal information. Following Europe's lead, Californian voters in 2020 passed the Privacy Rights Act, ensuring the "enforceable constitutional right of privacy for every Californian. Fundamental to this right of privacy is the ability of individuals to control the use, including the sale, of their personal information."[38]

Other countries may have additional regulations, and fines are steep. More importantly, customer sensitivity on this topic is paramount to building trust. Brands can avoid reputational, legal, and financial damage by adapting to regional privacy expectations and regulations. Protect customer data as the valuable asset it represents by protecting customer privacy, staying current on regulatory changes by market, and clearly communicating your customers' rights.

When Service Is Your Business: Cultural Hospitality

As the first rays of sunlight touch the Tokyo skyline, a sleek black sedan idles at the entrance of a luxury hotel. Mr. Yamamoto, a seasoned business traveler, slides into the backseat, adjusting his tie. The bell captain carefully stows his luggage in the trunk, then steps back. Hotel staff, dressed in crisp uniforms, cease all other activities to join him in forming a semicircle around the vehicle. As the car door whispers shut and the sedan departs, the entire staff group bows deeply in perfect harmony. This graceful, unified gesture of respect and gratitude leaves Mr. Yamamoto feeling valued.

"The bow is a remarkable cultural nuance," explains Sara Kearney, a seasoned hotelier after 25 years in global marketing and operations. "It isn't something we train staff to do," she admits. "The natural expression of their culture shows deep respect and appreciation and is always heartwarming to witness and to receive."[39]

The bow remains a touching gesture and takes place even in unlikely locations. I recall once leaving Narita Airport in Tokyo. As I was settling in for the long flight, I glanced out the window. On the tarmac far below, I noticed tiny-looking ground crew figures bowing as the massive gray machine around me rolled slowly away from the gate.

The emphasis on respectful greetings and farewells is not unique to Japan. In Bangkok, staff at the Mandarin Oriental Hotel greet guests with the traditional Thai *wai*. When visitors arrive, hoteliers welcome them with warm hospitality by pressing their hands together in a prayer-like gesture and bowing their heads slightly. "The *wai* is not just for guests," Kearney explains. "The genuine and heartfelt gesture is also used among friends, family, and work associates."

Over decades of working in hotels around the world, Kearney has countless stories of adapting the hospitality experience to cultural expectations. In a luxury hotel in Hong Kong, the sense of arrival is meticulously crafted. Staff assure no guest ever touches a front door handle. Regardless of the time of day or night, a doorman is always present to open the door, providing a seamless and luxurious entry. This ritual underscores the importance of the first impression, ensuring guests feel immediately welcomed and valued.

"Even at two in the morning, there is someone to open the door," Kearney noted. "It was a crucial touchpoint to make the experience distinct and memorable."

These practices are not only based on tradition, but the result of extensive research. Kearney and her teams worked to elevate and brand the customer journey by creating memorable touchpoints, and research showed the most critical part was giving guests a sense of welcome and comfort. "We found that the first and last impressions were the most lasting," she explained. "A warm greeting and a respectful farewell set the tone for the entire stay."

These culturally attuned greetings and farewells became integral components of the hotel guest experience around the world. Reflecting local customs and hospitality traditions, the gestures make each destination unique. Whether it is the bow in Japan, the *wai* in Thailand, the attentive doormen in Hong Kong, or the friendly staff in San Diego, these gestures reinforce the importance of cultural sensitivity to create lasting memories for guests.

Another insightful example of adapting service to cultural expectations is less visible to the customer. Few travelers recognize what goes into housekeeping at major hotels, much less how they differ around the world.

"Housekeeping has the largest team and operating budget of any hotel," explains Kearney, whose many roles included Executive Housekeeper. "It absolutely must respect the cultural standards of our guests."

"Guests in India expect not just cleanliness, but an experience that reflects the opulence and rich heritage of Indian hospitality," Kearney recounts. In luxury hotels in India, housekeeping adapts to the local expectations of grandeur and comfort by ensuring rooms are adorned with fresh flowers, silk cushions, and traditional Indian decor elements.

"Attention is paid to small details like arranging a tray of exotic fruits or setting up a traditional incense diffuser," Kearney adds.

The focus on detail rises to a whole new level in Japan. In the pristine corridors of Kyoto, an entire team of housekeepers moves with precision and purpose. Their task is not just to clean but to achieve a level of perfection that matches the high expectations of their Japanese guests.

"In Japan, cleanliness isn't just about being tidy; it's an art form," Kearney said. "Our housekeepers often work in groups, ensuring every corner is spotless and every item is in its precise place." Each room is a canvas, and every detail, from the crispness of the sheets to the placement of amenities, is meticulously crafted. The level of perfection in Japan was so high that they assigned fewer rooms to housekeeping teams to allow them to meet these expectations.

Housekeeping at the bustling Bangkok hotels reflects yet another culture's values: Thailand's balance of efficiency and hospitality. Housekeepers leave personalized notes, often accompanied by a small flower or a local sweet, to add a touch of warmth and personal connection. "In Thailand, hospitality is about creating a welcoming atmosphere," Kearney noted. "Personal touches like a handwritten note or a small flower make guests feel genuinely cared for."

From the attentive doormen at the front of the house to the operational network behind the scenes in housekeeping, these examples illustrate how the hospitality industry, whose very business is service, adapts to expectations across cultures. Each approach highlights the importance of cultural sensitivity in delivering exceptional service, illustrating the diverse values and preferences of guests from around the world.

Reflecting on these experiences, Kearney adds: "It's more than just meeting expectations. It's about creating an experience that resonates deeply with our guests, respecting their cultural values, and making them feel truly at home." Prioritizing cultural nuances across customer service touchpoints creates a sense that guests belong, an approach that not only enhances guest satisfaction but, by creating a desire to return, fosters tremendous guest loyalty, which builds brand value in return.

In today's diverse marketplace, strong brands adapt their services and customer relationship marketing to cultural expectations throughout the customer journey, from experiences and events to omnichannel service interactions. Making these connections more personal resonates emotionally with customers to foster appreciation, create loyalty, and drive brand value. In bringing their events to global customers, brands expand the canvases for their collections beyond Paris's Grand Palais and Milan's Galleria, to include islands in the Persian Gulf and the Sea World Culture and Arts Center in Shenzhen. With the knowledge, skills, and resources to adapt locally, the whole world becomes a source of inspiration.

But first, the brand must capture the customer's attention, so let's turn to the topic with the most creative license: adapting marketing campaigns to culture. Strong brands use marketing to engage in culture to create local meaning and emotional resonance. In the next section, we'll explore marketing frameworks that harness storytelling to drive awareness, engagement, conversion, and bottom-line results.

Summary

- **What is customer service?** Marketing services that bring the brand to life through personal experiences with staff.
- **Why adapt services?** Misunderstanding cultural expectations can offend customers and damage brand reputation, while culturally tailored services can transform even challenging situations into lasting brand loyalty.
- **How to adapt services?** Tailor brand services along the entire customer journey—from arrival experiences and communication styles to housekeeping standards, farewell rituals, and after-service excellence—to align with cultural values and expectations in each market.

The Global Digest

Chapter 7 Takeaways

1. **Cultural context is key:** Understand and adapt to local norms, values, and expectations around customer service. Brands that respect cultural preferences build trust and loyalty, creating meaningful connections with their customers.
2. **One size does not fit all:** Customize every aspect of service, from arrival to departure and after-service interactions, to meet customer expectations. Many cultures place high value on small gestures, which can significantly enhance the customer experience.
3. **Empower your frontline:** Educate frontline staff on your brand's history, values, and cultural nuances. Empower them to serve customers effectively by providing the tools and training needed to make informed decisions and deliver exceptional service.
4. **Build emotional connections:** Create experiences that resonate with cultural expectations to make customers feel valued. Emotional connections foster brand loyalty and encourage repeat business.

5 **Speak their language:** Hire multilingual staff and localize communications to effectively engage with diverse customers. Clear and customized communication is crucial in delivering excellent customer service.

6 **Honor local traditions:** Use meaningful local customs, such as bows in Japan or the Thai *wai*, to create authentic and memorable experiences for guests. These gestures demonstrate respect and cultural sensitivity.

7 **Tech-savvy engagement:** Utilize preferred local platforms and channels for customer engagement. Embrace technology that aligns with the local market to enhance the customer experience and streamline operations.

8 **Innovate branded services:** Develop service initiatives that reinforce your core brand identity and ethics. Consistency in values across all interactions helps build a strong and trustworthy brand.

9 **Respect privacy norms:** Adhere to local data protection regulations and cultural expectations around privacy. Staying attuned to new rulings ensures compliance and maintains customer trust.

10 **Measure beyond metrics:** Evaluate service initiatives based on both financial metrics and brand equity. Consider the long-term effects on customer satisfaction and loyalty, not just immediate financial gains.

References

1 N. Evason (2019) Saudi Arabian Culture–Greetings, Cultural Atlas. culturalatlas.sbs.com.au/saudi-arabian-culture/saudi-arabian-culture-greetings (archived at https://perma.cc/AXM9-7AUJ)

2 A. Bradford (2021) Step Inside Cartier's Dubai Mall Boutique, *The Kurator*, May 26. gulfnews.com/kurator/flair/step-inside-cartiers-dubai-mall-boutique-1.1621985077714 (archived at https://perma.cc/P26W-DCVA)

3 A. Bradford (2021) Step Inside Cartier's Dubai Mall Boutique, *The Kurator*, May 26. gulfnews.com/kurator/flair/step-inside-cartiers-dubai-mall-boutique-1.1621985077714 (archived at https://perma.cc/BY7R-YKYK)

4 A. Bradford (2021) Step Inside Cartier's Dubai Mall Boutique, *The Kurator*, May 26. gulfnews.com/kurator/flair/step-inside-cartiers-dubai-mall-boutique-1.1621985077714 (archived at https://perma.cc/ED4G-Q7HS)

5 Havas UK (2023) Research Finds Unprecedented Female Spending Power Drives Luxury Transformation, Little Black Book, October 23. lbbonline.com/news/research-finds-unprecedented-female-spending-power-drives-luxury-transformation (archived at https://perma.cc/QMH4-9WNL)

6 M. Iwasaki (2017) More Women Are Buying Jewelry for Themselves, S&P Global, October 17. www.spglobal.com/marketintelligence/en/news-insights/trending/0SwNryOWuNPGcjZshfGMRg2 (archived at https://perma.cc/DZ8H-6FD2); Havas UK (2023) Research Finds Unprecedented Female Spending Power Drives Luxury Transformation, Little Black Book, October 23. lbbonline.com/news/research-finds-unprecedented-female-spending-power-drives-luxury-transformation (archived at https://perma.cc/A887-P2X2)

7 Skyquest (2024) Luxury Jewelry Market Size, Share, and Growth Analysis. www.skyquestt.com/report/luxury-jewelry-market (archived at https://perma.cc/4CUK-EWKC)

8 M. Iwasaki (2017) More Women Are Buying Jewelry for Themselves, S&P Global, October 17. www.spglobal.com/marketintelligence/en/news-insights/trending/0SwNryOWuNPGcjZshfGMRg2 (archived at https://perma.cc/DZ8H-6FD2)

9 S. Friswell (2023) 5 Key Trends in Middle Eastern Luxury Retail, LuxuryDaily, February 17. www.luxurydaily.com/5-key-trends-in-middle-eastern-luxury-retail/ (archived at https://perma.cc/NZ89-7M4V)

10 M. Oluwole (2024) Interviewed by Katherine Melchior Ray, March 21, GoogleMeet

11 M. Oluwole (2024) Interviewed by Katherine Melchior Ray, March 21, GoogleMeet

12 A. Wendlandt and M. Fuchs (2011) Out of Public Eye, Arab Women Power Haute Couture, Reuters, October 5. www.reuters.com/article/lifestyle/out-of-public-eye-arab-women-power-haute-couture-idUSTRE7942YG/ (archived at https://perma.cc/U4MK-WKNT)

13 M. Oluwole (2024) Interviewed by Katherine Melchior Ray, March 21, GoogleMeet

14 M. Oluwole (2024) Interviewed by Katherine Melchior Ray, March 21, GoogleMeet

15 M. Oluwole (2024) Interviewed by Katherine Melchior Ray, March 21, GoogleMeet

16 Louis Vuitton Staff. A Legendary History, Louis Vuitton. us.louisvuitton.com/eng-us/magazine/articles/a-legendary-history (archived at https://perma.cc/X98Q-GEEV)

17 K. Israel (2022) Chanel Conquers the Island in Dubai for the House's Latest Cruise Collection, Wallpaper*, October 26. www.wallpaper.com/fashion/chanel-conquers-the-island-in-dubai-for-the-houses-latest-cruise-collection (archived at https://perma.cc/44W6-8Z9D); Chanel. Cruise 2024/25 Show Marseille. www.chanel.com/ee/fashion/collection/cruise-2024-25/ (archived at https://perma.cc/57ZV-YSRY)

18 M. Oluwole (2024) Interviewed by Katherine Melchior Ray, March 21, GoogleMeet

19 M. Oluwole (2024) Interviewed by Katherine Melchior Ray, March 21, GoogleMeet

20 M. Oluwole (2024) Interviewed by Katherine Melchior Ray, March 21, GoogleMeet

21 M. Oluwole (2024) Interviewed by Katherine Melchior Ray, March 21, GoogleMeet

22 W. Wu (2023) Dior Reprises Fall 2023 Show in Shenzhen, *JingDaily*, July 13. jingdaily.com/posts/dior-fall-2023-rtw-shenzhen (archived at https://perma.cc/VM29-SPJX)

23 W. Wu (2023) Dior Reprises Fall 2023 Show in Shenzhen, *JingDaily*, July 13. jingdaily.com/posts/dior-fall-2023-rtw-shenzhen (archived at https://perma.cc/4MS3-SS53); DaxueConsulting (2023) Bottega Veneta's China Success Story: Blending "Quiet Luxury" with Cultural Integration, September 5. daxueconsulting.com/bottega-veneta-in-china/ (archived at https://perma.cc/7F7G-2MEG)

24 P. R. Harris (2024) Success in the European Union Depends upon Culture and Business, *European Business Review*, December 1, 16(6). doi.org/10.1108/09555340410565387 (archived at https://perma.cc/839B-DRTP)

25 D. Rizzo (2016) Chinese Expectations of Customer Experience Are Developing Fast, LinkedIn, October 26. www.linkedin.com/pulse/chinese-expectations-customer-experience-developing-fast-dave-rizzo/ (archived at https://perma.cc/YAP6-WY8H); Viva City (2023) A Guide to Improving Chinese Customer Experience with WeChat Mini Programs, April 24. www.vivacityapp.com/wechat-news/improving-chinese-customer-experience-wechat-miniprograms (archived at https://perma.cc/G9M2-L7SH)

26 M. Oluwole (2024) Interviewed by Katherine Melchior Ray, March 21, GoogleMeet

27 Patagonia, Inc. (2024) Worn Wear. wornwear.patagonia.com/ (archived at https://perma.cc/LB6K-DFPW)

28 Archive Resale Inc. (2024) Hanna Andersson Preloved. preloved.hannaandersson.com/ (archived at https://perma.cc/AB32-XTJG)

29 Nordstrom (2022) The Nordy Pod: The Truth about Nordstrom's Legendary Tire Story, August 1. press.nordstrom.com/news-releases/news-release-details/nordy-pod-truth-about-nordstroms-legendary-tire-story (archived at https://perma.cc/S6YY-4DJB)

30 C. Heath (2020) What We Can Learn from Customer Service Cultures around the World, KnowledgeOwl, January 17. blog.knowledgeowl.com/blog/posts/global-customer-service-cultures/ (archived at https://perma.cc/7XG8-KK49)

31 Zendesk (2013) Brazilians Are the Most Demanding in Customer Service, November 11. www.zendesk.com/newsroom/press-releases/brazilians-demanding-customer-service/ (archived at https://perma.cc/8WHF-Y3VW)

32 Skale Club. Key Differences between Digital Marketing in Brazil vs USA – Commercial Service. skale.club/blog/key-differences-brazil-vs-usa/ (archived at https://perma.cc/388W-QTQ8)

33 DaxueConsulting (2019) How the Chinese Customer Experience Differs from the US, July 21. daxueconsulting.com/chinese-customer-experience-us/ (archived at https://perma.cc/K3W6-MLTR)

34 Economist Intelligence Unit (2010) Greater Expectations: Keeping Pace with Customer Service Demands in Asia Pacific, *The Economist*. https://graphics.eiu.com/upload/customerservice_DHL.pdf (archived at https://perma.cc/DY7X-SHJV)

35 Deloitte (2014) Delivering Superior Customer Experience in China: The Essential Ingredient to Building Customer Loyalty. www2.deloitte.com/cn/en/pages/consumer-business/articles/essential-ingredient-to-building-customer-loyalty.html (archived at https://perma.cc/3DTK-HZDN)

36 Greg. B. (2024) US vs. Japan – The Key Difference in Customer Support, TransCosmos, January 23. transcosmos.com/blogs/customer-support/us-vs-japan-the-key-difference-in-customer-support (archived at https://perma.cc/44UV-KKVE)

37 EDPS. The History of the General Data Protection Regulation. www.edps.europa.eu/data-protection/data-protection/legislation/history-general-data-protection-regulation_en (archived at https://perma.cc/QDZ2-WYRT)

38 The CPRA. The California Privacy Rights Act of 2020. thecpra.org/ (archived at https://perma.cc/G7H2-YC8Q)

39 S. Kearney (2024) Interviewed by Katherine Melchior Ray, July 17, GoogleMeet

Found in Translation

8

Brand Flexing Across Cultures

KATHERINE MELCHIOR RAY

Natura's Amazon Beauty

In the heart of São Paulo, busy urban life meets nature's calm embrace. The late afternoon sun filters between skyscrapers on Avenida Paulista, illuminating Parque Trianon's towering jequitibá trees. Benches crafted from jacaranda wood offer rest among ipê trees abloom with vibrant yellow and pink blossoms. Young professionals and university students gather along the avenue after emerging from subway stations that transport millions every day. Families pause to watch street performers as Portuguese, English, and Spanish mingle in the vibrant cityscape. As night falls on crowded bars, Avenida Paulista embodies the intersection of old and new, urban and tropical, uniting São Paulo's diverse inhabitants in a shared appreciation of their city's dynamic culture.

São Paulo is a city of contrasts, where vibrant graffiti art in Vila Madalena meets upscale boutiques. The floral aroma of jasmine blends with freshly brewed cafezinho, sizzling picanha, and sweet brigadeiros from food vendors. While the capital city boasts 30 Michelin-starred restaurants and Latin America's largest Fashion Week,[1] its towering skyscrapers on Paulista Avenue contrast with the lush tacuma palms of Brazil's most famous natural wonder—the Amazon Rainforest. In this dynamic metropolis, the spirit of Brazil comes alive—a place where the Amazon's rich biodiversity and the city's cosmopolitan flair create a truly unique cultural landscape.

The city's celebration of its natural beauty is mirrored in the ethos of companies like Natura, a local cosmetics brand that embraces Brazil's rich biodiversity. A pioneer in the beauty industry, Natura carved a niche 50 years ago by emphasizing natural ingredients and sustainable practices.

Born and raised in São Paulo, Fábio Luizari Artoni knew firsthand the unique blend of urban sophistication and natural beauty that defined his home city. As a child, he played endless futebol games at Ibirapuera Park, biking home through its winding paths, trying to out-pedal the setting sun. Family dinners featured dishes like *farofa* served alongside meat or fish. After earning a Master's degree in corporate reputation, Artoni sought a company committed to purposeful leadership, joining Natura for its dedication to Brazil's biodiversity.

Natura had thrived for five decades within Brazil, marketing natural and sustainably sourced beauty products, like jambu face cream and soap made from açaí and cocoa butter. After door-to-door sales propelled its domestic growth, Natura set its sights on international expansion.[2]

Natura's first foray onto the global stage in 2008 proved challenging. The company had strategically planted its green flag in two of the world's most iconic shopping districts: Paris's bohemian Latin Quarter and New York's trendy SoHo. Yet, these carefully chosen outposts failed to ignite international recognition; the brand remained a virtual unknown outside Brazil—its message lost in translation.

Elevated corporate expectations matched only the high-priced rents at those retail locations. Should Artoni target different markets or position the brand differently? Artoni needed to craft a narrative around the global fascination with Brazil and the Amazon Rainforest that could resonate with diverse international audiences, while staying true to Natura's roots.

The U.S., with its strong environmental movement and fascination with Brazil's rainforest, seemed promising.

"Americans love the Amazon," says Artoni. "They fight about it, they donate to it. You have more news about the Amazon in the U.S. than in the biggest newspaper in Brazil."[3]

Alternatively, Malaysia, with its growing middle class and interest in premium skincare, offered a test case for expanding to millions of consumers throughout Southeast Asia.

"The opportunity in Malaysia was better than the U.S. at the time," Artoni notes. With less competition, Natura was more likely to succeed. And yet, while people were familiar with Brazil, the Amazon positioning didn't resonate.

"Malaysia itself has some of the biggest rainforests in the world. They have Borneo, their own equatorial rainforest," Artoni explains, "so they're less interested in the Amazon."

Artoni faced the challenge of communicating one global brand to these two vastly different cultures. Artoni and his team identified three core pillars of Natura's positioning in Brazil to focus and prioritize brand attributes for testing market resonance:

1. **Amazon origin**: Natura's natural and sustainable ingredients sourced from the Amazon
2. **Relationships**: The importance of community and connections (based on Natura's door-to-door sales approach)
3. **Care**: Caring for one's beauty as a pathway to caring for others.

Initial tests showed all three were powerful and relevant in both markets. However, Artoni knew that trying to communicate all aspects of these pillars might result in a diluted message.

"If I expect to have the customer know all aspects of these pillars, I might end up with three or more different brands around the world," he explained.

Balancing global consistency with local relevance required careful study. They developed two brand positioning options with different weighted mixes of these concepts. Artoni recognized that the best solution for all markets might mean an imperfect solution for some.

"The brand propositions we tested may not have been the best specifically for Malaysia or for the U.S.," he admitted. "But we had to talk about these three pillars in a way that makes sense in both markets."

Through qualitative analysis and digital testing, Natura developed a global brand concept that could be adapted locally. The campaign featured the Amazon as a backdrop, emphasizing natural, sustainable ingredients from the rainforest. As consumers became more familiar with the brand and its products as they moved through the conversion funnel, Natura translated the Amazon messaging and product focus differently in each country.

"The digital world supports this adaptation well," says Artoni. "You can do hundreds of tests, get feedback, and apply real-world learning outside of focus groups."

In Malaysia, Natura emphasizes skincare products, leveraging ingredients like Fevillea to promote increased hyaluronic acid in face creams. In the U.S., body lotions take center stage, with products featuring tucuma from the Amazon. This strategy of a "brand halo concept" allows Natura to maintain a consistent global image while tailoring its product offerings to local preferences.

Artoni's approach proved successful. Today, Natura's presence in over 110 countries and $22 billion valuation point to the power of thoughtful global marketing adaptation. Natura skillfully capitalized on the products' Brazilian "country of origin" to craft an authentic narrative that resonates worldwide. When people hear "Brazil," it's often the lush rainforest that springs to mind, rather than São Paulo's towering skyscrapers. Natura brilliantly tapped into the more widely recognized ecological association as a foundation of its brand story.

Artoni's strategy for Natura offers a masterful case study on how to brand global, adapt local. In this chapter, we break down key aspects of this approach to juggling brand positioning across cultures; explain powerful, but tricky, double-edged global brand and marketing concepts; and share ideas for localizing marketing campaigns to help manage the critical balance between global consistency and local communication for creating value.

Brand Storytelling across Cultures

The attributes within a brand's positioning offer a rich menu for creative ideation across cultures. (For a refresher on brand positioning, see Chapter 2.) The first rule is to remain authentic and true to the brand's core values. But as we saw with Natura, those values can be dialed up or down depending on how they resonate across cultures. The notion of resonance, therefore, is another key aspect of successful global branding. Strong brands ignite emotional connection by playing into culture, which varies around the world. Moreover, culture is always evolving, so brands need to stay relevant as markets shift. Various concepts help marketers deftly harness culture, as the real-life stories in this chapter illuminate.

Like culture itself, a brand reflects the collective programming of its actions. (For a refresher on culture, see Chapter 3.) However, while culture evolves organically, brands actively and intentionally develop programming across the organization and beyond. Building brands globally requires both intellectual agility, to understand and lean into the top lines of cultural currents, and marketing dexterity, to integrate messages aimed at different rational and emotional needs that, together, turn target audiences into loyal customers. The marketing funnel offers a convenient ladder for managing these layers as it drives customers into the brand from awareness to conversion. Creating powerful brand storytelling across cultures transforms ideas into bottom-line sales results. If this sounds like fun, it is.

Country-of-Origin Effect

One of my favorite concepts that influences brands perception across cultures relates to where the brand is from. We've emphasized how important it is to understand your brand, to know its origin story and brand values. Why? Because not only does that help anchor the brand in its unique and authentic narrative, but a brand's *country of origin* is a powerful tool in shaping consumer perceptions of quality and value.

The "country-of-origin effect" describes how a product's perceived national source shapes consumer attitudes and purchasing decisions.[4] This can stem from where a brand is founded, where a product is made, or where significant value is added. Consumer opinions—whether positive or negative—are influenced by these associations, affecting perceptions of quality, value, and desirability.

In the Natura example, Artoni understood the brand's attributes in its home market and leveraged positive global perceptions of Brazil's natural beauty and rich biodiversity. Geographic mystique affects perceived value, allowing brands to capitalize on their geographical roots.

Swiss watches, renowned worldwide for precision and craftsmanship, enable Swiss watchmakers like Rolex to command premium prices. French perfumes, synonymous with elegance and sophistication, make the "Made in France" label a mark of desirability. Japanese automobiles, celebrated for reliability and advanced technology, benefit from Japan's reputation for engineering excellence. These associations reflect long-standing cultural priorities. The perception of superior quality means consumers are willing to pay more, creating a powerful competitive advantage.[5] Thus, country of origin serves as a potent marketing signal, akin to price. Yet, while marketers can set pricing, they cannot control where goods are made. The power of global marketing is to recognize this unconscious bias and decide strategically how to highlight it.

Remember the old adage, "The further from Rome, the stronger the Faith"? The same is true for country and brand association, but don't pull out your prayer beads too quickly! This truth is powerful yet double-edged, with a potential downside when a product's origin negatively impacts consumer perception. Harvard Business School professor Rohit Deshpande calls this the "provenance paradox," where, for example, electronics made in developing countries may be perceived as inferior, regardless of their actual quality, and can't charge a fair price.[6] Wines from regions not traditionally known for winemaking might be undervalued compared to their French or

Italian counterparts. When Chile began selling its quality Cabernet Sauvignon wines abroad, it had to overcome a negative geographic perception. Companies must carefully navigate these views, balancing the benefits of promoting their origin against potential prejudices.

Recent findings show these stereotypes are weakening in our increasingly global marketplace. As more brands become international powerhouses, global stature itself is beginning to indicate quality more strongly than the "Made in" mark. Studies show that while country-of-origin associations remain influential, they are less impactful than perceptions of a brand's global presence itself.[7] This shift underscores the importance of wisely leveraging country of origin to drive the broader strategy of building global brand recognition.[8]

Shiseido: The Face of Japanese Beauty

Like Artoni, marketers need to define their brand attributes in the home market to determine how they resonate across culture. It's not enough for a brand to be simply known in different parts of the world; it must be recognized consistently for its unique qualities. Having multiple brand dimensions enlarges your marketing toolkit to leverage alternative messages to consumers in different locations or at different times. A caution—while cultural adaptation is important, too much variation dilutes the brand.

In the 1870s, as Japan emerged from 200 years of isolation, the Meiji Emperor initiated reforms encouraging interaction with the West.[9] Arinobu Fukuhara founded Shiseido in 1872 as a Western-style pharmacy in Tokyo's Ginza, introducing cosmetics that modernized Japanese beauty standards.[10] In 1888, after the tradition of blackening women's teeth was outlawed, a custom known as *Ohaguro*, Shiseido launched a scientifically designed toothpaste as a healthier alternative to damaging powders.[11] Shiseido's later innovations in skincare, formulating the anti-aging hyaluronic acid, perfume, and makeup, cemented its reputation as a beauty pioneer. Fukuhara's son, Shinzō, who studied photography in New York and Paris, incorporated art and culture into the Shiseido brand, with its stylized camellia logo as early as 1915.[12]

In the 1970s, when Japan was better known for high-quality electronics than cosmetics, Shiseido expanded the business into the U.S. and Europe. Breaking into Western markets proved difficult for the brand. The subtlety of Japanese art often puzzled Western audiences. In the U.S., Shiseido's avant-garde, aspirational image clashed with its competitive pricing strategy, confusing consumers and weakening its premium positioning.[13] Despite these challenges, Yoshiharu Fukuhara, Shiseido's president and grandson of the founder, defended the brand's approach, stating, "If this image seems too sophisticated... too bad. I think that the American market is a sophisticated market."[14]

In 2017, I was hired as a consultant and later as CMO to build Shiseido's prestige brands internationally. While Shiseido had grown into a global beauty powerhouse, 75 per cent of its revenue came from Asian countries, where Japanese aesthetics were better understood.[15] Korean beauty was surging internationally with the catchy phrase "K Beauty."[16] Meanwhile, Shiseido, the grande dame of Asian skincare, needed to define the qualities of what would become "J Beauty."

Global studies confirmed the Shiseido brand's fragmented identity. Functional and emotional benefits of even award-winning products were unclear. The most positive brand attributes were recognized by only the smaller markets. The brand had a global marketing problem.

Based on this data and internal research, we began to refine our positioning. We clarified our core attributes with a diverse, regionally representative team: high-quality products, research and innovation, culture, and relationships. A Japanese colleague highlighted the holistic approach to beauty through multi-step skincare routines that engage the senses—texture, touch, color, scent, and sound—as reflecting the Shinto belief in the energy of nature. Ultimately, we distilled the essence of Shiseido's Japanese beauty as a fusion of art and science, anchored in the brand's history and expressed through *Omotenashi*, or deep respect for self and others.

We drew on the brand's Japanese heritage to enhance our marketing strategies, highlighting our rich archives and hosting cultural performances in various markets. By unmasking the hidden qualities of Shiseido's Japanese beauty—a harmonious blend of art and innovation—we created a cohesive brand identity that resonates worldwide.

History Is Not Only for School

Frameworks like heritage and country of origin build emotional value for brands. Strategically marketing a brand's history transforms its heritage into powerful, competitive differentiation. Narrating history goes beyond recounting the past; it anchors, deepens, and broadens the brand. In the luxury sector, history serves as proof of a brand's timeless appeal and long-lasting value derived from decades of commitment to craftsmanship and innovation. A rich heritage allows brands to justify premium pricing and cultivate deep loyalty by offering more than just products—an experience rooted in tradition, provenance, and culture.

Marketers must select the historical elements that align with the brand's core values. How a brand curates these stories anchors its authenticity and provides inspiration for maintaining future relevance. For Shiseido, innovation was spurred by new markets, new ways of seeing the world, and new expressions, combined with relentless research and development. Shiseido has been synonymous with Japanese culture and its evolving definition of beauty and women's roles in society for over 100 years. Connecting with important cultural and historic movements, heritage stories create brand value and deepen its appeal for wider audiences.

Bernard Arnault, founder and chairman of the world's largest luxury holding company, LVMH, says they don't conform to traditional marketing. In a forum at Oxford University, he explained the company does not analyze customer desires and tailor their products accordingly. Instead, he explains, they innovate freely, creating new products which may sometimes fail, but which, when successful, set trends that customers eagerly follow.[17]

In reality, this approach is itself a sophisticated marketing strategy, designed to leverage exclusivity and aspiration to maintain Louis Vuitton's premium positioning in the luxury market. By claiming they "don't do marketing," Arnault reinforces the brand's image as authentic and driven by artistry, rather than commerce.

I can attest Louis Vuitton engages in marketing. The company appointed me Vice President of Marketing for Louis Vuitton Japan. What Arnault is describing is actually their approach to product development and brand positioning. In contrast with reactive, consumer-led product marketing, Louis Vuitton emphasizes innovation and creativity, using market research to get inspired. They lead trends, rather than follow them. This requires taking measured risks with new product launches. The approach aims to shape consumer desire rather than respond to it and positions the brand as a tastemaker and industry leader.

Running marketing for one of the world's top brands is no ordinary job. As I often explained to my teams, my guiding principles for leading a global brand are clear: our first priority is always, *always*, to protect the brand. The brand is supreme, larger and lasting longer than our business, and measured in long-term value versus daily, monthly, and annual sales. In a fiercely competitive industry, others are always trying to borrow your cache or bring you down. Our second job is to stay *a half-step ahead* of the market: A full step may be too far ahead of cultural resonance, but if you're not pushing the brand forward at the edge of culture, you leave room for competitors to outmaneuver you and claim the future. This tricky balance—protecting while pushing—is the true art of leading the world's most powerful brands.

Our Louis Vuitton teams spent a great deal of time creating consumer demand by building brand value through connecting to culture. In addition to supporting product launches and new store openings, we initiated content, campaigns, and events to connect the brand to both French and Japanese cultures. As you'll recall from Chapter 1, we had a department called "Patrimoine," or cultural heritage, dedicated to preserving and communicating the brand's history. We worked to connect Louis Vuitton's history to the modern customer by crafting a cinematic series that celebrated the antique trunks' global stories and cultural significance. In a Tokyo studio, we arranged each trunk with reverence, treating them as cultural artifacts rather than mere products. With dramatic lighting reminiscent of a theater stage, the resulting imagery evoked a timeless elegance that bridged past craftsmanship with contemporary storytelling. The book invited customers into stores not just to shop, but to engage with the heritage and artistry that defined the brand. It was a powerful reminder that connecting products to cultural narratives can transform a transaction into an emotional experience.

Marketing heritage through history is not just about preservation, but about evolution, ensuring that the brand's narrative adapts while maintaining its core identity. This approach turns historical legacy into a continuous competitive advantage, showcasing how a deep appreciation of history can be a powerful tool in crafting compelling and lasting brand stories.

Infusing Gucci's Icon Amor with Love

Gucci is another brand that understands the power of cultural storytelling and innovation. A century before Lady Gaga and Adam Driver brought Gucci's glamor-studded, tragedy-lined story to the silver screen, the brand was founded in 1921 in Florence, Italy, where it earned a reputation for exquisite leatherwork and equestrian products. During World War II, when leather was scarce, the brand showcased its ingenuity by creating the iconic bamboo handle—a testament to Gucci's ability to adapt creatively in challenging times.

When I joined Gucci in Japan in 2008, the company was preparing for the following year's new, exclusive jewelry launch, an annual tradition set to coincide with a peak sales period during Golden Week each spring. However, frequent use of Gucci's interlocking GG logo in recent designs had begun diluting the impact of the iconic symbol. Consumers were growing tired of the predictable offerings, leading to a two-year decline in sales. It was clear we needed a fresh approach.

The challenge was real: The ring, featuring a heart along with the famous GGs, was already in production. The teams in Italy would, however, work with me around the product. I needed to reposition this product from a repeat lookalike to an original Gucci creation. Nothing, aside from those GGs, spoke to Gucci the brand and its Italian heritage of design and craftsmanship. I thought of featuring the brand's creative director, Frida Giannini, but she was busy redesigning the brand's flagship store in Rome.

The word "love" felt too English, too American, too trite. I wanted, somehow, to leverage Italy, the brand's country of origin. Italy, after all, is the birthplace of romance, from the passion of Dante's sonnets to the iconic love stories of *la dolce vita*. In Italian, love is *amore*, or *amor*.

Looking at that word, the idea struck me immediately. I realized "amor" is the exact opposite, the mirror reflection of Roma, the Italian name for its capital city. I found our new name and concept: Gucci Icon Amor, an exclusive creation by Frida Giannini in honor of the Roma flagship store redesign.

To illustrate the connection between "amor" and "Roma" and to evoke Gucci's Italian heritage of handmade craftsmanship, we cleverly photographed the rings on a stone bridge in front of the Roman Colosseum. The shoot set contemporary elegance amidst Italy's storied past, with the rings glittering against ancient cobblestones graced by the feet of everyone from Roman centurions to modern-day lovers roaming the streets. We added pink and white gold options to make it a collection and launched an integrated marketing, PR, and retail campaign to bring the story to life. In-store displays and sales training infused Gucci's rich history into every customer interaction, and an online microsite with a countdown to the launch date built anticipation.

The results were remarkable. Not only did sales meet expectations, but they surpassed previous records from two years earlier. The success demonstrates how effectively storytelling can connect people to culture and deliver emotional value for a brand. Gucci Icon Amor stands as a shining example of how leveraging history and heritage can turn marketing challenges into opportunities, creating intimacy with audiences to reinforce a brand's iconic value.

Balancing the Brand Fulcrum

The Brand Fulcrum is a strategic framework I developed to maintain a brand's vitality and relevance over time by balancing opposing yet complementary values (Figure 8.1). A fulcrum, used for balance, helps visualize the extremes of a brand's identity—tradition and authenticity on one side, innovation and trend on the other. Gucci is a prime example of how a brand can successfully navigate this balance. Known for over a century for traditional craftsmanship, working with family-owned factories in Italy, Gucci also reflects the fashion zeitgeist with trendy designs. Tom Ford's daring, provocative creations of the 1990s or Alessandro Michele's eclectic, inclusive styles of the 2010s exemplify how Gucci has stayed fresh without losing its heritage. Stores may feature the classic bamboo bag alongside Michele's wild, mixed prints—an exciting juxtaposition that keeps the brand dynamic.

The fulcrum ensures a brand doesn't become too classic and conservative, or too flirty and fleeting. By pushing both edges, brands can expand their range and appeal, blending heritage and craftsmanship with edgy, avant-garde innovation. This elasticity creates a sense of friction that drives excitement and market relevance, ensuring that the brand evolves while staying true to its core identity. The Brand Fulcrum serves as a powerful tool for building brand relevance and value in an ever-changing marketplace.

The Art of Campaign Localization (Without Losing the Core Brand Identity)

The above ideas—the country-of-origin effect and its counterpart, the provenance paradox; the value of history and heritage; and the Brand Fulcrum—are all frameworks that bring the brand's intrinsic values to life across cultures.

Figure 8.1 Brand Fulcrum

- ✔ **VALUE**: Creates emotional meaning
- ✔ **RANGE**: Achieves wide appeal
- ✔ **ELASTICITY**: Displays energy and adaptability
- → **RELEVANCE**: Ensures the brand remains fresh, pertinent, and meaningful to its target audience

They rely on cultural perceptions to anchor and illustrate brand values. Other ways to create value across cultures focus less on building the brand from the inside out, and more on adapting marketing by localizing campaigns, copy, imagery, influencers, and media.

Greg Hoffman, former CMO at Nike and author of *Emotion by Design*, insists that marketers should aim to communicate not only the rational value of products but also their emotional value. This ensures brands are not merely seen as commodities, and that the audience is willing to pay beyond the medium price point in a category:

> *"To effectively communicate the rational value, we found it effective to write product attribute descriptions from a global center of excellence, leveraging proximity to where innovations and product designs are created—often months or even years in advance. This approach maintains consistency in product details, ensuring the story strengthens as it approaches the market. To deliver emotional value, we must enable our audiences to see themselves reflected in our brand stories, allowing local teams to tailor these narratives."*[18]

Anchoring Stores in Culture

As Hoffman observed, when people see themselves in the brand, they derive deeper, more personal value, and local teams are often best suited to tailor those topics. Brands are increasingly collaborating with local artists and architects to create physical spaces that embody both their global identity and local cultural significance.

Louis Vuitton's long history in Japan exemplifies this strategy. When establishing their first standalone store in Tokyo's Ginza district in 1981, they enlisted renowned Japanese architect Jun Aoki. Evoking the brick structures symbolic of Ginza's Meiji era, his design seamlessly blended Japanese heritage with French luxury. When Louis Vuitton embraced local artistry, Japanese consumers felt honored and it deepened their connection to the brand.

Starbucks has embraced such localization in Japan, creating unique outlets that honor local history and culture. In Kyoto, a Starbucks occupies a traditional *machiya* townhouse from the Taisho period (1912–1926), complete with tatami floors, *zabuton* cushions made from local kimono fabric, and *tokonoma* display spaces. This store received the Kyoto Scenery Award for its preservation of tradition alongside contemporary coffee culture.

In Hokkaido, Starbucks repurposed a centuries-old warehouse, preserving its wooden flooring and staircase while offering views of Hakodate Bay. The outlet in Aomori Prefecture occupies a former division commander's residence from 1917, blending Western and Japanese design elements.

Even in less historic settings, Starbucks demonstrates cultural sensitivity. In Saitama Prefecture, the café resembles a traditional warehouse with a locally sourced cedarwood exterior and a tiled roof. Inside, repurposed *fusuma* sliding panels serve as wall art, while bench cushions feature local Kawagoe *tozan* kimono fabric.

According to Starbucks Coffee Japan CEO Takafumi Minaguchi, "Our unique store designs perform very well both financially and for brand development." Minaguchi and I had worked together earlier at Louis Vuitton Japan, so I have no doubt he was instrumental in that development. He continues, "One of our brand missions is to be close to each community, so unique stores with locally sourced art and handcrafted material are important brand expressions. Our partners (Starbucks employees) love how relevant stories from each unique location help them connect one on one with our customers."[19]

Budweiser's British #DreamGoal

You may think of Budweiser as the quintessential American brand. If so, their U.S. marketing campaigns have done the trick—ads featuring thirsty cowboys in boots and handsome cowgirls in blue jeans, meeting up at the local bar to crack a cold one after a hot, dusty day on the ranch. As any NFL fan knows, it's not the Super Bowl without a Budweiser commercial.

In 2013, Jennifer Anton moved to England as Brand Manager for Budweiser in the U.K. Her challenge: Make Budweiser as relevant and sexy in the U.K. as it is in the U.S. Having led innovation and global brands in the U.S. beer industry, she was determined to increase Budweiser's brand awareness and market share against the well-established local brands Carling and Carlsberg.

High-profile global sponsorships certainly helped, such as the NFL, the FIFA World Cup, and the MADE music festival with Jay-Z and Rihanna. These premiere sports and music events reinforced Budweiser's American values—optimism, energy, a sense of togetherness, and the pursuit of the American dream. Focus groups and surveys revealed that consumers viewed these characteristics positively and they were universal values that resonate across borders.

The most valuable local marketing initiative in the U.K. was the Football Association Challenge Cup (FA Cup), which Budweiser had sponsored for three years. Yet, only one year after Anton arrived, Emirates won the FA Cup's title sponsorship and, along with it, Budweiser's most valuable asset for connecting with U.K. consumers. How could she come up with a campaign to celebrate the hugely popular sport of football without a local sponsorship?

Anton convened an emergency meeting with cross-functional teams and agencies to devise a new local plan to bring the brand to life. They revisited discarded ad campaign concepts and brainstormed new ideas; from them, #DreamGoal was born, a campaign celebrating extraordinary goals by everyday players in Sunday leagues.[20] The campaign partnered with Sky Sports media, creating ads that looked like amateur footage with professional commentary, inviting the public to "Send in their Screamers." Plastering the campaign nationally across retail, pubs, local parks, and football fields generated widespread buzz.

The campaign quickly went viral. Players across the U.K. flooded Budweiser's site and social media with their Dream Goal submissions. The climax came when the winning goal was aired nationwide and celebrated by league elites, after which the champion Northern England player was treated to a VIP experience at that year's FA Cup.

#DreamGoal not only won awards but also secured Budweiser's place in the hearts of British consumers.

"Dream Goal was a win," explains Anton, "because it did what Budweiser does best, using its positioning as the King of Beers to shine a light on and celebrate others. Staying true to both the heart of the brand and understanding our U.K. consumer so perfectly made it a standout campaign."[21]

Under great pressure and time constraints, the team's innovative approach demonstrated how making a brand's core values resonate authentically with local audiences is key to building brand value across culture.

Emotional Essence across Cultures

Whether customers are sweating it out or spritzing it on, brands that connect locally deliver results.

Think of the last time you bought perfume or saw a perfume ad. Were you interested in specific product attributes? Was the ad communicating ingredients or the number of ounces in a bottle? Or were you motivated by pleasure, some emotional desire evoked by the scent, the bottle, the imagery, or the name?

Our sense of smell is connected to our limbic system, which regulates emotion and memory.[22] This forges emotional connections especially important for fragrances, which are gifted more than other luxury categories.[23]

However, the deeply emotive power of scent also presents a challenge, as the notion of "pleasure" varies greatly across cultures.[24] Fragrance marketing demands a nuanced cultural understanding to cultivate visceral desire across vastly different markets.

According to Morin Oluwole, formerly Meta's Director and Global Head of Luxury, "Perfumes are anchored in emotion, even more so than other luxury products, so they have high liquidity for cultural adaptation."[25] This fluidity requires brands to navigate a delicate balance between global consistency and local customization.

Certain markets, like the Middle East and Asia, demand more extensive adaptation through imagery, model and product selection, and styling. Oluwole recounts working with luxury brands in the Middle East to ensure Ramadan-timed marketing materials resonated with the market without risking cultural appropriation. This included incorporating holiday symbols into marketing content and even tailoring scent preferences.[26]

Aligning global and local strategies can pose challenges. Oluwole found that luxury brands in the Middle East prepared for Ramadan months in advance, yet often received marketing campaign content weeks or sometimes just days before this key period began.

Oluwole emphasized the importance of providing cultural context to headquarters, even when it meant delivering difficult feedback. "Global brands tend to be receptive to on-the-ground feedback related to cultural nuance around issues like styling and skin exposure, especially if they want to stay competitive," she says.[27]

Global campaigns tend to feature one brand ambassador, but may choose a different celebrity for specific market preferences. For example, CHANEL and Louis Vuitton are known to adapt their global brand campaigns in Asian markets with popular K-pop stars as their brand ambassadors.[28]

The beauty industry has taken this localization approach to new heights, particularly in China. Rather than relying on attractive female models, brands have embraced fresh-faced male stars as marketing ambassadors. These young idols, propelled by popular talent shows, command large female fan bases eager to support the brands they represent.

The strategy has paid dividends: when singer-actor Xiao Zhan partnered with NARS Cosmetics, the brand's sales skyrocketed 200 per cent, generating over $11 million.[29] Xiao Zhan, known as China's "King of Luxury," now fronts three leading beauty brands. Similarly, rapper Jackson Wang joined fellow K-pop star Lisa from Blackpink to serve as a male ambassador for MAC Cosmetics.

This trend illustrates additional opportunities to brand global and adapt local. What might seem unconventional in one market can drive success in another. Recognizing cultural differences and adjusting our approach reveals the subjectivity of our own assumptions. Balancing global brand imperatives requires applying emotional intelligence to marketing strategies. As the global landscape evolves, the key to building brand value lies in leveraging culturally relevant trends. Successful brands seamlessly blend universal brand narratives with local insights to create emotional connections that resonate in diverse cultures.

Interview Insight: Eclat

Romance and Radiance across Cultures

Sweden-based Oriflame, Europe's largest direct-selling beauty company, works with over three million independent consultants in 60 countries.[30] Reflecting its Scandinavian roots, Oriflame's beauty philosophy celebrates natural radiance and elegance, empowering women to embrace their authentic beauty. Oriflame communicates new products to this global network via catalog, while the affiliates determine their own promotion to consumers.

In between two stints at Natura, Fábio Luizari Artoni chose to work abroad to experience different cultures and understand their business challenges. Joining Oriflame as its Global Director of Fragrances in its Swedish headquarters, Artoni reflects on the contrast with Natura in Brazil, "We were based in the smallest market, driving business for 35 other countries."

In 2015, Oriflame prepared that year's largest launch for the flagship fragrance, Eclat, across three culturally diverse markets. The goal was ambitious: getting over 50 of their sales consultants in the top three markets of Russia, Poland, and Indonesia to purchase at least one bottle within the first 30 days.

"As our biggest launch of the year," explains Artoni, "we needed to ensure strong adoption by our 1.2 million sellers in these key markets for Eclat, whose name means 'luminosity' in French."

They were going to put Eclat on the cover of that month's catalog, but how to position Eclat to market one fragrance successfully to all three markets?

If we use the C.A.G.E. framework discussed in Chapter 3 to evaluate the three countries, Russia and Poland prove closer geographically and culturally to each other than either country is to Indonesia. Both Russia and Poland are Christian countries, whereas Indonesia is a predominantly Muslim nation.[31] Indonesia is a collectivist society, with strong emphasis on family and relationships within a social group.[32]

Artoni confirms these cultural themes bore out in Oriflame's research and discussions with consumers: "We saw common storytelling potential for Russia and Poland, given their geographical and cultural proximity. For women there, fragrances were about attraction, feeling beautiful and alluring—a way to express self-esteem."

Indonesia, however, presented a challenge.

"In Indonesia, it was also about power and self-esteem, but expressed differently," Artoni continued. "In this Muslim, family-driven society, it was more about bringing positive energy and connecting people." Indonesian consumers wouldn't identify with the same kinds of emotional appeals as their Russian and Polish counterparts.

To solve this brand challenge, the team created one global brand positioning centered on self-esteem and empowerment, with consistent global pricing, but tailored the visual storytelling to each market's cultural values. Oriflame featured the same Parisian setting in front of the Eiffel Tower with an elegant model basked in soft pink lighting, but adjusted her clothing and expression in two separate catalog images. The European versions featured an attractive, confident woman in sleeveless summer dresses. In one image, she is looking at the camera from behind, over her bare shoulders as if beckoning a man to follow; in another, she gently rests her head and nude arms on a man's shoulder.

For the Indonesian market, the same woman appears solo, in personal reflection, her shoulders covered in a soft, feminine silk blouse. Self-esteem, in this context, is expressed through inner radiance and spiritual connection, bringing one's best self to the world.

The launch exceeded expectations, with Eclat achieving over 50 adoptions among sales consultants across all three markets.

At Oriflame's Swedish headquarters, Artoni knew their success was in large part due to the diversity of his global team and getting locals involved in the decisions. With 350 people from 33 different countries operating from one of Oriflame's smallest markets, the team at the Swedish headquarters showed deep appreciation for cultural differences and knew how to ask the right questions about new markets. They first set clear expectations on which elements were open for local adaptation and insisted everyone distinguish between their subjective preferences and data-driven insights.

"The diversity of the team brings a lot of value," reflects Artoni. "Whether it's nationality, gender, orientation, or religion, the more diverse a team is, the more open it becomes to listening and understanding other cultures. A diverse team is better equipped to navigate cultural challenges and perform in global markets." We will soon dive into the topic of teamwork when we put all of these ideas together in the final section.

In this chapter, we explored how to adapt marketing both from the inside out through cultural brand storytelling and from the outside in by localizing campaigns, imagery, communication, and store design. From beers to bags, frappucinos to fragrances, there are countless ways to blend existing elements with local flavor. Successful marketing adapts to diversify the consumer experience across markets. With more brands than ever investing in a digital presence to merge offline and online experiences, more and more companies can reach customers globally. However, as we discuss next in Chapter 9, adapting a digital go-to-market business is very different from building a global brand.

Summary

- **What is adapting marketing to culture?** Tailoring marketing strategies to resonate with target audiences by creating emotional connections that align with their cultural values. Different markets embody unique traditions, preferences, and expectations, so successful brands adjust their campaigns, products, and messaging to reflect and respect these regional differences.
- **Why adapt marketing to culture?** Meeting the unique needs and expectations of diverse markets increases brand relevance, expands brand reach, and drives growth in competitive global environments by creating emotional connections to cultural preferences of diverse audiences.
- **How to adapt marketing to culture?** Visit the markets and involve local teams to understand the target audience. Then, strategize how best to leverage cultural perceptions in brand storytelling, imagery, messaging, and store design, collaborating with local artists, ambassadors, and more!

The Global Digest

Chapter 8 Takeaways

1 Marketing's global tightrope: Successful brands find the delicate balance between maintaining global consistency and adapting to local market needs. This requires staying true to core brand attributes while understanding and integrating local cultural values.

2 **AI insights:** Large language model platforms allow brands to rapidly test and gather insights for adapting marketing strategies across cultures. This agility enables companies to gather real-world feedback outside traditional focus groups and quickly apply learnings in rapid iteration.

3 **Top-of-funnel brand halo:** Creating one unified campaign for consistent messaging worldwide drives brand awareness and maximum return at the top of the conversion funnel. As consumers learn more, content can adapt to cultural preferences along the conversion funnel through narrative, imagery, and product offering.

4 **Culture is king, queen, and empire:** Strong global brands maintain relevance by continuously adapting their storytelling to culture. As culture is always evolving, leaning into those layers of emotion keeps brand values current.

5 **Rooting in heritage:** A brand's history and heritage are powerful tools for creating authenticity, competitive differentiation, and long-lasting value. Not just luxury brands but all brands can expand into this cultural playbook and leverage the power of the passage of time.

6 **Country-of-origin prism:** A brand's country of origin can significantly shape consumer perceptions of quality and value to influence purchasing decisions. Strategically highlighting a brand's geographical roots allows brands to command premium prices for competitive advantage.

7 **The provenance paradox:** While a product's origin might boost its appeal, it can also lead to negative perceptions if the country is not generally associated with high quality. Understanding which aspect is at play allows brands to dial this powerful symbol up or down.

8 **Global branding creates quality impression:** In an increasingly globalized marketplace, a brand's global stature can signify quality more than its country of origin, emphasizing the importance of a strong international presence.

9 **Balance the brand fulcrum:** Strong brands integrate seemingly opposing themes, such as tradition and innovation, to enrich the brand's range, depth, and vitality. The Brand Fulcrum framework ensures brand relevance and value in an ever-changing marketplace.

10 **Diverse teams, global success:** A diverse team brings a wealth of perspectives and cultural insights, making it better equipped to navigate the complexities of global marketing and adapt strategies to resonate with local audiences.

References

1 RT Staff Reporters (2024) Michelin Guide 2024: 21 Restaurants in Rio de Janeiro and São Paulo Awarded Stars, *The Rio Times*, May 21. www.riotimesonline.com/michelin-guide-2024-21-restaurants-in-rio-de-janeiro-and-sao-paulo-awarded-stars/ (archived at https://perma.cc/6ZSM-D2WZ); Folhapress. São Paulo Fashion Week, Google Arts & Culture. artsandculture.google.com/story/sC3A3o-paulo-fashion-week-folha-de-sp/PgWBW1gPMLd_Og?hl=en (archived at https://perma.cc/N22Q-K8JQ)

2 C. S. Kogut, P. E. H. Boldrini, R. Cotta de Mello, and L. Fonseca (2022) Natura Goes Shopping: The Case of an Emerging Market Multinational, *Revista de Administração Contemporânea*, 26(6). doi.org/10.1590/1982-7849rac2022210103.en (archived at https://perma.cc/ZA8Z-8GUE)

3 F. Artoni (2024) Interviewed by Katherine Melchior Ray, June 5, GoogleMeet; October 2, email

4 Management Study Guide Content Team. Country of Origin Effects on Marketing: How Brands from Certain Countries Score over the Others, Management Study Guide. www.managementstudyguide.com/country-of-origin-effects-on-marketing.htm (archived at https://perma.cc/4XLW-442Z)

5 A. Cristea, C. Gabriela, and S. Roxana-Denisa (2015) Country-of-Origin Effects on Perceived Brand Positioning, *Procedia Economics and Finance*, 23. dx.doi.org/10.1016/S2212-5671(15)00383-4 (archived at https://perma.cc/B2MK-MRVW)

6 S. Silverthorne (2010) Milwaukee Chocolate? Overcoming the Provenance Paradox, CBS News, December 2. www.cbsnews.com/news/milwaukee-chocolate-overcoming-the-provenance-paradox/ (archived at https://perma.cc/A9AH-5LX2)

7 D. Holt, J. Quelch, and E. L. Taylor (2004) How Global Brands Compete, *Harvard Business Review*, September. hbr.org/2004/09/how-global-brands-compete (archived at https://perma.cc/83DZ-CEA4)

8 D. Holt, J. Quelch, and E. L. Taylor (2004) How Global Brands Compete, *Harvard Business Review*, September. hbr.org/2004/09/how-global-brands-compete (archived at https://perma.cc/U8V5-ZGH8)

9 J. Huffman (2003) The Meiji Restoration Era, 1868–1889, Japan Society. japansociety.org/news/the-meiji-restoration-era-1868-1889/ (archived at https://perma.cc/D3UF-A69X)

10 L. Gumpert (2000) Face to Face: Shiseido and the Manufacture of Beauty, 1900–2000, Grey Art Museum New York University. greyartmuseum.nyu.edu/exhibition/shiseido-091500-102800/ (archived at https://perma.cc/SA2K-SLW8)

11 Shiseido Team (2022) History, Shiseido. corp.shiseido.com/en/company/history/ (archived at https://perma.cc/TDY2-KWRL)

12 The British Museum. Fukuhara Shinzo. www.britishmuseum.org/collection/term/BIOG187400 (archived at https://perma.cc/B3AZ-5M8R)

13 A. Aktar and S. Raper (1995) Shiseido's Patience Pays Off in Europe; U.S. Is Next Target, *Women's Wear Daily*, September 29. wwd.com/feature/article-1146647-1754155/ (archived at https://perma.cc/74TP-DWW7)

14 A. Aktar and S. Raper (1995) Shiseido's Patience Pays Off in Europe; U.S. Is Next Target, *Women's Wear Daily*, September 29. wwd.com/feature/article-1146647-1754155/ (archived at https://perma.cc/B3UV-WHX4)

15 Shiseido Team (2022) Integrated Report 2022, Shiseido. corp.shiseido.com/report/en/2022/pdf/report-en.pdf (archived at https://perma.cc/6M99-T6PU)

16 M. Russon (2018) K-beauty: The Rise of Korean Make-up in the West, BBC News, October 20. www.bbc.com/news/business-45820671 (archived at https://perma.cc/L23N-4QUR)

17 Oxford Union (2016) Bernard Arnault – Full Q&A – Oxford Union, YouTube. www.youtube.com/watch?v=EhNKy5yNIgs&t=2s (archived at https://perma.cc/2BJE-4ZGH)

18 G. Hoffman (2024) Correspondence with Katherine Melchior Ray, June 19, email

19 T. Minaguchi (2024) Correspondence with Katherine Melchior Ray, August 22, email

20 C. Ainsley. Budweiser: Dream Goal, ThisisCraigAinsley. thisiscraigainsley.com/budweiser (archived at https://perma.cc/YPJ3-LWPQ)

21 J. Anton (2024) Correspondence with Katherine Melchior Ray, July 7, email

22 C. Walsh (2020) What the Nose Knows: Experts Discuss the Science of Smell and How Scent, Emotion, and Memory Are Intertwined – and Exploited, *The Harvard Gazette*, February 27. news.harvard.edu/gazette/story/2020/02/how-scent-emotion-and-memory-are-intertwined-and-exploited/ (archived at https://perma.cc/LT36-5UH3)

23 J. Wenskus (2023) The Top-Gifted Beauty Item During the Holidays, Beauty Packaging, December 18. www.beautypackaging.com/contents/view_experts-opinion/2023-12-18/the-top-gifted-beauty-item-during-the-holidays/ (archived at https://perma.cc/J47M-GL86)

24 H. Evanschitzky, O. Emrich, V. Sangtani, A. Ackfeldt, K. E. Reynolds, and M. J. Arnold (2014) Hedonic Shopping Motivations in Collectivistic and Individualistic Consumer Cultures, *International Journal of Research in Marketing*, September, 31(3). doi.org/10.1016/j.ijresmar.2014.03.001 (archived at https://perma.cc/4N3W-WHJW)

25 M. Oluwole (2024) Interviewed by Katherine Melchior Ray, June 11, GoogleMeet; October 6, email

26 S. DiGuiseppe (2023) A Haute Look at Van Cleef & Arpels' Stunning New Alhambra Collection: The Alhambra Carnelian, *Haute Living*, June 19. hauteliving.com/2023/06/a-haute-look-at-van-cleef-arpels-stunning-new-alhambra-collection-the-alhambra-carnelian/732083/ (archived at https://perma.cc/SX4N-S5YU)

27 M. Oluwole (2024) Interviewed by Katherine Melchior Ray, June 11, GoogleMeet; October 6, email

28 C. Tai. (2023) From Jackson Wang, to Wang Yibo: How K-Pop's Chinese Stars Become China's Favorite Brand Ambassadors, *Jing Daily*, January 23. https://jingdaily.com/posts/ethnic-chinese-kpop-stars-china (archived at https://perma.cc/3PDN-BAGC); C. Tai (2023) K-pop Group RIIZE: Louis Vuitton's Newest House Ambassadors, *Jing Daily*, December 13. jingdaily.com/posts/rising-k-pop-group-riize-is-louis-vuitton-s-newest-house-ambassador (archived at https://perma.cc/C2KG-S2XQ)

29 D. N. Le. (2023) 8 Chinese Male Idols Who Became the Face of Beauty Brands: From Xiao Zhan and Hong Kong's Jackson Wang to TFBoys' Roy Wang and "Uncle Star" Huang Bo, Repping for Nars, Mac, Shiseido and More, *Style*, July 10. www.scmp.com/magazines/style/celebrity/article/3227112/8-chinese-male-idols-who-became-face-beauty-brands-xiao-zhan-and-hong-kongs-jackson-wang-tfboys-roy (archived at https://perma.cc/BA4J-7GRR)

30 Oriflame Team (2019) This Is Oriflame, Oriflame. investors.oriflame.com/en/this-is-oriflame (archived at https://perma.cc/QG39-4BFB)

31 Pew Research Center (2017) Religious Belief and National Belonging in Central and Eastern Europe, May 10. www.pewresearch.org/religion/2017/05/10/religious-affiliation/ (archived at https://perma.cc/WTX5-9K44)

32 K. C. Stirling (2024) 5 facts about Muslims and Christians in Indonesia, Pew Research Center, March 28. www.pewresearch.org/short-reads/2024/03/28/5-facts-about-muslims-and-christians-in-indonesia/ (archived at https://perma.cc/3F5F-WSKU)

How Global Is Your Website? 9

Digital Marketing Across Cultures

NATALY KELLY

High-Speed Tech Localization at Scale

When you think about adapting digital experiences for local customers, what's the first thing that comes to mind? Many people think about how hard it is to translate content, not only adapting messages, but conveying the right meaning. Indeed, that work is difficult. Images, however, are often considered more universal in nature—or so we might mistakenly think. I learned a lesson the hard way on this topic while overseeing the launch of not only a local website, but a new international office for HubSpot, a leading marketing automation and customer relationship management (CRM) platform company where I worked for eight years.

But first, let's rewind. Prior to joining this high-growth tech company, I was well known for my expertise in globalization, localization, and international business. I had led numerous globalization projects for Google, LinkedIn, and NetApp as a consultant; advised foreign governments; and presented before the European Commission as a subject matter expert. I had written on these topics for *Harvard Business Review*, and my expertise was frequently cited in *The New York Times*. I served as an adjunct professor in Middlebury Institute's graduate degree programs in localization, a feeder program for Silicon Valley's top tech companies.

But every business's path to international growth is different, and some companies simply move faster than others. Already a public company when I joined, HubSpot was in what tech companies call "hyper-growth" mode, sustaining double-digit growth rates at an already impressive size. We were known for being big and fast.

Today, nearly half of the company's revenue comes from customers outside of the U.S. HubSpot serves more than 205,000 businesses in 135 countries, with 7,500 employees across 14 global offices.[1] But when I joined in 2015, we were very early in this journey, with less than 20 per cent of revenue coming from foreign markets. We had international employees, but in English-speaking markets only (Ireland, Australia, Singapore).

I was no stranger to global websites. I had worked as a Spanish translator for websites in the earliest days of the internet, when we had to make translations by editing HTML code ourselves. I had also worked at a software company that developed the technology behind complex, international websites such as Tesla, Slack, Canva, Pinterest, British Airways, and others. But it was not until my job at HubSpot that I created a website for a new country and language at turbo-speed, leading me to experience one of the most professionally embarrassing moments of my life.

I joined the company as Vice President (VP) of Marketing, excited to be part of HubSpot's world-class marketing team. At the time, HubSpot was inspiring marketers all over the U.S. to embrace "inbound marketing," a form of content marketing online that involves blogging, search engine optimization (SEO), and aligning digital content offers with the different stages of a buyer's journey to convert them into customers. Our marketing team was cutting-edge, pushing the limits of digital marketing. The Latin American marketing team, which reported to me, set records in website traffic growth with the internet's most popular and fastest-growing marketing blogs in Spanish and Brazilian Portuguese. We were innovating and breaking boundaries in digital marketing every single day.

But, when I was asked to become VP of International Operations and Strategy, tasked to launch our first office in a non-English-speaking country, I found it hard to resist such an offer. I loved international business and enjoyed cross-functional work. I was eager to help the company become a global success.

"Sign me up!" I said with delight. As is typical in high-growth tech companies, I did not really know what I was getting into. When I learned we'd be setting up this new office in Japan, a jolt of fear hit me. Japan is a notoriously difficult market for American companies to crack. I knew from experience that many companies rush the process, blundering into Japan in ways that don't map to the needs of the market. Was our newly IPO'd, fast-growing Boston-based scale-up really ready for this?

Many digital-first companies think that with a company website accessible to people around the world, they're global. It's a mirage; the closer you get to serving foreign customers, the more complicated it becomes. A true global brand doesn't just appear everywhere—it resonates with diverse audiences by adapting its customer experience to local culture and laws. The mentality of speed over perfection can blind tech companies into stumbling across international tripwires. For disruptive software companies in particular, "market pull" can cause them to move very quickly into a new market. I gained firsthand experience in the messy realities of going global at a breakneck pace, while trying to follow best practices on how to brand global, adapt local for digital marketing.

"When do we want to have the office live?" I asked hopefully. My boss replied that it was in the budget for September, trying to offer reassurance on the financial front. But my heart skipped a beat. That was seven months away. I did some reverse mental math. We'd have only two quarters to adapt legal contracts to local employment laws, set up bank accounts and payroll, find an office location in Tokyo, hire local staff and an expat to move to Japan to run the office, localize the website… My head was spinning as I worked backward through all the logistics that would need to happen by early September 2016.

"Got it!" I said, reflecting the typical can-do attitude we espoused in HubSpot culture. We knew how to get things done. We had great people on the launch team. "Two quarters is practically a lifetime here," I told myself. And then, as my mindset moved between starry-eyed dreamer and feet-on-the-ground operator, I remembered… it wasn't just two quarters I was bound by—it was also two trimesters. I was in my first trimester, with our baby due at the end of August. Worse, I had suffered seven miscarriages getting to this pregnancy. I buried those thoughts in the back of my brain, donned my rose-colored glasses and told myself, "I'll be having both a real baby, and a work baby, all in such a narrow time span. Surely that must be good luck in some part of the world!"

Dialing up the heat further, I remembered our founder and CEO Brian Halligan had lived and worked in Japan early in his career. He knew the culture well, had many Japanese friends and had published a best-selling book in Japan, *Marketing Lessons from the Grateful Dead*,[2] which sold even better there than in the U.S. He also sat in the cubicle next to me in our Cambridge office. "No pressure for Halligan's company to do well in Japan, right Nataly?" I said to myself with irony.

Nonetheless, with the energy and enthusiasm one musters to survive in the world of high tech, I took on this new assignment. I tried to make light of the pregnancy stress, joking at every roadblock that we had to find a way to get it done: The Tokyo office *had* to open before my baby arrived (cue a belly pat to drive home the point).

I made fast friends with the Japanese trade organization, JETRO, which helps companies set up operations in Japan.[3] From free office space to complimentary accounting services and legal contract support, this Japanese government agency was an absolute godsend. After our first meeting, we Americans questioned why they were being so helpful. Was all this support really free? We wondered aloud if they would send us a bill.

That was my first of many lessons on cultural differences doing business in Japan. In the U.S., we say, "The customer is always right." In Japan, the saying is, "The customer is God." And that is precisely how JETRO treated us: Better than we expected or felt we deserved.

While I appreciated this level of attention, it also alarmed me a little. HubSpot was a scrappy, move-fast-and-break-things tech company. We had phrases like "GSD" (get shit done) written in huge letters on our office walls. While we had a strong record of success in our home market, I felt nervous about our cavalier company's ability to adapt so swiftly, especially if our customers in Japan expected a more polished and mature, white-glove customer experience.

Differences in Employment Culture

When my JETRO contact learned we needed to hire 12 employees in six months, he blinked rapidly. He had never seen a foreign company hire so many people so fast in its first hiring wave in Japan. That was when I hit my first big roadblock: the concept of *lifetime employment*. In Japan, the majority of the workforce rarely, if ever, leave their first employer. While attitudes are changing, most employees in Japan expect to remain employed by the same company for their entire life.[4]

In the U.S., HubSpot could easily recruit fresh talent in 3–6 months, as our employer brand—especially in the Boston area—was strong. In Japan, we had no reputation because we were not in the market. The time required to build an employer brand to attract talent hadn't gone into our planning assumptions, and yet, headcount costs were budgeted for September. I began to wonder if I had accepted Mission Impossible.

To complicate matters further, we needed to find proficient (near-native) bilingual speakers in English to communicate with their American counterparts. People who met this description *and* had the necessary technical skills represented less than 1 per cent of the entire population, and guess what? Most of those people were already happily employed by tech giants such as Google and Facebook—*for life*. All of my other plans for the office launch hinged on getting such people hired by a specific date.

Through our colleagues in America and in Singapore, we managed to identify talent and convince them to take the risk to join an unknown foreign employer in a country where such companies are assumed to fail. There is often great shame in Japan over losing a job, bringing disappointment and embarrassment to the family, so the risk for these individuals was high. Through a Western lens, a business failure is no one person's fault, but in Japan, a person may become associated with that collective failure and become less employable as a result.

As my pregnant belly kept growing, we kept working around such blockers to check off the tasks on my launch plan. A critical step was making two early hires with overseas experience, fluent in English and willing to take risks alongside us. One was Masan (Masakatsu) Kosaka, a Japanese localization specialist. The other was Shohei Toguri, a Japanese marketer.

With no local recruiter to help find a localization specialist, I got creative. I took to LinkedIn to search for the perfect candidate. When I saw Masan's profile with a non-traditional picture of him snorkeling, it made me smile. We often hired employees with quirky profiles and interesting hobbies at HubSpot. But most importantly, he had experience working with other American tech companies—Oracle, Google, Dell, and many others—so he was familiar with risk.

I sent him an InMail, hoping our lack of a recruiter would not be a red flag. Surprisingly, it worked in my favor. "It was the first time a senior leader of a well-established tech company contacted me directly expressing interest in my expertise, which made me feel honored," Masan explained. "I was drawn to the company's unique culture and business model. HubSpot was unlike any of my previous experiences with foreign companies, so the opportunity handpicked by the senior leader to lead Japanese localization made it an offer I couldn't refuse."[5]

Masan and Shohei would work closely together as a team to get our content marketing machine working for HubSpot in Japan. Together, they made a huge difference helping us prepare the office launch and accomplish the many moving interdependent steps on my task list.

When Easy Peasy Is Anything But

Towards the end of our six-month window, we were ready to localize and launch the Japanese website. While I had studied Japanese in college, I knew my one-semester introduction was insufficient to adapt the website into native Japanese. Nonetheless, I felt confident leading this task. Not only had I been involved in dozens of much more complex global website projects, I managed the team localizing web, product, and marketing content into other languages. What's one more language? Easy peasy, I thought.

Not at all. To start with, Japanese has different character sets. We did not even own the needed font, so we purchased it and added it into all systems with customer-facing text. Masan was provided with the same standard equipment as employees in other offices. But because our keyboards lacked Japanese, he couldn't do his job. While we outsourced translation to a local agency, Masan needed to adapt all the content as it came in. Much of the terminology HubSpot used was simply untranslatable. Concepts required not only translation, they had to be *explained* to be even partially understood.

For example, HubSpot was famous for "inbound marketing," activities like blogging and SEO content that seek to attract new customers. But in Japan, we quickly learned that this term meant "marketing to Chinese tourists."[6] It seemed like nearly every marketing concept required creative explanation. It was taking a hundred times longer than any other language, yet the terms still didn't sound right to a native ear.

Then came my most embarrassing "ignorant American" moment of all, reminding me that localizing a website isn't easy, no matter how much experience you have.

A Picture Is Worth a Thousand Words

Late one evening, I stood weary from another long day across a 12-hour time zone and trying to sit my bulging body in the zany bean bag chairs peppering our tech-friendly office. I was cranky from balancing the joys of pregnancy with burning the candle at both ends in meetings with my colleagues in Singapore and Japan as well as in Boston and in Europe. And I had a two-year-old at home.

My partner on the brand team localizing the website, Dmitry Shamis, said, "Nataly, we have a problem." I leaned over his monitor, trying not to hit him in the head with my enormous belly. "They have no good photos of Asian models. Nearly all of the models are white." Our shoulders dropped.

We looked for different photo image sites specializing in Asian models but found very few offerings from our search location in the U.S. We needed to get the images added ASAP, as the office launch was only a few weeks away. "Pick the ones you think are best for now, Dmitry. We can always swap them out later," I said, knowing our fast-moving company would be making constant changes to all of our websites anyway.

When I woke up the next morning, Dmitry had added the photos and sent me the link. With Masan's wizardry combining the translations with the new images, the site looked good to me. I checked the local time for Tokyo. Apologizing for another late-night request, I notified Shohei and Masan to take a look at the latest version. Email sent. Laptop closed. Time to embark on my commute from the Boston suburbs into Cambridge to begin the American portion of my workday.

When I got to the office, a message popped up on my screen. "Nataly, can we speak now?" Uh-oh. My new team member in Japan was still awake. And online. And wanted to have a call. This didn't sound good. I fired up the Zoom.

"Hey Masan, what's wrong?" I asked in my direct and informal American style, hoping he was bicultural enough to tell me whatever I needed to know. He politely but bravely stated, "Nataly… I don't know how to tell you this. But the images we have on the website, the people in the images? They are… not Japanese."

So sank the heart of this international expert who, at that moment, did not feel worthy of the title. I had authorized photos of models described as "Asian" in our mad rush to get the website up. But these models were from countries as glaringly different from Japan as Italians are from Finnish people. "We are such dumb Americans, myself included," I admitted, apologizing to Masan, who had seen worse.

"So, how do we fix this?" He shared his screen and showed me a selection of local Japanese stock image sites. But the websites did not accept foreign credit cards. There were hurdles in our way at every turn.

I ran downstairs to go through our checklist with my Boston colleagues at our weekly Tokyo office launch meeting. Most of our tasks, including the hardest ones, were now complete: Healthcare and other local benefits created in line with local standards; core staff and salespeople hired; new territories mapped in systems; currency and local payment support added; foreign exchange tracker prepared for quarterly evaluation to inform price adjustments; payroll steps complete; local tax strategy done; launch party being organized by our MBA intern and culture team; ex-pat housing obtained; flights for executives booked; press release sorted. The list of tasks went on and on, but we were coming to the end of the process.

Then it was my turn to share an update on the website, which, given my experience, everyone assumed was easy and I had under control. I tried not to show my panic. "We have a couple minor issues before we finalize the website, but we're nearly ready," I reported, taking care to strike the right tone—accurate but not alarmist—despite very real stress. I didn't want to panic them, me, or my baby.

Everything Old Is New Again

Back upstairs at my desk, I had an idea. On our U.S. website, instead of paying for stock images, we featured HubSpot employees. We took pride in doing things differently with the motto, "When they zig, we zag." When customers visited the office or our annual conference, they would recognize specific employees. The popularity of these online photos led to an internal joke of being "HubSpot famous." What if I could make our new Japanese employees locally famous too?

Once again, I got creative. I reached out to business contacts who had worked in Japan who helped me find an available photographer in Tokyo. In just a few days, we had authentic photos for HubSpot Japan's new website shot in our new office. The setting with our HubSpot orange walls helped anchor our employer branding. Thinking outside the box and leveraging personal connections not only helped new hires feel involved, but replicated an element of our culture. Some of those photos remain on the Japanese HubSpot website today.

My daughter came into this world on August 31, 2016. By that day, our website was ready and every task on my list for the Tokyo launch had a satisfying check mark by its side. We officially announced our new Tokyo operations to the media on September 8, 2016.[7] I somehow birthed a child *and* a new market for a tech company in the same two-week period. In spite of the difficulties along the way, I knew they were both important beginnings.

Busy with my new baby, I wasn't able to join the Tokyo launch party. I didn't need to. I cared about planting the seed for a new business to sprout and grow for many years to come. Not only did our Tokyo office open on time, but so did our Japanese digital presence, which would endure—*and deliver for us*—all day, every day.

Globalization: Local Experiences on Steroids

As my experience in Japan shows, delivering an online digital experience in a new country and language isn't easy. Greeting the online visitor is the first step of the process. But how do you know which language to greet them in, or what country they're from, when you're a global brand with a hundred or more possibilities to choose from?

Many websites figure out the answer to this question using a technique called *geolocation*. The company can auto-detect a user's language and country from the very first moment when a user visits their website. Settings in the visitor's website browser can route them seamlessly to the most appropriate online experience for their anticipated country and language. Should this auto-detection strategy fail, the user can manually choose a preferred region and language from a "global gateway" menu, marked by a globe icon discreetly tucked at the top or bottom of the homepage.

It's important to remember that making the website available in another language does not automatically adapt a digital product. Take the example of Adobe, well known for its web design and photo manipulation. Adobe makes its top-selling website and marketing content available in up to 100 languages. However, other Adobe products are sold in 35 languages while the newest releases are available in only five.[8]

The number of languages offered for the various software, technical documentation, and marketing materials are also different. For example, Adobe Experience Cloud software is localized into nine languages. Meanwhile, the corresponding documentation is available in 12 and the related marketing materials in 17. This is quite common, because sometimes people are perfectly happy to use a software product in their second language, but prefer that the documentation for how to use it be available in their native language instead, to help them with clarifying technical questions. Adding additional complexity, Adobe has more than one website to localize. It has many.[9]

Let's take a look at a relatively "easy" market such as Canada. For an American company like Adobe, accommodating online users in neighboring Canada should be simple, right? *Not exactly*. The core Adobe website doesn't have just one version for Canada but two: one for Canadians who speak French, and one in English. After all, they both need to pay in the Canadian dollars. Canadian customers need to be directed to the specific version of software localized for Canada. In fact, the Canadian government requires some companies to provide French-language offerings in order to do business in Canada.

Despite all the effort of creating the French-Canadian website, it can't be leveraged by Adobe customers who speak French in other parts of the world. Not only are there linguistic variants, but Canadian users have different needs from customers accessing Adobe from France. Similarly, if you speak French but hail from Belgium, Switzerland, or Luxembourg, you want to access unique French-language experiences relevant for your country, which means that users can access not just one, but *five* distinct French website experiences from Adobe.com.

Europeans are often multilingual and cross borders easily. Let's imagine your company has a customer originally from Germany who now lives in Belgium. You can display options for a Belgian website experience in French,

Dutch, or English, but this customer's native language is German. Should you display the German website for Germany, even if the product the customer wants isn't sold in Belgium? Or, should you display the Belgian website in English, in the hope that your customer can speak it as a second language? The answer: Let the user decide! Give your website visitors all of these options, so they can choose based on their own preferences.

While the complexity of this scenario might sound surreal, it's a reality companies contend with every day to provide a digital experience that is both globally accessible and locally relevant. The majority of people on the earth speak more than one language. But they can only live in one culture at one time. In the online world, as people switch between languages and move from place to place, they expect their experiences to be easily and instantly adapted. As a result, global brands need to take all these scenarios of real-life combinations into account. Not just at the beginning of the experience, but at every step, for every click, and with each and every line of copy along the way.

Catering to so many potential users of a global website, across so many different combinations of languages and countries (known as "locales"), to provide an identical experience is not the end goal—that's a fool's errand. After all, users in different markets have different needs.

If you have a monolingual website for just one country, you can roll out the same red carpet to welcome your visitors over and over. But if you have a global website that needs to account for diverse and divergent local experiences, you'll need to build an ever-changing, technicolor dream coat instead.

Weaving a High-Tech Tapestry

In the age of Google Translate and AI tools, can local experiences be "activated" with the simple click of a button? Not exactly. Building an ever-changing technicolor dream coat requires high-tech artisans. They must operate extremely advanced software tools, invisible to the average person, that create the ever-changing patterns on the coat to adapt to the local wearer's needs. While paying attention to the tiniest of fibers in every single thread, they must also obsess over how the coat adapts and changes, making sure it fits perfectly, feels comfortable, and looks good.

The experts planning and executing all of this—a small army of people at Adobe and across a network of external vendors—are a combination of linguists and engineers. Thousands of different translators in-house and freelance are involved in adapting and reviewing Adobe content. Additionally, thousands of engineers are taught to write code world-ready from the start. While the work is highly cross-functional in nature, the majority of these efforts sit within a function at digital companies referred to as "globalization."[10]

Globalization encompasses far more than just translating content, creating local experiences, and ensuring the code is adapted for international needs. It begins with defining the strategy for adapting the digital offering as the global brand expands into local markets. That takes a team of highly specialized people with deep technical expertise, as well as strategic skills.

Jean-François Vanreusel, a Belgian living in California, has worked on the globalization team at Adobe for more than two decades. He works hand in hand with Ankush Sharma, heading globalization engineering at Adobe, and Priscille Knoble, who oversees international strategy and product management. Vanreusel and his team pioneered "continuous localization" solutions at Adobe, to ensure that the product could be released in multiple languages even while being developed and deployed in markets all over the world.[11]

The sheer volume and diversity of experiences Adobe must offer have grown in complexity over the years, and so has the team itself. As Vanreusel points out, "When I joined Adobe we had nearly 2,000 employees and now we're at about 25,000. We once offered just a handful of key products people know, like Acrobat, Illustrator, and Photoshop. But the portfolio has grown, and we now deliver more than 100 products. We've had to evolve with the product assortment."[12]

While adding a language or a currency to your website may seem minor at first, once a brand begins to offer an online experience to customers in new countries and languages, it is making a long-term commitment that extends far beyond what it might have initially envisioned.

Secrets of the Best Global Websites

The work of Vanreusel and his colleagues showcases Adobe's commitment to global accessibility and local experiences. In fact, year after year, Adobe is recognized as the top global consumer technology website in the world by the *Web Globalization Report Card*, an independent third-party assessment managed by global design and research expert John Yunker of Byte Level Research.[13]

My experience at HubSpot reveals that many companies expend enormous effort to translate their website. But how important is it, to offer your website in local languages in order to build a global brand?

To put it plainly, "Failure to support the language of customers in a country in which you do business shows a lack of respect," Yunker explains. "It may not be offensive, but it's poor practice." Surprisingly, some brands succeed globally in spite of not doing a great job at language support. Yunker points to Apple as an example, despite its tremendous success as a global brand, "Apple customers based in Japan or Italy will land on a localized website that relies on the same global template and design system."[14]

According to Yunker's research, Apple has lagged behind other consumer brands such as Toyota and NIVEA in global reach. The Apple website supports 37 languages. While this may sound like a lot, it is less than consumer brands like Toyota, at 54 languages, and NIVEA at 45, and far less than peer tech companies like Google or Facebook, which each support more than 100. "In the end, Apple has the means to support 100 or more languages but chooses not to," Yunker points out. "This is unfortunate because it leaves a good portion of the world underserved."

Not all companies can be as comprehensive in their language support and user interface as these highly global mega-brands. On average, the top 25 websites support an average of 58 languages.[15] Not all businesses need to support so many languages, but Yunker's research over the years shows that to remain competitive, top global brands are adding more languages than ever before, with the average number of languages on the world's top 150 websites rising from 12 in 2004 to 34 two decades later.[16] As digitization increases, language gaps are closing, and the world is literally becoming a smaller place.

But the number of languages a website supports is not the only thing that matters for the report. Yunker conducts detailed assessments of global websites to determine the winners each year. Here are the four key components of Yunker's scoring matrix, showing that striking the balance between a unified global brand identity while adapting to local cultures and languages isn't easy:[17]

1 **Global reach:** A perfect score requires 50 or more languages, not counting English for the U.S.

2 **Global navigation:** It's not enough for brands to simply offer localized experiences. They must also make it easy for users to find and access the right content if they want to switch their language or country at any point in their website experience.

3 **Global/mobile architecture:** Because usage scenarios differ by country, online experiences must also cater to users on mobile devices.

4 **Localization and social:** Websites don't need to make all content available for every language and country combination, but they need to provide positive and equitable experiences, including tie-ins to locally relevant social media.

What are some of the other things that the very best global websites have in common from a brand perspective?

- **Clean and simple design.** Because global websites are inherently complex, design needs to be extremely simple. As Yunker advises, "Global design is less design. The look and feel should be distilled to the most basic and globally relevant elements." Examples include the logo, design template, and design system. "The global design template is generally free of any embedded images or text, so that each country and region is free to develop and localize content," he advises. "The goal is to balance global consistency with local flexibility." Simple can be hard, especially for companies with a complex matrix of teams and employees across the world.
- **Flexible templates that allow for local flavor.** Yunker's research highlights Google, Philips, and Wikipedia as companies that do a good job streamlining their websites. "The underlying global templates of all three sites are free of photographs of people—the photographs we see on Wikipedia are provided by the content creators themselves. Companies that struggle with global templates include Honda and Coke—two legacy brands with globally distributed and independent teams. Their internal lack of centralization makes it especially challenging for their many local websites to come together on a common architecture. This can lead to a global experience that feels disconnected. The sooner a company can embrace global templates the better off they are in the long run."
- **Avoiding global taglines.** One surprising aspect of the best global websites is to avoid adapting a single slogan to all markets, like trying to make a circle fit different squares, triangles, and ovals around the world. Even Nike failed to take "Just Do It" global. Per Yunker, Nike initially tried to localize the famous slogan, but found it impossible to convey the meaning in so few words across many countries and languages. They ultimately left the slogan in English, which works in some markets, but not all.

- **Featuring local faces.** Yunker points to NIVEA as a brand that cares not only about offering the various languages its customers speak; the company adapts its visuals as well. "NIVEA is a company that very early on invested in hiring local models to promote their facial and skin products around the world," Yunker explains. "This may seem obvious today, but you'd be surprised how many global companies resist going the extra mile to hire local talent to promote their products in each country they do business."[18]

As you can see from the examples in this chapter, adapting a global website for local purposes is a complex undertaking. Localization is nuanced, with plenty to learn along the way. While it might seem tempting to ask any person at your company bilingual in the local language to help launch the website in that market, there is no replacement for hiring localization experts. Businesses such as Adobe and HubSpot have sizable localization teams consisting of subject-matter experts, engineers in software workflows, custom-built infrastructure, and automation. All of these people work collectively behind the scenes to shape every online experience for a new market. Furthermore, to be considered a global player, the bar on how many languages and countries should be supported is getting higher each year.

Summary

- **Does a local website make you a global company?** Providing customers with the right online experience to meet their local needs is the key to success, but this requires ongoing commitment well beyond the website.
- **How many languages is enough to be global?** The number of languages required depends on the business goals, but top brands are adding more languages each year to remain competitive in multiple local markets.
- **How should you adapt a website for a local market?** Localizing a website, and indeed any digital experience, takes ample attention to detail, including consideration for images, language, currency, culture, product availability, and many other local nuances. Finding the right local talent is an important first step.

The Global Digest

Chapter 9 Takeaways

1. **Speak your customer's language:** Communicating with your customers in their native language is a basic sign of respect for doing business.
2. **Consider the country:** It's not enough to just translate the words on a website. Every aspect and action within the experience must take into account the user's country and expectations.
3. **Give it time:** Adapting a website takes time, but businesses have specific timelines and financial targets. Build in sufficient time to define and design a high-quality local experience.
4. **Understand the local customer:** Creating a local digital experience requires understanding cultural differences beyond language, such as visual preferences and employment norms. A successful global strategy requires managing these nuances to positively impact customer perception and brand acceptance.
5. **Customer service needs vary:** Some markets have higher standards for customer service. The time it takes to learn about these standards, and establish a brand reputation from scratch, are often underappreciated (see Chapter 7).
6. **Localization involves far more than text:** Localization requires adapting concepts and cultural references that may not have direct equivalents. Be creative to convey company-specific terms or industry jargon in ways that resonates with local audiences.
7. **Lean on people who know the market:** Missteps in cultural understanding, such as using non-Japanese Asian models on a Japanese website, can significantly harm a company's image. It's crucial to involve locals in content selection.
8. **Assess corporate cultural differences:** High-growth tech companies often operate with a "move fast" mentality, which may clash with markets that prioritize thoroughness and tradition. Adapting a company's approach to meet local expectations while maintaining core values is essential for global brand success.
9. **Use creativity under pressure:** When taking high-growth businesses into new markets, you have to be inventive and occasionally scrappy. You may even need to leverage professional contacts in your and your team's networks.

10 **Embrace lessons learned:** International market expansion is fraught with unexpected challenges but overcoming them leads to business and professional growth and pride. Success requires cultural sensitivity, flexibility, and a willingness to learn from mistakes.

References

1 HubSpot Communications (2024) HubSpot Expands Reach for Top Talent Globally with New India Office, HubSpot Company News, April 24. www.hubspot.com/company-news/hubspot-expands-reach-for-top-talent-globally-with-new-india-office (archived at https://perma.cc/LD2J-WUZ5)

2 D. Meerman Scott (2011) Japanese Language Edition of Marketing Lessons from the Grateful Dead, December 8. https://www.davidmeermanscott.com/blog/2011/12/japanese-language-edition-of-marketing-lessons-from-the-grateful-dead.html (archived at https://perma.cc/N9QM-TL5P)

3 JETRO. About Us. www.jetro.go.jp/en/jetro/ (archived at https://perma.cc/4ERQ-GRAG)

4 M. Inoue and B. Dooley (2020) A Job for Life, or Not? Class Divide Deepens in Japan, *The New York Times*, November 27, updated 18 May 2021. www.nytimes.com/2020/11/27/business/japan-workers.html (archived at https://perma.cc/JA2B-XD6E)

5 M. Kosaka (2024) Correspondence with Nataly Kelly, October 23, email

6 J. L. Borile (2024) The Yen Effect: The Rise of Inbound Marketing Against a Weaker JPY, *The Aix Post*, January 7. aixpost.com/trends/the-yen-effect-the-rise-of-inbound-marketing-amidst-a-weaker-jpy/ (archived at https://perma.cc/U4FG-6ZHL)

7 N. Eberle (2024) HubSpot Opens Japan Office with a Week of Celebration and Content, HubSpot Company News, April 24. www.hubspot.com/company-news/hubspot-opens-japan-office-with-a-week-of-celebration-and-content (archived at https://perma.cc/C8XF-KXZ6)

8 I. Boonen (2024) Lessons in Localization: Adobe's Globalization Strategy, Nimdzi Research, September 8. https://www.nimdzi.com/ lessons-in-localization-adobe/ (archived at https://perma.cc/BB5Q-DP7W)

9 I. Boonen (2024) Lessons in Localization: Adobe's Globalization Strategy, Nimdzi Research, September 8. https://www.nimdzi.com/lessons-in-localization-adobe/ (archived at https://perma.cc/J8FZ-TDCM)

10 I. Boonen (2024) Lessons in Localization: Adobe's Globalization Strategy, Nimdzi Research, September 8. https://www.nimdzi.com/lessons-in-localization-adobe/ (archived at https://perma.cc/QG4C-LDFZ)

11 I. Boonen (2024) Lessons in Localization: Adobe's Globalization Strategy, Nimdzi Research, September 8. https://www.nimdzi.com/lessons-in-localization-adobe/ (archived at https://perma.cc/AW5Z-CP2G)

12 A. Rey. Evolution of Localization from an Internal to External Function, Global Ambitions Podcast. globalambitions.net/evolution-of-localization-from-an-internal-to-external-function/ (archived at https://perma.cc/F9QP-CMFQ)

13 J. Yunker (2024) The 2024 Web Globalization Report Card, Byte Level Research. bytelevel.com/reportcard2024/ (archived at https://perma.cc/KV37-47ZG)

14 J. Yunker (2024) Interviewed by Nataly Kelly, September 25, email

15 J. Yunker (2024) Interviewed by Nataly Kelly, September 25, email

16 J. Yunker (2024) The 2024 Web Globalization Report Card, Byte Level Research. bytelevel.com/reportcard2024/ (archived at https://perma.cc/W75K-LSPL)

17 J. Yunker (2024) The 2024 Web Globalization Report Card, Byte Level Research. bytelevel.com/reportcard2024/ (archived at https://perma.cc/W75K-LSPL)

18 J. Yunker (2024) The 2024 Web Globalization Report Card, Byte Level Research. bytelevel.com/reportcard2024/ (archived at https://perma.cc/W75K-LSPL)

Adding Complexity 10

Building a Global B2B Brand

NATALY KELLY

In this chapter, we explore how business-to-business (B2B) companies *brand global, adapt local*. Business-to-consumer (B2C) and B2B marketers have more in common than not. When expanding internationally, the core concerns of tailoring the offering are similar in both settings. B2B companies seeking to enter new markets must adapt their value proposition, messaging, and customer service standards. To do so, they need to consider the same variables reviewed in this book, such as language, behavior, and culture differences; after all, they are individuals in one business serving individuals in another.

But building a global B2B brand has some important differences. B2B contracts apply to many people, so the services are broader, longer lasting, and more expensive. Along with regulatory and compliance concerns, the higher hurdles in B2B sales require building trust with the customer through client relationships and brand equity over a long lifecycle, as opposed to driving short-term transactions. Business customers want to ensure they will get the support they need, so they expect salespeople, support staff, customer service reps, and others to speak their language and live in their country (or at least in their time zone). Therefore, B2B brands seeking to build foreign markets should prioritize local actions to anchor and promote the brand, while simultaneously forming a legal entity, opening an office, and hiring local staff. These aspects of B2B marketing add additional complexity and nuance to going global.

Let's look at an example from one of India's largest, most diversified, and respected conglomerates, the Tata Group. In India, the Tata Group has been recognized as a symbol of reliability, trust, and social responsibility since its founding in 1885.[1] But until recently, the brand was little known in many foreign countries. To extend its presence and respect internationally, one division designed an innovative global sponsorship strategy that highlights its technical expertise in performance and captures the attention of local business customers in multiple target markets.

It's a Marathon, Not a Sprint

Tata Consultancy Services (TCS), an Indian multinational IT firm, has taken a fascinating approach to building trust with its business buyers over the long term by developing a portfolio of marathon sponsorships that anchor the company in specific cities like Amsterdam, London, New York, and Mumbai. According to Abhinav Kumar, Global Chief Marketing Officer at Tata Consultancy Services, beyond the sponsorship, TCS uses its tech expertise to enrich the participant experience, designing and managing mobile apps for the marathons. The company's app for the New York City marathon alone was downloaded half a million times.[2]

By integrating itself into the cultural fabric of its key markets via tech-driven experiences at local sporting events, TCS reinforces its credibility and builds trust among a broad array of local stakeholders including clients, potential clients, and the communities. The company's intent is for executives and decision-makers in local markets to view TCS as a locally rooted, global brand they can trust for their IT solutions.

It's not easy for a foreign B2B brand to build awareness and trust in a new market. As the saying goes, Rome wasn't built in a day, and neither is a multinational B2B brand. While it takes time and perseverance, TCS is succeeding by investing in operations and marketing in local communities all over the world. Over the past 14 years, TCS's brand value has multiplied an incredible 8.3 times to $19 billion.[3]

When the Customer Is a Committee

Each time you target a new local market, you inevitably add business complexity. While individual consumers make purchase decisions on their own, business contracts usually require approval from several cross-functional stakeholders.

Because of the number of people involved in the decision, B2B marketers need to market the brand and build trust across a target organization, whose buyers have different needs based on roles, purchasing authority, titles, and seniority. To ensure the entire company can address them effectively, marketers in B2B train their own staff on the needs of these different people by creating "buyer personas." It's not easy to convince different buyer personas with similar tactics or channels. They consume different media, engage in different social channels, and attend different conferences and events. They have different needs so, sometimes, even their goals conflict. Compared to B2C marketing, which uses various attributes to segment one target, selling a B2B product or service requires a similar level of segmentation across multiple audiences with different needs. Managing the marketing and messaging to each person in the decision-making process becomes complex. Multiply that by as many local markets as your business ambition and you quickly realize that B2B global marketing is global marketing on steroids. The complexity expands beyond marketing to the entire go-to-market strategy, encompassing sales, customer success, and more.

For this reason, B2B brands need to think strategically about which markets to target before investing. In addition to the numerous decision-makers for B2B, the scope of services is larger, contract prices are substantial, and sales cycles take much longer, so the business risks are often greater. In light of such considerations, B2B marketing investments can take much longer to yield. It's not easy to back away from a new local market after investing for months, hiring local employees, and making customer commitments. It takes long-term tenacity for a B2B company to grow brand presence and carve out market share in any new market. So, when you decide to expand a B2B brand into new countries, you're not just investing marketing money—you're multiplying layers of complexity on a process already rife with complication, nuance, and decision matrices about which investments to make on which channels and with which campaigns to satisfy multiple stakeholders.

Building Global Brands for Businesses versus Consumers

Let's explore the multiple factors affecting how taking a brand global differs when selling to businesses compared to when targeting consumers.

Localized Value Proposition

B2B customers seek solutions that directly address their business challenges, but the challenges themselves vary widely across industries and regions. Therefore, like B2C, it's essential for B2B brands to adjust their value propositions to local market demands. What resonates with customers in the U.S. may not be relevant in Europe or Asia due to differences in the business itself, technological maturity, regulatory issues, or business culture. B2B companies need to invest in market research to understand the unique needs and pain points of each market and then localize their product features, sales strategies, and messaging accordingly.

For example, HubSpot rolled out its new global tagline, "Grow Better," designed to convey that companies could grow in better and easier ways with our software. When planning with our local Japanese marketing team, we discovered that this tagline, even when perfectly translated, wouldn't resonate very well with our customers there. Japan's aging population meant that Japanese business priorities were not just growth. A higher near-term priority was digitizing their operations to ensure smooth business continuity. Their goal was not to grow "better." Rather, it was more specific—to grow in a way adapted to the reality of their aging population. We could not translate the tagline directly into Japanese because it did not make sense. Instead, working with our local Japanese marketing team, we used the transcreation process, which requires a deeper and more flexible level of cultural adaptation. We decided on phrasing to convey "smarter growth" instead, a far more tailored angle for the local market. Thanks to tight coordination between our domestic marketing team in the U.S. and our local marketers overseas, we caught this early, enabling us to *brand global, adapt local*.

Familiarity and Credibility in B2B

For B2B companies, establishing credibility is crucial. Unlike consumers, who make purchases routinely as part of everyday life, businesses are committing larger sums with long-term implications, so they are far more risk averse in making decisions. You can mitigate this challenge by building brand trust in the marketplace. (See Chapters 3 and 11 for more on trust.) Investing in local relationships, partnering with established businesses, and building a physical presence significantly impact the success of a B2B brand's international expansion.

While B2C brands may focus on "air cover" brand plays, such as mass marketing and brand awareness, B2B brands need to go "feet on the ground" first—network extensively with industry leaders, participate in local trade shows, and provide references from existing customers. The more tightly interconnected a given market, the more this tendency holds true. Many businesses find local partners and leverage the trust their clients have in them for a fast foothold in a new market. Other businesses may choose to acquire local competitors for a quick entry. Traditional marketing plays and direct channels cost less but take time to build brand awareness, credibility, and trust.

For instance, SAP, the global enterprise software giant, uses a partnership-driven strategy to build many of its relationships in new markets. In countries like India, SAP partners with local technology firms to co-develop and integrate solutions tailored to regional business needs. This not only builds trust among potential customers but also allows SAP to leverage local partners' reputations. SAP is further expanding its presence in India by focusing downmarket on smaller businesses.[4]

Building channel partnerships is extremely common in B2B software in particular because businesses have existing relationships with local software implementation providers and resellers they know and trust. For such large purchases that may be mission-critical for a business, having a local partner is an incredibly important market-entry strategy.

Longer Sales Cycles

With B2B sales processes, the purchase usually requires involvement from multiple decision-makers across different levels of an organization. Examples of the types of people involved might include procurement teams, technical evaluators, and executive sponsors. Each of these stakeholders may have their own unique criteria for selection. The criteria can vary greatly not only from company to company, but from country to country. For example, in some regions, formal requests for proposals and extensive due diligence are standard, while in others, informal relationships and local networks are more important. Differences in negotiation style are important to navigate—in some countries, discounting is a basic way of doing business, while it's viewed negatively in others. Without a thorough understanding of the nuance involved in local sales customs, B2B companies can struggle to close contracts, even if they have a superior product, service, and marketing.

Salesforce, the dominant global company offering customer relationship management (CRM) software, knows this very well. The company successfully expanded across the globe by changing its sales approach for different markets. Founder and CEO Marc Benioff has written extensively about the company's entry into the Japanese market in particular. When Salesforce entered Japan, the company encountered a culture that prized personal relationships and trust. As Benioff explained, "There is a Japanese belief that business is temporal, whereas relationships are eternal. That's true. One day you compete. The next day you partner. One day someone is your subordinate; the next day he or she may be your superior."[5]

Salesforce wasted no time applying this important lesson. In Japan, they prioritized hiring local salespeople with deep personal connections and robust networks. They updated their messaging to emphasize security and compliance to match local expectations. And importantly, they began building a strong partner network. This relationship-driven approach helped them overcome the longer sales cycles in Japan and gain traction in a market that traditionally favored local software competitors.

Regulatory and Compliance Differences

B2B companies in healthcare, finance, and government face far more stringent regulations than those in B2C. Like the governments that design them, regulations differ significantly from one country to another, requiring businesses to thoroughly research local laws and adapt their offerings. Failure can result in lost opportunities, financial penalties, and legal issues. Just like in B2C, B2B brands must ensure that their products meet local compliance requirements, such as data privacy laws in the European Union (the General Data Protection Regulation, or GDPR) or specific product certifications in Asia.

Microsoft's cloud services expansion is a classic example of adapting to different regulatory requirements. In Germany, Microsoft partnered with Deutsche Telekom to operate its cloud data centers, allowing customers to store data locally while ensuring compliance with strict German data protection laws. This partnership enabled Microsoft to overcome regulatory barriers and establish a strong local presence, setting itself apart from competitors that could not meet these compliance demands.[6]

Localized Support and Training

B2B customers often need ongoing support, training, and other resources to effectively use a product or service, which require much greater business investment than meeting the service needs of individual consumers. This means localizing technical documentation, customer support channels, and training materials to reflect the language and business practices of each region. Additionally, B2B companies may need to provide on-site training or custom implementation services to accommodate the specific needs of larger organizations.

We saw this exact trend play out at HubSpot. We required all of these pieces to deliver our software and ensure customers' success in English-speaking markets, but the need for these offerings in other countries and languages was perhaps even more important. The difficult thing about all of this is that the needs of each market are very different, so what you decide to localize may look different in every country.

Employer Branding and Local Talent Acquisition

Attracting the right talent in a new market can be a significant challenge for B2B companies. Unlike B2C companies, where most hiring focuses on sales and customer-facing roles, B2B brands often need to build teams of technical experts, industry specialists, and people with strong local business connections. Establishing a strong employer brand helps attract skilled professionals who can navigate the complexities of local business environments, making the company more competitive in each market.

As we saw in the HubSpot example in Chapter 9, it can be hard hiring the first "landing team" required to set up an initial office in a new country because you do not yet have a strong local employer brand. And in each new market, you basically start again from scratch. With zero halo effect, employer branding is incredibly important in B2B. When going into a new market, a B2B company might need to rely more heavily on third-party recruiting agencies because the negotiation styles and methods of hiring vary from country to country too.

Pricing and Contract Negotiations

B2B pricing strategies often require flexibility to account for different local market dynamics such as economic conditions, competitor pricing, and customer expectations around service levels and customization. Unlike B2C pricing models that are relatively standardized, many B2B companies may need to offer custom pricing and payment terms based on factors like contract volume, length, implementation needs, and local payment practices.

However, many B2B software companies that sell globally do not adapt their pricing much; this is because of increased cost and risk from the operational complexity of currency fluctuations, invoicing in local currency, accepting local payments, collections on local markets, and so on. To reduce complexity, many B2B software companies charge the same price, and in some cases they do not even offer any sort of local payment method, let alone pricing in local currencies. But when they fail to provide these allowances, companies often see an organic iteration emerge in the form of discounting.

In markets where the price-to-value relationship is strong and similar to the ratio in the domestic market, minimal discounting takes place. But, if a business fails to take into account comparative pricing and negotiation customs, local salespeople may discount the product heavily due to different local negotiation traditions or because the cost is simply too high. Not only that, in some markets, a customer has to pay an additional local tax when buying from a foreign company and might expect to see this credited in the form of a discount.

These areas highlight some of the ways in which B2B brands must manage far more than just a global marketing effort in order to successfully navigate the unique challenges of global expansion. In fact, focusing on marketing too early can be an enormous waste of time and money if you do not first focus on deep market understanding, local relationships, customized offerings, and regulatory compliance.

Now, let's look at how some of these examples mentioned above play out in real life.

From Boston to the World

As mentioned in Chapter 9, I worked at HubSpot during some of the company's highest growth years. We transformed from a Boston-based startup with a successful initial public offering (IPO) into a global tech unicorn with a valuation of $1 billion and customers in more than 100 countries. We maintained double-digit growth rates to hit $2 billion in revenue. But this success did not come by accident. While we executed on our Japan office launch at a breakneck speed, HubSpot very carefully and intentionally designed the overall international expansion strategy needed to achieve this success. And once we committed to that strategy, we moved very quickly to execute.

Because of the high complexity of taking a B2B brand global, all businesses must consider both the long-term opportunity and the up-front costs. The cost of going into new markets is not just monetary. There's also the opportunity cost. The trade-offs between investing in international growth with its additional complexity at the expense of other priorities were high on the radar for Brian Halligan, HubSpot's co-founder and CEO. In an article for *Harvard Business Review*, he explained that an important part of a growth strategy is knowing when to say "no" and when to say instead "not now."[7] Investing in international growth was low on HubSpot's priority list, until it later became an important part of the business's growth strategy. Early on, the company needed to stay focused on building strong product–market fit for its core buyer persona, marketers at mid-market companies within its domestic market of the U.S.

In 2015, I was hired at HubSpot as part of a deliberate strategy to capitalize on the higher international growth rates the company was seeing. As Vice President (VP) of Marketing, I initially focused both on Latin America and marketing localization for all of HubSpot's content, multimedia assets, and campaigns globally, in all non-English markets. As the company's success in foreign markets grew, I moved into a VP of International Operations and Strategy role to additionally oversee expansion strategy and execution, and then into a VP of Localization role as the complexity of our globalization needs evolved. All three roles represented both an honor and a challenge, but in each role I oversaw localization of the company's marketing content, websites, community, software, and all communications destined for local users, customers, and prospects.

Go-to-Market Complexity

To comprehend the complexity of taking a B2B brand like HubSpot global, it's important to understand how a company goes to market. B2B software companies use diverse approaches in a multi-threaded approach. The simplest way such companies go to market is to hire salespeople. Another thread is product-led growth, in which users sign up on the platform for free with purchase options surfaced to them automatically. Customers have options to upgrade, purchase add-ons or additional products, and renew without talking to anyone. While these product-driven actions are automated, the business usually depends on human touchpoints to move the process along. Customers often need reassurance that the software will help them accomplish their goals.

Companies using product-led growth strategically leverage volumes of data in product development. They know exactly when customers log onto the software and how to steer them towards conversion. They understand how customers derive value and guide them towards unlocking increasingly expensive tiers.

The product and marketing teams work together on the flow and content enabling user-driven upsell and cross-sell actions. The product team monitors usage patterns to determine perceived value and create hypotheses about which actions will encourage additional purchases. Then marketers design communication in the app and via email to trigger such actions.

Imagine the complexity required to coordinate this process across multiple languages. The behaviors that matter in one market are not always the same in another. Therefore, the communications and campaigns must vary too. Not all flows and comms are needed in all languages. At HubSpot, that's how my localization team played a critical role in enabling the company's international expansion.

Adapting the User Interface

When taking a software product global, what matters most is localizing, with extreme care, the user interface where your customer's clients interact daily while honoring the brand guidelines. A user interface is composed of many different display options, dictated by lines of code, that appear based on the user's actions. That code has text within the interface such as menu items, messages, prompts, and data. Each piece of content needs to be localized for each market's needs, meaning they're not only translated, but rewritten, adapted, or completely changed.

Painstakingly, one string at a time, human translators use the latest and greatest high-tech software in this process. Even so, the work does not happen automatically. Every line of code which is important to users' actions needs human review to ensure not only that the meaning is conveyed properly, but that the localized strings do not break anything. This quality assurance is then reviewed by people familiar with the product to ensure that the various strings appear live as expected. A series of automated checks and tests are run before the code is published.

At HubSpot, my localization team was responsible for this work on many millions of words in multiple languages each year. Engineers shipped code updates in the form of software strings thousands of times per day, requiring the corresponding updates in all of our 14 languages within one to two days, before the engineers could release the work. Only then could it appear within the customers' user interface.

This was complex work because we had a specific brand voice in English, known for being fun, light-hearted, and entertaining. The product teams writing code had a computer bot help them write with a consistent brand voice in English. Named BethBot after Beth Dunn, the early HubSpot product leader who masterminded the distinctive HubSpot voice, this automatic bot kept the code on brand.[8]

Without a BethBot in other languages, we developed terminology databases (known as termbases) in each language to apply consistent terms and phrases. My team worked closely with Beth to develop tailored brand voice guidelines in each language to ensure that this spirit would carry over as we produced localized code.

Support and Knowledge Base Localization

In modern software development, the product is released continuously, with small changes to lines of code taking place many thousands of times per day. When updates take place in web applications, a team of technical writers is alerted of any significant changes to adjust the corresponding technical documentation. In B2B, businesses use technical documentation to understand how to implement the software and teach internal users how to use it. This support content is also accessed directly by users with questions about its use or needing to troubleshoot specific problems unanswered within the interface.

In the case of HubSpot, the online knowledge base, where the product's technical documentation was stored, consists of many thousands of articles. As daily changes to the user interface were made, we updated these articles in English. After software automatically detected those changes, we fed those segments into our translation tools to update all 14 of HubSpot's core languages. We used a combination of advanced machine translation technologies, including original machine learning engines we had built and trained ourselves.

Local Onboarding, Training, and Academy Content

It's not enough to create a knowledge base for customers and users to troubleshoot on their own. New users require specific content for onboarding to begin learning the software and more to become proficient. Onboarding content is often provided in many different forms such as emails, slides, visuals, web pages, videos, and more. At HubSpot, my team was responsible for localizing this content as well.

There's more. We designed additional content for our professional services team to deliver and train customers on various topics. As our training staff spoke different languages, these training assets needed to be localized.

Similar content was used by another group called HubSpot Academy. Academy content could be accessed via online courses with slides, scripts, videos, audio files, quizzes, forms, and yet another user interface with its own software that required localization. Customers found the massive amount of Academy content extremely helpful, but it was by far the most time-consuming and costly to localize.

Unique, Locally Relevant Marketing Content

Marketers on all the many HubSpot marketing teams were constantly creating new content to be localized. The most important marketing efforts requiring localization were product launches, as they came with large numbers of multimedia assets and content. Each time a product is launched or updated, it requires documentation for accompanying assets and new sales pitch decks.

In addition, the localization team handles core web content such as landing pages, call-to-action buttons, slides, visuals with embedded text, ebooks, and toolkits. As marketing teams regularly created dozens of emails, blog posts, and social media assets, localization worked hard to adapt campaign assets for marketing campaigns. Let's not forget case studies, customer proof, competitor battle cards, and many other assets marketing teams produce for salespeople to transform leads into actual business.

Partner, Developer, and App Ecosystems

Many B2B companies use a channel strategy to go global, so this program, too, requires extensive localization for other countries and languages. As HubSpot derives 40 per cent of its business from an agency partner channel, we had to localize on an ongoing basis the partner versions of the user interface, enablement assets, newsletters, and more.

HubSpot has diverse partners whose needs for content differ. Education partners have different needs from resellers, and the various levels of partners within each program have different needs and expectations. Often, specific needs for content assets in each language vary by geography too.

In addition, B2B tech companies cater to the needs of developers seeking to use application programming interfaces to integrate the software with other business systems. This means the localization team also supports the developer relations team, providing access to its developer site, documents, and newsletter.

Because HubSpot had many partners developing apps that integrate with its services, my team also worked closely with the product leaders who built the app marketplace to globalize the entire user interface. This included both the public-facing version as well as the one displayed upon login. The requirements entail localizing all of the listings for every app, but not all apps had their user interface available in all languages. We created different workflows and taxonomies so users on both sides understood which apps were offered in each language.

Legal, Financial, and Security Content

Legal content, too, needs to be translated by B2B companies, such as terms of services for both the master service agreement and partner agreement. Each time we added a new legal entity, the large numbers of legal documents required for B2B contracting needed to be updated in all languages. Since the binding language of most agreements is in English, some B2B companies provide "courtesy translations" for reference purposes only. Because legal content is highly specialized, this type of content requires certified legal translators for each language.

When customer payments are due, the accounting team reaches out with its own set of automated email workflows reminding customers to pay. All communications needed to be localized into all core languages, especially in situations where product users were happy using the English version of software, but the payment team did not speak English. My team translated all of those communications, as well as renewal reminders and other automated emails and in-app messages related to billing and invoicing.

Sometimes emergencies happen, as we all experienced during the Covid-19 pandemic. When something goes wrong or systems are down, users need to be notified right away. At HubSpot, my team was part of an emergency communications group to make sure that anytime an issue might affect customers, we could ensure speedy translation followed by human review, knowing urgent communications can be risky.

Measuring the Value of Localization

One of the hardest parts of expanding internationally for B2B is helping others understand why localization matters and why not all localization matters equally. Markets are not all at the same stage of business maturity, so not all markets require the same depth and types of content. Often, foreign market teams want all content that their domestic team enjoys until they learn how much it would cost the company. Providing all they want all at once would cost more than all of the salaries of all of the staff combined in that market.

To prove the value of localization, HubSpot measured the value of everything in terms of its impact on recurring revenue growth. When speaking with executives, I highlighted revenue growth from countries whose languages we supported compared to those we did not. I always had the following numbers ready:

- Global revenue growth (total, worldwide)
- International revenue growth (from markets outside the U.S.)
- Non-English revenue growth (from non-English international markets)
- Supported language revenue growth (from languages supported by localization).

As we grew the brand globally, it was important to assign the costs of localization to the company's overall return on its investment and to the team making it happen.

Did those investments pay off in the long run? When I joined HubSpot in 2015, less than 20 per cent of its revenue came from outside of the U.S. Nearly 10 years later, according to the Q2 2024 earnings call transcript, HubSpot's international revenue represented 47 per cent of total revenue, and its growth far outpaced domestic growth. People from every function across many offices joined forces to make that happen. But most would be unable to do their jobs if it were not for a world-class localization team, continually working alongside them, powering the massive HubSpot content engine quietly in the background to brand global, adapt local.

Along the way, standing at the forefront of international expansion and local adaptation, I built the most global team in the company, hiring and managing teams of professionals located in Colombia, France, Germany, Ireland, Japan, Scotland, Singapore, and the U.S. I had the privilege of launching offices in three new countries (Colombia, Germany, Japan) in as many years. As I would come to learn, the people you hire in new markets are essential to ensuring your brand global, adapt local strategy.

Global Progress over Local Perfection

Even if your brand has flawless translations and localizes content to look and feel locally "native," there is still no guarantee that your company will succeed in a local market. Why? Often, the underlying strategies, models, and frameworks that led to the development of content for your domestic market are not applicable to a new market, and an entirely different strategy is needed. When fast-growth companies go into new markets, they often "don't know what they don't know" until they build up local market knowledge specific to their products and services. When companies are in a rush to grow, this often results in their trying to fit a square into a circle.

In B2B tech firms in high-growth, fast-paced environments, especially with software disrupting traditional business solutions, demand from outside a company's domestic market is often extremely high. Businesses seek emerging technologies in the global marketplace to help them grow faster and operate more efficiently. They often embrace new tech solutions as fast as possible, even if the software and services are not fully localized.

The majority of B2C products are one-off purchases to be enjoyed for a short duration of time. If not consumed, like foodstuffs and cosmetics, the items can be returned or resold, making the risk of the purchase considerably lower than B2B. In contrast, the risk and time horizon associated with a B2B purchase is often much higher—it's not just a purchase to be used for a day, week, or year—it's a long-term business investment. It's also a budget line item of five, six, or seven figures, attracting the attention of a watchful CFO or procurement officer, who expects results.

When your website serves as a global gateway, especially in B2B tech, a desirable product can attract customers worldwide. Many tech companies experience market pull as demand finds them. Therein lies the challenge: Do you wait until your strategy is perfect, or serve eager customers now and adapt along the way? Most companies choose "progress over perfection," recognizing that B2B is complex, and international growth adds further layers.

As we saw in the previous chapter, B2B tech companies can't fully tailor every aspect of the customer experience for each local market before entering. Even with unlimited budgets, there simply isn't enough time if hordes of customers stand behind the door of your digital storefront waving money for what you're offering. The key is adapting just enough to meet market demands, which is especially challenging as the software evolves daily. B2B companies propelled by global growth rarely have the time to craft unique strategies for every market they're entering simultaneously.

Asking the Right Question

We were eager to read the latest feedback from our global customer survey. As a software company based in the U.S. selling to customers at small- and medium-sized businesses, our standard survey to the small- and mid-sized business users of our software was the net promoter score (NPS).[9] The survey design itself is simple. It asks, "How likely would you be to recommend our company to a friend?" Software users reveal their satisfaction levels by ranking their answers on a scale from 1 to 10.

We translated this question into multiple languages to enable all of our customers around the world to respond, along with the follow-up question, "Why did you give us this score?" We back-translated the answers to those questions into English to understand the reasons behind the scores and planned to analyze the data to uncover the trends.

The German score stood out, as it was significantly lower than other countries. When I looked further at individual user responses and the lowest outlier scores, I noticed one German respondent had given us the worst possible rating. Yet this very same business recently renewed its subscription. I checked our CRM software. The customer success manager in our Berlin office said this customer was happy with our service and recently purchased multiple add-ons. He had joined a recent user group meet-up and attended a training session at our office. He had even voted our German support articles as "helpful."

So, his low NPS score really did not add up. Why would he actively engage with us if he was so unhappy? Why would he score us so low but continue to subscribe to our services? When I checked his responses in the free-form text box, the answer became abundantly clear. He had written, very logically, "I would not recommend this software to a friend, because I do not have any friends who need this type of software."

At that moment, it became glaringly obvious that we were an American company with home market blinders on. We were asking a question, but with an intent that he did not share. At a minimum, we were asking the question in a way he didn't understand. The problem wasn't the language barrier. The words in German had been translated accurately by my team of expert translators, and he clearly understood the words themselves. What we at the company level had failed to take into account was that, like many users in that market, he might have never before seen an NPS survey, so the framing of the questions did not make sense to him.

Something as simple as selecting a survey methodology can trip up companies when serving many different audiences with varying cultural needs. It's critical to phrase questions appropriately and know that *how* people score varies across cultures, even if their satisfaction levels are quite similar. This is a complex undertaking. Marketers must shape every single aspect of the customer experience in order to build trust with an array of buyers with different needs based on titles, roles, purchasing authority, and seniority. Welcome to the complex world of international B2B marketing.

Local Sprints in a Global Straight Jacket

During my HubSpot interview, the hiring team asked me for examples of "best-in-class" B2B tech companies with strong global brands. I answered honestly: I don't believe any B2B company truly excels at building a global brand or delivering a local experience, especially compared to B2C brands. I easily cited examples of B2C brand campaigns that authentically reached new markets and drove success. In B2C, products are often developed specifically for local markets, allowing brands to enter new regions swiftly after conducting initial market research.

With B2B software, the starting point is different; it's like sprinting into a new market while wearing a global straight jacket. Product and engineering teams typically control the product itself, leaving B2B marketers with limited influence. At HubSpot, I was fortunate to oversee product localization, giving me more sway over the local software experience. Yet, even with this scope, many changes required extensive re-development, making swift adaptation challenging. B2B marketing leaders often have limited control over product adaptations and are usually distant from key international strategy decisions, so my broader role in driving local impact was an uncommon privilege.

When selling a constantly evolving product, you're not introducing a finished, market-specific solution. Instead, you're forced to take a product that's still changing and deliver a local experience across more diverse communication touchpoints into many markets at once. In B2B tech, global success relies less on upfront planning for a grand market entry and more on agility—how effectively a company adapts in real time across diverse markets. This requires ongoing commitment to tailoring the local experience as the global product evolves while accepting that, in B2B, adapting local is never perfect. It is also never done.

Summary

- **What makes B2B global expansion more complex than B2C?** While both share the need to adapt to cultural differences and navigate regulations, B2B global expansion faces more complex challenges due higher price points, longer sales cycles, and a more diverse set of decision-makers involved in every single sale.
- **Why is it important to build local relationships in B2B markets?** In B2B markets, trust and local relationships are essential, as businesses tend to be risk averse and rely on personal connections for long-term purchasing decisions.
- **How do B2B companies brand global, adapt local?** B2B companies must adjust their value propositions to meet regional business priorities and regulatory requirements of local markets. This includes adapting product features, pricing, sales, messaging, and customer success efforts, and in the case of digital offerings, they must do so while their product is rapidly evolving.

The Global Digest

Chapter 10 Takeaways

1 **Acknowledge B2B complexity:** Selling to businesses often involves multiple stakeholders with varying needs, making it more complex than selling directly to individual consumers.

2 **Adapt local marketing strategies:** B2B brands must adjust their marketing strategies for different buyer personas across various channels, increasing the complexity of global expansion.

3 **Focus on trust and relationships:** Establishing credibility in local markets through partnerships and relationship building is critical for B2B success, especially in relationship-driven cultures.

4 **Expect longer sales cycles:** B2B sales involve navigating complex processes and long sales cycles that vary by region, requiring a deep understanding of local business practices, laws, and regulations.

5 **Localize the value proposition:** What works in one market may not resonate in another; adjusting the value proposition to local needs is essential for success.

6 **Navigate local regulations:** B2B companies must adapt to local regulatory environments, as failure to comply with regional laws can severely impact business opportunities.

7 **Tailor support and training:** With many more stakeholders involved, B2B services must provide a wide array of localized support, training, and technical documentation to ensure customers across different regions can effectively use the product.

8 **Consider cultural differences:** Translating basic customer communications such as surveys is about more than just language accuracy; cultural context and understanding play a crucial role in the effectiveness of the feedback you receive.

9 **Use diverse go-to-market strategies:** B2B companies often adopt diverse go-to-market approaches, such as product-led growth or direct sales, which all require adaptation to meet local customer expectations across diverse markets.

10 **Measure the different types of international impact:** B2B companies may support different markets and languages to varying degrees. Measuring the impact of localization investments helps determine the relative value of these efforts to the global business.

References

1 Tata Consultancy Services. Tata Sports Timeline. www.tata.com/newsroom/heritage/tata-sports-timeline (archived at https://perma.cc/8SAP-FQV6)

2 Tata Consultancy Services. TCS NYC Marathon Technology. www.tcs.com/who-we-are/sports-sponsorships/tcs-nyc-marathon-technology-app (archived at https://perma.cc/MTK5-YAYK)

3 A. Bapna (2024) Why Tata Consultancy's Long-Term Sponsorship Strategy Is a Marathon, Not a Sprint, *The Drum*, April 26. www.thedrum.com/news/2024/04/16/why-tata-consultancy-services-long-term-sponsorship-strategy-marathon-not-sprint (archived at https://perma.cc/Z6XY-HV76)

4 B. Parmar (2023) SAP's India cloud growing over 50%, to focus on smaller businesses: India MD, *The Economic Times,* October 10. economictimes.indiatimes.com/tech/information-tech/saps-india-cloud-growing-over-50-to-focus-on-smaller-businesses-india-md/articleshow/112086682.cms (archived at https://perma.cc/5ETX-6PEB)

5 M. Benioff (2009) *Behind the Cloud: The Untold Story of How Salesforce.com Went from Idea to Billion-Dollar Company—and Revolutionized an Industry.* Jossey-Bass, Hoboken, New Jersey

6 Deutsche Telekom (2015) Deutsche Telekom to Act as Data Trustee for Microsoft Cloud in Germany, November 11. www.telekom.com/en/media/media-information/archive/deutsche-telekom-to-act-as-data-trustee-for-microsoft-cloud-in-germany-362074 (archived at https://perma.cc/7H5V-7Y6B)
7 B. Halligan (2018) The Art of Strategy Is about Knowing When to Say No, *Harvard Business Review*, January 26. hbr.org/2018/01/the-art-of-strategy-is-about-knowing-when-to-say-no (archived at https://perma.cc/KM3L-6GKD)
8 C. Baxter-Reed (2023). Rolling Out Brand Voice Guidelines at HubSpot with Bethbot. Acrolinx Podcast. Interview with Beth Dunn, July 26. www.acrolinx.com/blog/rolling-out-brand-voice-guidelines-at-hubspot-with-the-bethbot/ (archived at https://perma.cc/FS5C-4G8F)
9 Bain & Co. History of Net Promoter. www.netpromotersystem.com/about/history-of-net-promoter/ (archived at https://perma.cc/KD9P-EACQ)

PART FOUR
Connecting the Global Dots

The Two Most Important Words in French

11

Building Teams across Cultures

KATHERINE MELCHIOR RAY

When in Rome

What are the two most important words in French?

As one of my favorite icebreakers, the answer is not what you think. Guesses normally include:

"*Merci beaucoup.*"

"'*S'il vous plait.*' Oops, that's three!" students say.

Hmmmm, people mumble. "'*Bonjour*' is only one…"

I smile, and show them photos of French colleagues greeting one another with air kisses to spark an idea in their puzzled minds—and *still* my students can't pop the cork on the mysterious bottle.

So, I tell them a story. I was working in Paris for the parent company of Uniqlo, Fast Retailing, helping them grow their French fashion subsidiaries, Comptoir des Cotonniers and Princesse Tam Tam. The Japanese team had flown into Paris to review the next collection of women's lingerie for the Princesse Tam Tam line. French designers had carefully hung samples of lace bras with matching panties in fall's new colors on rolling racks in the showroom headquarters, across the street from the Louvre museum. When the six male Japanese managers entered in their black suits, the French female designers quickly extinguished their cigarettes and stood up, smiling nervously.

The lead manager walked over to the rack at eye level and began to review the collection. The others trailed behind him, each finding a place to inspect the various bras, briefs, and culottes. As they compared notes in Japanese, I joined them, eager to listen in.

After about 10 minutes, I returned to the French team, who had not moved, their faces stone cold with anticipation.

"It's ok," I tried to comfort them. "They recognize the beautiful stitching and designs. But, they feel the color palette is too dark and autumnal; they believe you need more pastel-like colors."

No reaction, which is unusual for the passionate French.

"Katherine!" one woman began in a loud voice. "That's *not* the issue. How can we begin to discuss the collection when they do not even say *Bonjour*."

The two most important words in French are *Bonjour, Monsieur* or *Bonjour, Madame*. What may seem a formality in some cultures is oxygen in others. In this scenario, especially as the Japanese came from the parent company, it was important for them to acknowledge those in the room. The French women were waiting to be shown respect with what they viewed as a simple greeting.

When I explained this to the Japanese, they were surprised. They explained that they assumed the French designers were on their team, part of the larger company. Both France and Japan are hierarchical cultures, where respect and formal communication are extremely important. However, Japan also has a dual orientation of inner and outer circles, which change based on context. In Japan, it is customary to say *Good Morning* with *Ohayo*, or *Ohayo Gozaimasu* if the person is senior to you. In France, regardless of whom you're speaking to, *Bonjour* is *de rigueur*—required by etiquette. Even to the person in a kiosk selling newspapers, especially to service providers, you should greet them with *Bonjour, Monsieur* or *Bonjour, Madame* to show respect.

When I lived in France working for the French fashion brand Façonnable, purchased by Nordstrom, I learned this the hard way. I was expected to *Bonjour* every member of the company. Without it, I might encounter a cold shoulder, apathy, or resistance to business plans.

I thought I had figured it out by saying "*Bonjour*" to everyone, anytime I encountered them in the hall or the lunch *cantine*. Unfortunately, it was not so easy. Rather than engendering respect, I appeared a cultural buffoon, which I discovered only when someone replied dismissively, "*Re-Bonjour*," meaning "We already said *Bonjour* today." Thereafter, every single day, I learned to track whom I had and had not yet *Bonjour*'d.

While these anecdotes may seem silly in some cultures, they are table stakes in others. International business demands cultural fluency to work effectively across communication codes and conventions. In order to help Fast Retailing expand its French brands and set the company up for continued business success, I organized team workshops on cultural understanding and communication alongside the brand expansion plans.

Relationships matter in marketing, and they matter in organizations. As seen in the last chapter on B2B and throughout this book, understanding your customers' values, speaking their language, and prioritizing their cultural preferences builds trust in the brand. But achieving this isn't solely the responsibility of the marketing department; it requires the collective effort of the entire organization. Marketing may take the lead in acquiring new customers, but the most profitable and sustainable growth comes from keeping those same customers loyal and satisfied. This means every department must share the goal of enhancing customer satisfaction.

Creating a corporate culture that truly places the customer at the heart of every decision goes far beyond simply assembling a diverse team. It's about building cohesive international teams that transcend departments, languages, and cultures, all working together towards a shared purpose. When each team member, regardless of their role, consistently delivers on brand values tailored to local markets, every customer interaction becomes meaningful. This, in turn, fosters customer loyalty which builds brand value.

As today's workplace grows more interconnected, global success depends on building high-performing teams that collaborate effectively across cultures. In this chapter, we explore how to align these teams with shared goals and values. By fostering genuine relationships and teamwork, you can drive innovation and build a culture that truly puts the customer first. So, *bonjour* to you, reader—and *bon voyage*!

Conducting an Orchestra: The Case for Diversity

People are often a company's greatest asset, with about 40–70 per cent of its revenue directed to salaries and associated costs.[1] Teams are composed of individuals, with each person bringing their unique skills, talent, experience, and personality.

Diverse teams offer powerful advantages. A 2015 McKinsey report, which analyzed over 350 public companies, found that those in the top 25 per cent for ethnic and racial diversity in management were 35 per cent more likely to deliver financial returns above their industry average.[2] This underscores the direct link between diverse leadership and superior performance. Building teams that reflect a variety of perspectives isn't just a moral or ethical imperative—it's a business strategy proven to drive results. Teams with diverse perspectives provide a wider range of cultural insights and increase objectivity by pointing out blind spots or questioning others' facts. Through discussion and clarification, the team actually gets smarter and produces greater innovation. (We'll talk more about the positive individual impact in Chapter 12.)

When I refer to diversity, I mean all kinds: ethnic, racial, gender, cultural, sexual orientation, age, religion, personality, global experience, and more. In the U.S., diversity is sometimes assumed to focus on inclusive practices for BIPOC (Black, Indigenous, and People of Color) for many good reasons. However, global diversity casts a much wider net to create understanding and equity for all. Internationally diverse teams help build globally equitable organizations.

BOX 11.1 BRAND GLOBAL, ADAPT LOCAL FROM RECRUITMENT TO REVIEWS

Creating a high-performing international team begins with thoughtful recruitment and team composition. Allying with the human relations department assists not only in recruiting for diversity, but in helping to orchestrate the symphony of talent. In any team or organization, aim for a balance of skills, experiences, and cultural backgrounds that align with your global marketing objectives. It's easy to fall back on the education and upbringing we know from our own culture, but working internationally requires actively embracing people with different education and experience. Look at it as an opportunity to learn more about the behaviors and values in other cultures and how our own background may be only one form of expertise in a rich and varied world.

Global performance reviews are crucial for aligning employees with the company's core values while ensuring equitable advancement. However, just like marketing initiatives, these reviews must be flexible enough to account for local cultural nuances in management and evaluation. While it's important to uphold consistent standards globally, leadership styles, initiative, and feedback preferences vary across regions, and so should how employees are graded. Shape global teams with human resources using the same approach as *brand global, adapt local.*

This being said, diversity alone is not enough. The group needs to be developed into a high-performing global team, so its rich and varied perspectives as well as talent can broaden and personalize market insights to deliver innovative solutions for a global audience. The capability to harness the power of diversity must be built into the organizational fabric.

Think of it like a sports team. In soccer, or football to a large portion of the world, teams rely on forward strikers for speed and precisional excellence, wing players for crossing abilities, defenders for their tackling effectiveness, and goalkeepers for their reflexes and size. They need to all be physically and mentally strong, while leveraging one another's individual skills with excellent communication. Just as a great coach develops this teamwork on the field, a strong global leader builds a high-functioning business team across cultures.

Customer-Centricity as a Collaborative Purpose

In the late 1990s, as a hotel corporation expanded its global footprint, it faced the challenge of maintaining customer service consistency across diverse cultural contexts. Recognizing that traditional classroom-style training was not enough to foster the deeply ingrained, customer-focused culture they aspired to, the hotels partnered with Northwestern University to reimagine customer relations as more than a new technology platform, but as a business process owned by every employee.

The centerpiece of this initiative was deceptively simple: a small notebook. In training sessions around the world with hotel staff, international marketing, and communications teams, employees received these notebooks to record their observations or overheard customer needs. If an employee heard guests alighting the elevator mentioning their anniversary or needing more shampoo, they were empowered to act on them, to call housekeeping themselves to ensure the guests' needs were promptly met.

Sara Kearney, who spent 25 years in global marketing and hotel operations, explains how this initiative created shared ownership for the customer experience across all levels and departments. It increased cultural sensitivity and awareness by encouraging employees to pay close attention to guest needs and preferences. Employees in every location felt empowered to take initiative and make decisions that would positively impact the guest experience.

"We were trying to translate marketing into experience and bring that mindset and responsibility to every employee," says Kearney.[3]

The notebook initiative wasn't just about individual actions; it was about creating a customer-centric culture, where every employee owned the customer experience. Keeping customers happy became a common goal across departments. As a shared sense of intimacy with the customer resonated across regions, traditional silos between departments and hierarchies broke down. Daily team meetings became forums for sharing observations, insights, and best practices.

Over time, a wealth of detailed, personalized information allowed the hotels to build comprehensive customer profiles. These profiles enabled the company to identify high-value, loyal customers and surprise them with personalized gestures—a practice that became known as "random acts of kindness." A couple celebrating their anniversary might find a surprise bottle of wine in their room. At a birthday meal in the hotel restaurant, the server might offer a guest's favorite chocolate cake.

By empowering employees across roles, regions, and cultural backgrounds to contribute to the customer experience, the company created not just satisfied customers, but a truly customer-centric culture. This approach to customer service profoundly impacted how the hotels built and managed their international teams, creating a unifying sense of purpose that transcended cultural differences.

The Collaborative Economy

You can't get global work done in a vacuum. How you work together, therefore, is critical. Today's workplace is more collaborative than ever. Over the past few decades, managers and employees are spending 50 per cent more time collaborating.[4] In a competitive landscape, collaboration allows teams to imagine audacious initiatives, solve complex problems, innovate rapidly, respond more quickly to change, and serve customers more seamlessly. Doing this globally requires an even higher level of collaboration to overcome distance, language, time zones, and culture.

To leverage the benefit of teamwork, you need to create a supportive environment to build the right capacity and skills. It may seem surprising, but the more people feel comfortable sharing their emotions, exposing a bit of vulnerability, the more productive the team is. When Google sought to identify how to make its teams more productive, it learned surprising findings about team dynamics.[5] After analyzing hundreds of teams, Project Aristotle discovered that the key to a team's success wasn't the mix of individual skills, but rather how team members interacted, respected one another, and contributed to the group. Psychological safety—the belief that individuals can take risks, voice their opinions, and ask questions without fear of embarrassment or punishment—emerged as the single most important factor.

Teams with high levels of psychological safety were more likely to leverage the collective intelligence of their members, leading to higher innovation and productivity.

Fostering psychological safety can feel uncomfortable, especially in a professional setting where vulnerability is often seen as a weakness. Admitting mistakes, asking for help, or expressing uncertainty may seem counterintuitive in workplaces that value competence and confidence. Yet, Google found that when team members feel safe enough to expose themselves, they become more connected, willing to share ideas, learn from one another, and collaborate. You can imagine this can be particularly challenging in global teams, where cultural differences may further complicate how vulnerability is perceived. Yet, encouraging openness and emotional safety is critical for building trust and helps bridge cultural gaps to cultivate successful collaboration in diverse teams.

We return to the topic of trust, which we explained in Chapter 3 is a critical element in a brand's relationships with its customers. A company that creates trust internally among its teams is more likely to foster trust with the customer in every brand experience.

You may recall from our definition that trust is comprised of three parts: shared values, open communication, and a history of promises kept. While easy to understand, this is hard to implement, especially across diverse cultures. If a team agrees to certain ways of working, communicates with one another openly and honestly, and shows over time they can rely on each other, trust grows. All three are critical and must be practiced. Trust takes time to build, but is easy to lose.

Communication is important in all three aspects of trust. Yet, in wake of the Covid-19 pandemic, our increased reliance on digital communication works to erode our simple conversation skills.[6] As the Pew Research Center noted in 2020, "The less interpersonal trust people have, the more frequently they experience bouts of anxiety, depression and loneliness."[7] And, according to the World Health Organization, loneliness continues to increase among young people all over the world.[8] The good news is small talk is one of the easiest ways to begin to build relationships. We simply need to focus on it more, especially in international business. Those first few minutes of a Zoom call where you check in with each other, or maybe make a joke to break the ice—those minutes are more important than you think.

To help integrate new colleagues in Japan, Nataly created a simple "coffee chat" program in which people could pick topics they had in common—food, music, art etc. They were randomly assigned a colleague to meet in quick 15-minute chats. Called the *tomodachi* (friends) program, the initiative helped ensure that people get to know each other before relying on them for work. The program continued for years and eventually became popular globally.

For those working in Anglo-Saxon countries, like the U.S., Germany, the Netherlands, and Australia, this might not seem obvious. These cultures prioritize transactions more than relationships, as we saw in Chapter 3 on cultural preferences. Working in those cultures emphasizes getting things done quickly and efficiently. Many other countries around the world place a higher priority on building relationships first.[9] This is a critical and foundational aspect to global business and to building global teams.

If you are traveling for an important business meeting to a country that places a high priority on relationships, especially if it's a first meeting, consider arriving the night before. Sharing a meal together the day before discussing work details begins to build a relationship on which business is more easily transacted. I have found people in many countries feel much more at ease collaborating and are open to negotiate if they feel comfortable with someone ahead of time.

The first step to building collaborative working relationships across diversity is to recognize what we know, what we know we don't know, and what we don't know we don't know.

Develop an Open Mindset

Diverse teams need to begin by acknowledging there is a lot to learn about others. Curiosity requires humility. That can be challenging for powerful, disciplined brands built by strong marketers with audacious campaigns and effective negotiation skills. I joined Nike as General Manager of Women's Footwear in the U.S. While my role was U.S.-focused, my strong international background pulled me into discussions about global strategies for women. In the late 1990s, Nike had not yet made a shoe from a women's last, the three-dimensional mold of a foot used to shape shoes, engineered a maximum-support sports bra, or sold its products in department stores.

In the U.S., we were just launching the breakout campaign, "If You Let Me Play," that presented the facts about women and sports. Rather than highlighting the glory of female athletes, the ad sent a powerful message encouraging girls' sports. Young girls of different ages shared statistics on how sports make them stronger, increase their self-confidence, protect them from diseases, and help deter depression. At that time, girls and young women were not permitted to participate in organized sports as much as men and were still needing to ask for opportunities.[10]

I thought within Nike, we got it—we understood different audiences want different things.

And yet, I found myself often explaining internally that women athletes want products made for their bodies—embracing how they run, walk, shoot, and score—designed for their tastes and sold where they shop. In Japan, decades before the country fielded the gold medal for Women's World Cup Soccer, I had to encourage the head of global footwear to listen to the local team explain how women in Japan were not likely to respond to such a bold American ad campaign of empowerment.

Nike is not alone. I have found many U.S.-based companies wrongly assured that the way it works in the home country is how it should work overseas. Rather than discussing how to tailor offerings to different customers, many companies spend too much time debating the need to adapt. Call it the paradox of plenty—where companies with large domestic markets are blinded by local success and lose the objectivity necessary for adapting to a new market.

This blind spot is not as common in companies headquartered in smaller countries, like many in Europe and Asia. One day, it dawned on me why. While it could be false confidence or ignorance, executives in American companies are physically far from global markets and seldom speak foreign languages. The U.S. is blessed by a huge and diverse domestic market, but it is also isolated by two vast oceans and, with its neighbors across its longest border, shares a language. European and Asia-based companies, in contrast, are surrounded by countries with different cultures, different languages, and, in Asia, different currencies. That geographical reality often translates into greater recognition of the need to understand and adapt to other countries and cultures, so they can focus their energies on doing just that.

Lower the Waterline in Teams

Leading an international team requires a high degree of emotional intelligence, adaptability, and determination. Your teams will only be as successful as you set them up to be. To leverage the benefit of diversity, you must establish common ground for understanding and collaboration. You need to build appreciation for different ways of working and foster an environment for people to perform their individual best towards shared goals.

Remember the expression "lower the waterline" from Chapter 3? It's a way of proactively understanding foreign cultures' unspoken or hidden values. This approach applies equally well to building cohesive teams from diverse cultures. Help them develop awareness, understanding, and cross-cultural communication skills.

As the leader, establish a forum and guidelines to develop a shared vision and mission, articulating values and rules of engagement collaboratively with the team. Having local teams co-create the culture ensures they feel reflected and included from day one. Reduce misunderstandings by building the culture around explicit and direct communication. This process helps everyone understand their own cultural subjectivity and find common ground. The brand can serve as your guide. The most successful marketing organizations align their team dynamics with their brand's values, creating consistency across both internal collaboration and customer-facing activities.

When it comes to defining goals, global marketing teams need to balance brand, business, and team objectives. These goals might include building a premium, innovative brand; increasing customer lifetime value; or expanding into new markets. Achieving these goals requires prioritizing marketing skills such as customer-centricity, creativity, and data-driven decision-making.

Encourage everyone to be authentic, speak honestly and transparently, respect diverse opinions, support others, and embrace constructive criticism. Investing in such team-building goes a long way. Spend time to explain that practicing these explicit rules of engagement lowers the waterline of hidden assumptions across diverse backgrounds. Emphasize the importance of building trust in diverse teams and outline its three components as a critical basis of premium performance. Prioritizing authenticity encourages people to be themselves and to feel comfortable sharing even wild ideas, some of which may work outrageously well. Supporting one another allows people to take risks because embracing vulnerability and accepting failure are critical elements for empowering creativity. Working in complex, fast-moving, global industries with rapid market changes is high-pressure, hard work, so building team skills in communication and collaboration helps manage conflict and improve resilience for challenging times.

Lead with Cultural Intelligence

Among the leadership skills required to manage globally diverse teams is cultural intelligence (CQ). Building effective international teams starts with the same open and empathetic approach towards foreign audiences in the marketplace: curiosity, humility, and active listening. The explanations of CQ and the cultural dimensions model explored in Chapter 3 provide useful frameworks for understanding how cultures differ along key axes such as individualism versus collectivism, long-term versus short-term orientation, and power distance.

Effective leaders flex their style to accommodate different cultural expectations around authority, decision-making, and feedback. For example, team members from hierarchical cultures like India, China, France, Malaysia, and Arab countries may expect more directive leadership, whereas those from egalitarian cultures like the U.S., Canada, and Australia may want more participative decision-making processes. Similarly, it is not easy to balance communication needs when a team is composed of people from direct and indirect cultures. Recognizing these differences and understanding how to code-switch helps leaders tailor their management style and foster an environment where all members feel valued and understood. They need to embrace that diversity and create a new, shared culture with explicit values where everyone learns to adapt.

Language is one of the most powerful tools for bridging cultural differences because it reflects how we interpret the world, which is deeply influenced by culture. For example, in Japan, the term *sonkei* is often translated as "respect," but it also implies obedience. When you show *sonkei* to someone in authority, it's expected that you follow their lead without question. This contrasts with English, where respect doesn't necessarily mean agreement, and it's common to respect someone's opinion while disagreeing with them. Learning to speak multiple languages is an undervalued asset in English-speaking countries, but it is extremely valuable for building teams in international business, and in a career, as we'll see in Chapter 12.

Communication is more than just words—nonverbal cues are equally crucial and can vary widely across cultures. In India, nodding is a common nonverbal cue that can easily lead to misinterpretation. A head nod might seem like a sign of agreement to Westerners, but in India it often indicates that the person is listening, without necessarily implying agreement or consent. In Latin America, gestures like putting an arm around someone is seen as a sign of warmth and friendliness, but to someone from a culture where physical touch is unprofessional, it might feel overly familiar. These subtle differences in nonverbal communication can cause misunderstandings if their intent is not recognized for what it is, and what it is not. (More examples can be found in Chapter 12.)

As social psychologist Devon Price writes, "If a person's behavior doesn't make sense to you, it is because you are missing a part of their context."[11] Gaining that context often requires reaching out, engaging in small talk, and listening. These brief, friendly exchanges create a positive social dynamic which have been shown to make people feel good.[12] By bridging social barriers, these informal chats also signal a desire to build a relationship which improves emotional well-being.

Anticipate these differences by learning about the codes and conventions of the groups you're working with. Even without knowing the language, you can understand meaning through gestures and behavior, as nonverbal cues often reveal true intentions and motivations. Beyond physical movements, pay attention to who arrives at a meeting first and last, where people sit, greetings, and the order in which people speak. Be aware of these expectations and manage them thoughtfully. Absorb as much information as possible. Practicing focused presence or mindfulness helps your brain become more attuned to new meaning in the behavior of other cultural groups. And, if you're part of the dominant culture, help others to adapt quickly by pointing out nuances that may not be familiar to them.

Relationship building varies greatly across cultures. Some cultures prioritize them more than others. After many years of international work, I've come to value relationships highly for improving collaboration and cultivating meaningful professional bonds. I recommend visiting your colleagues in person and spending time outside the work environment—whether sharing a meal or visiting their communities. This not only deepens your relationship but also exposes you to their culture. In many countries, this simple, enjoyable effort can significantly enhance work collaboration.

How people solve problems is another sensitive cultural touchpoint. In direct cultures like Germany and the Netherlands, feedback is straightforward, which may seem harsh to more indirect cultures, such as Japan and Brazil. The U.S. presents an interesting case, with strong regional differences: New Yorkers are direct, Southerners are friendly and welcoming, and the West Coast leans friendly but cautious, sometimes called passive aggressive. Additionally, since jobs often provide healthcare and employees can be easily fired, many Americans hesitate to speak frankly at work. With the U.S.'s reputation for being direct and straightforward, this dynamic can confuse people from other countries.

When working with others across cultures, you may encounter conflicting expectations. A common question I often hear is, "How much should I adapt?" Should you adjust to their style or stay true to your own? The answer lies in learning to "culture flex" to meet your goals. Adapting to their behavior can improve relationships by making the other party feel more comfortable, but sacrificing important values can be personally uncomfortable; or worse, if the behavior appears unnatural, it can create suspicion and distrust.

Like all aspects of global work, finding the right balance between adaptation and authenticity is an art that requires knowledge and skill. The more experience you gain, the more adept you'll become. You'll probably read a few rooms wrong before you learn to read them right—I certainly did! By expanding your cultural understanding, emotional intelligence, and adaptability, you'll expedite the learning curve and strengthen your toolkit for any situation. Keep in mind that markets and cultures are always evolving, and to succeed, we must evolve with them.

BOX 11.2 CROSS-CULTURAL COMMUNICATION RULES

Clear communication is the lifeblood of any successful team, but it becomes even more critical in a cross-cultural context. To overcome language barriers and cultural differences, consider implementing the following strategies:

1. Establish a common working language with explicit communication that encourages translations and clarifications. Words do not carry the same meaning across cultures.
2. Use plain language and avoid colloquialisms, idioms, or complex jargon which don't translate well.
3. Provide written summaries of key discussions, as people may be more comfortable reading a language than speaking it.
4. Become culturally intelligent in nonverbal communication differences across cultures.

Developing emotional and cultural intelligence to understand and navigate these verbal and nonverbal nuances is essential for reducing conflict and fostering collaboration in international teams. The ability to distinguish between innocent misunderstandings and meaningful disagreements allows teams to focus on addressing the most critical issues. A deeper layer of emotional intelligence—empathy—has become increasingly recognized as crucial for success in diverse, global teams.

As Yale professor Marissa King explains in her book *Social Chemistry*, strong social connections are powerful predictors of cognitive functioning, resilience, and engagement.[13] Teams that foster friendships perform better, and people who have supportive co-workers enjoy better work–life balance and lower stress levels. Interestingly, recent research shows a promising trend: empathy, particularly among younger generations, is on the rise. A 2024 study revealed that empathy among young Americans has been increasing since 2008, nearly returning to the high levels seen in the 1970s.[14] This upward trend offers valuable insights into how developing empathy can help build stronger, more compassionate teams, which is vital for success in diverse, international settings. As emotional intelligence improves, so does the teams' ability to work harmoniously across cultures. This growing emphasis on empathy reflects the increasing importance of social and emotional skills in a globally connected world, where understanding and relating to diverse perspectives is crucial for collaboration.

Starwood Builds Empathy and Trust in Global Teams

The best way to practice cultural intelligence skills is visiting your colleagues around the world. As we saw in Chapter 5, Starwood President and CEO Frits van Paasschen went even further by moving his executive team to work from China for a full month. Working with his local teams on the ground helped to build the social capital needed to build a global mindset and implement international standards.

While living in China, he'd scheduled a meeting with the headquarters in Connecticut for July 5 at 9 am. It had not dawned on him that meant 9 pm on July 4, when the Americans would be eating hot dogs and hamburgers to celebrate their national Independence Day holiday. That moment made the U.S. team reflect on the number of times they had unintentionally scheduled calls during Chinese New Year or other culturally important days for the China team. While the U.S. headquarters felt comfortable declining that July meeting with their American CEO, the China team likely felt pressure to accept invitations that conflicted with their personal lives. Imagining the China team stepping away from their families during important cultural holidays strengthened van Paasschen's resolve to demonstrate mutual respect and understanding between Starwood's local and global teams.

This sensitivity to local considerations went a long way in building trust between Starwood headquarters and Chinese executives. Joint problem solving between local and global teams fueled Starwood's growth both within China and abroad. The collaborative approach was instrumental in Starwood's success and its eventual acquisition. In 2016, Marriott bought Starwood for $13 billion, becoming the world's largest hotel chain. Marriott was attracted to Starwood for its strong hotel brands, its broad geographic footprint in Asia and the Middle East, and its robust loyalty program—all bolstered by van Paasschen's commitment to China.[15]

Tommy Hilfiger Unites Teams on Purpose

While Starwood built trust by embedding its leaders within the local culture in China, Tommy Hilfiger took a different but equally impactful approach to foster empathy and mutual respect. Rather than bridging time zones, they sought to unite their global teams around a shared purpose, empowering employees to connect with the brand's core values.

As President and Chief Brand Officer for Tommy Hilfiger, Avery Baker understood the importance of getting people from a company headquarters out to local markets and vice versa.

"It's a luxury," she acknowledges. "Not every company can do this, but real-life interactions cannot be underestimated."[16]

In a time of working from home, limited business travel, and reduced expense accounts, how do you create a meaningful corporate culture beyond in-person?[17] Companies are not always willing to swipe the company card to mingle over cocktail hour, and since the Covid-19 pandemic, employees are not always willing to attend. As one administrator remarked to the *Wall Street Journal*, "I don't want to put in eight, nine, ten hours and go out and have a beer—to talk about work for another four hours."[18] Many working parents and caregivers simply can't do that. And research suggests that company social events can be uncomfortable for minority members of diverse teams.[19]

Companies, therefore, have to get creative in designing initiatives and events that engage employees, enhance company culture, and bring the company purpose to life. Baker's team at Tommy Hilfiger did exactly that by handing the microphone back to employees.

First, they redefined the company's purpose. The heart and soul of the Tommy Hilfiger brand was always inspired by the courage to express one's personal twist, certainly in fashion, but also in culture at large. The brand champions the drive to dream, to dare, and to reinvent the status quo.

By spotlighting the pioneering steps taken to build the brand throughout its 35-year history, Baker's team illustrated how courage is a core part of the company's values. Courage means questioning established norms and pushing boundaries. It means truly embracing individuality in fashion, work, society, cross-cultural connection, and the collective experience. Tommy Hilfiger encourages bold optimism, taking steps to create a world and a future where everyone is welcome. To bring this purpose to life for every employee in stores, factories, and offices around the world, the company asked its entire global population to consider what "Courage to…" means to them and to create a short talk on this theme.

The company partnered with TED, an organization that hosts expert speakers at professional events (and top videos garner over 40 million views on YouTube). During a one-year period, they staged a selection process of several rounds, from written submissions to three-minute "elevator pitch" events hosted in each region. Winners would receive individual speaker training from TED executives and present at a stand-up event to be streamed across all of Tommy Hilfiger's markets.

"We had hundreds of people submitting from all around the world," Baker says. She flew to Japan for a selection round and was heartened by how many people felt safe enough to present their ideas—especially in a foreign language—to thousands of their peers.

Sixteen finalists received personal coaching from trained TED executives to develop and prepare their talks for public delivery. Under dramatic lighting on a grand stage in Amsterdam, the winners finally spoke to over 1,000 Tommy teammates in the audience and 10,000 more employees live streamed around the world.

They weren't just talking about overcoming career obstacles or learning to better manage emails; topics ranged from parenting to gender identity and political dissent. The winners came from all over the world, including India, Japan, and Latin America. One woman spoke about launching an adaptive clothing brand after watching her differently abled son struggle with zippers; another discussed fashion as a form of protest. One man made the case for the circular economy, while another encouraged everyone's role in overcoming oppression.[20] All ideas reflected the individuals' personal perspective on what courage means to them.

Rooted in Tommy Hilfiger's brand purpose, the initiative wove the global community together around innovation steeped in human potential. TED@Tommy invited team members to step into the spotlight, sharing their passions with bold vulnerability. By pushing the boundaries of their own assumptions and facing some of the world's greatest challenges, they unlocked fresh perspectives and creative solutions. As they stood on stage before their peers, each individual found personal meaning in the brand's purpose. The collective openness fostered a deep sense of team unity with the brand's core values, the vital thread that bound them together.

"It was one of the most magical things I've been fortunate enough to be a part of," reflects Baker. "People came up to me months and years later to thank me for the opportunity to speak; some say it changed their life."

The most unified global marketing teams are inspired by their brand values and celebrate their diversity to encourage creativity and collaboration.

These teams ignite each person's unique potential while embracing differences in language, communication, and behavior. When team members feel both inspired and connected, they can build a global brand by adapting initiatives to their local cultures. Regardless of their role, each interaction becomes impactful, enhancing customer loyalty and driving brand equity. Being part of such a dynamic, global team offers more than professional growth; it's an opportunity to broaden one's perspective and connect with our shared humanity.

In the final chapter, we'll explore how to build a global career to immerse oneself in new cultures and work environments, creating experiences that profoundly shape our worldview and expand our sense of self.

Summary

- **What is global teamwork?** Cross-cultural groups of professionals who collaborate across borders, languages, and cultural differences to create and implement effective global strategies.
- **Why build global marketing teams?** To leverage diverse perspectives, gain deeper market insights, increase innovation, and create marketing campaigns that deliver on the brand promise and resonate across cultures.
- **How to build a global team?** By fostering cultural understanding, promoting inclusive practices, developing emotional intelligence, establishing clear communication strategies, and harnessing cutting-edge technology to dissolve boundaries and bridge the gaps.

The Global Digest

Chapter 11 Takeaways

1 **Bonjour or bust:** Never underestimate the power of a simple greeting. In some cultures, it's the gateway to respect and collaboration.

2 **The innovation catalyst:** Embrace cultural diversity as a powerful asset to drive creativity and innovation in global teams.

3 **Cultural intelligence, your competitive edge:** Develop and nurture cultural intelligence within your team. Understand the nuances of communication, gestures, feedback, and decision-making styles to "culture flex" or even "language flex" between cultures.

4 **Empathy is the new currency:** In global teams, empathy is non-negotiable. Understanding others' perspectives not only boosts morale, but also drives performance.

5 **Psychological safety nets:** Innovation thrives when teams feel safe. Cultivate an environment of psychological safety to unlock your team's full potential and encourage open communication across cultures.

6 **Leadership chameleon:** Adapt your leadership style to accommodate different cultural expectations, balancing direct with participatory approaches.

7 **The communication compass:** Establish clear, explicit communication rules to improve understanding and reduce unspoken assumptions across cultures. Agree to discuss disagreements to find common ground and build meaningful connections.

8 **The trust toolkit:** Trust is a bedrock of effective teams. Establish shared values, open communication, and keep your promises. Remember that trust takes time to build—and only a moment to destroy.

9 **Holidays are not global:** Build social capital with your international colleagues by taking the time to understand and honor both their personal and professional lives.

10 **Creating a unifying purpose:** Shared personal passion is a powerful unifying force. Build global teams around personal narratives that embody a brand's higher purpose to unite people across diverse cultures.

References

1 Paycor (2022) The Biggest Cost of Doing Business: A Closer Look at Labor Costs, *The Business Journals*, May 1. www.bizjournals.com/bizjournals/news/2022/05/01/the-biggest-cost-of-doing-business.html (archived at https://perma.cc/HQ5A-93R8); Deloitte Development LLC (2017) Labor Spending or Overspending. www2.deloitte.com/content/dam/Deloitte/us/Documents/human-capital/us-cons-workforce-costs-are-hiding-with-laborwise.pdf.pdf (archived at https://perma.cc/2L9H-ZFS3)

2 D. Rock and H. Grant (2016) Why Diverse Teams Are Smarter, *Harvard Business Review*, November 4. hbr.org/2016/11/why-diverse-teams-are-smarter (archived at https://perma.cc/P8AA-CS3A)

3 S. Kearney (2024) Interviewed by Katherine Melchior Ray, July 17, GoogleMeet

4 R. Cross, R. Rebele, and A. Grant (2016) Collaborative Overload, *Harvard Business Review*, January–February. hbr.org/2016/01/collaborative-overload (archived at https://perma.cc/GTK5-LMBG)

5 C. Duhigg (2016) What Google Learned from Its Quest to Build the Perfect Team, *The New York Times Magazine*, February 25. www.nytimes.com/2016/02/28/magazine/what-google-learned-from-its-quest-to-build-the-perfect-team.html (archived at https://perma.cc/G47D-U46X)

6 L. Rainie and A. Perrin (2020) The State of Americans' Trust in Each Other amid the COVID-19 Pandemic, Pew Research Center, April 6. www.pewresearch.org/short-reads/2020/04/06/the-state-of-americans-trust-in-each-other-amid-the-covid-19-pandemic/ (archived at https://perma.cc/S4QH-K4JV)

7 L. Rainie and A. Perrin (2020) The State of Americans' Trust in Each Other amid the COVID-19 Pandemic, Pew Research Center, April 6. www.pewresearch.org/short-reads/2020/04/06/the-state-of-americans-trust-in-each-other-amid-the-covid-19-pandemic/ (archived at https://perma.cc/6MNP-PT5B)

8 S. Johnson (2023) WHO Declares Loneliness a "Global Public Health Concern", *The Guardian*, November 16. www.theguardian.com/global-development/2023/nov/16/who-declares-loneliness-a-global-public-health-concern (archived at https://perma.cc/833H-FFWK)

9 Watershed Negotiations Team. Country List of Cultural Characteristics, Watershed Negotiations. www.watershedassociates.com/learning-center-item/country-list-cultural-characteristics.html (archived at https://perma.cc/MKS7-AYPZ)

10 M. V. Yarbrough (1996) If You Let Me Play Sports, *Marquette Sports Law Review*, 6(2). scholarship.law.marquette.edu/cgi/viewcontent.cgi?article=1150&context=sportslaw (archived at https://perma.cc/L7C4-QXH9)

11 A. Sale (2021) How to Make Your Small Talk Big, *The New York Times*, May 1. www.nytimes.com/2021/05/01/opinion/sunday/covid-lockdown-social-small-talk.html?action=click&module=Opinion&pgtype=Homepage (archived at https://perma.cc/4SDF-JU22)

12 S. Flamisch (2021) Here's Something You Never Thought You'd Miss: Office Small Talk, *Rutgers Today*, February 11. www.rutgers.edu/news/heres-something-you-never-thought-youd-miss-office-small-talk (archived at https://perma.cc/Y9DD-2WWD)

13 A. Beard (2020) True Friends at Work, *Harvard Business Review*, July–August hbr.org/2020/07/true-friends-at-work (archived at https://perma.cc/Y2P5-URWC)

14 Lilly Family School of Philanthropy (2024) Empathy among Young Americans on the Rise, Indiana University Indianapolis, May 10. philanthropy.indianapolis.iu.edu/news-events/news/_news/2024/empathy-among-young-americans.html (archived at https://perma.cc/79ZZ-BQYA)

15 Marriott International (2016) Marriott International Completes Acquisition of Starwood Hotels & Resorts Worldwide, Creating World's Largest and Best Hotel Company While Providing Unparalleled Guest Experience, September 23. news.marriott.com/news/2016/09/23/marriott-international-completes-acquisition-of-starwood-hotels-resorts-worldwide-creating-worlds-largest-and-best-hotel-company-while-providing-unparalleled-guest-experience (archived at https://perma.cc/6FD7-42NC)

16 A. Baker (2024) Interviewed by Katherine Melchior Ray, April 23, GoogleMeet

17 S. R. Kelleher (2023) Business Travel Will Never Bounce Back to Pre-Pandemic Levels, Studies Say, *Forbes*, April 24. www.forbes.com/sites/suzannerowankelleher/2023/04/24/business-travel-comeback/ (archived at https://perma.cc/UJA7-UFL8)

18 L. Ellis (2022) Americans Are Breaking Up with Their Work Friends, *The Wall Street Journal*, August 17. www.wsj.com/articles/forget-work-friends-more-americans-are-all-business-on-the-job-11660736232 (archived at https://perma.cc/H2WQ-6PBY)

19 Knowledge at Wharton Staff (2013) Is the Party Over? The Unintended Consequences of Office Social Events, Knowledge at Wharton, March 27. knowledge.wharton.upenn.edu/article/is-the-party-over-the-unintended-consequences-of-office-social-events/ (archived at https://perma.cc/C32J-USVT)

20 B. Rumuly, B. Greene, C. Catlett, C. Hunt, D. Chen, and L. A. Trujillo (2017) "The courage to…" The talks of TED@Tommy, TEDBlog, November 15. blog.ted.com/the-courage-to-the-talks-of-tedtommy/ (archived at https://perma.cc/2952-F4XH)

Expanding Horizons 12

Building a Global Career

KATHERINE MELCHIOR RAY

Discovering the World in a Bowl of Risotto

> *"We may not do everything right, but we know how to do food!" my Italian colleagues exclaimed. In Milan, warming up leftovers in the office microwave is unheard of. With that and the encouragement to join in for a communal lunch, I saw firsthand how food, community, and work culture were different from anything I had known. It was an eye-opening experience where a simple thing like warming risotto over the stove with colleagues became a window into a way of life.*[1]

Jennifer Anton began her career in consumer goods in Chicago with global companies Unilever and MillerCoors. Unilever felt like completing a second Master's in Business Administration, opening her eyes to an international network of colleagues and experiences. In Rotterdam, she met colleagues from the United Arab Emirates (UAE) who explained how the city of Dubai was ambitiously transforming into a global capital of skyscrapers in the desert. While working for MillerCoors, when colleagues from the SAB Miller team in Africa explained how they distribute beer to remote townships, she realized how little she knew about business, marketing, or the world outside her U.S. home.

"How could I be a global marketer if I've only lived in the U.S.?" she asked herself. "How will I learn to empathize and understand global perspectives if I never leave?"

Driven by curiosity, Anton made the bold move to Italy, with her husband and young daughter, where she eventually learned the value of sharing a bowl of risotto at lunch.

From there, she moved to London, where she continued to manage businesses across Europe, the Middle East, and Africa for major brands like Budweiser, Revlon, Tory Burch, and La Perla. In each of these roles, she found herself surrounded by individuals who spoke multiple languages and brought different cultural perspectives.

"It was humbling to be outside my comfort zone. And the discomfort was transformative: It helped me grow as a marketer and a person. Had I stayed in the U.S., I would have been always measuring other countries on my normal. Even when I thought I was humble, I felt confident in the false knowledge that my way was better."

Anton evolved from that ingrained belief of being right to seeing the world from a multitude of perspectives: "Becoming a global marketer has been one of the most rewarding decisions of my career. Stepping out of the familiar and immersing myself in different cultures was the best decision I ever made. Working for brands that have deep emotional meaning across the globe, and being part of their growth, has been a fulfilling journey."

"People who want to become global marketers should take the time to leave their home country for at least three to five years. Force yourself to learn and be uncomfortable. Only then will you be ready to lead a global brand."

"Great brands—and great global marketers—connect people. They transcend borders, bringing emotion and a sense of oneness, no matter the borders that separate us. They appreciate the differences as beautiful and enriching and incorporate those into local executions."

Anton's experience teaches us that choosing to work in a foreign culture not only enhances professional skills but also leads to immense personal growth through an expanded and more nuanced understanding of the world. The first step in building a successful global career requires a willingness to step out of one's comfort zone, seek the adventure of an international experience, and embrace cultural differences. In this chapter, we explore why people choose to work abroad, how they overcome the challenges, and, most importantly, what lessons they learned. With today's remote work, many of those lessons can be gained without moving abroad by cultivating a global mindset from working in global teams and frequent long-stay travel. Still, full cultural immersion offers uniquely transformative experiences, so we share ideas and considerations for taking that leap.

The Promise: A Global Mindset

Working internationally expands one's possibilities further than the eye can see. While people go to work in foreign countries for many reasons—work opportunities, family reasons, and curiosity—all agree that the experience is transformational. Immersing yourself in a foreign culture, where the room you live in, the food you eat, the language you speak, and the behavior around you are all different, disrupts your routine. If your life was a steady stream of work, weekend activities, and holidays, nothing will be the same. And nothing can be taken for granted. Living in a state of constant discovery—realizing things are not what they seem—changes your perception, expanding your understanding of the world and your place within it.

It's not easy. People have concerns about what and whom they're leaving behind and if or how they will fit in and gain support in a strange place. Leaving to work in a foreign country is not like traveling there. You leave your routines, friends, and family behind, while in front of you, you have business objectives, deliverables, and team dynamics to manage in a foreign culture. Take comfort in knowing those concerns are the seeds of new growth. Like anything hard, it takes time. How you act in one culture may not work well in another. You make mistakes. You will be challenged. With those trials, you advance; you learn new ideas, new perspectives, new skills, and you gain patience with others and with yourself.

Every single person I interviewed expressed overwhelming appreciation for the experiences and especially the personal growth, which made them more open, more aware, more instinctive, and more objective. In fact, working with people who are different from you challenges the brain to overcome its regular thought process to sharpen its performance. You learn to process information more carefully.[2]

So, in addition to uniquely memorable experiences, people who work internationally gain invaluable skills in critical thinking from listening carefully with humility and empathy. Most importantly, they develop a greater awareness of the nuances and beauty of the world in which their own identity shifts and expands. This global mindset illustrates the truth of subjectivity: perception is one's reality until it appears otherwise.

That's why this book approaches global marketing from a global mindset, with a strategic approach that leans heavily into culture as it evolves to build cutting-edge relevance and value across multiple markets. To brand global, adapt local, you need to understand and value deep cultural insights. Living, working, and spending extended time in another culture provides this opportunity.

Global Work Is Hard

John Rowe is no stranger to the thrill and challenge of global work. As the former Director of Wieden & Kennedy's Tokyo office in one of the world's largest and most competitive advertising markets, John led high-stakes campaigns in a culture vastly different from his own.

What drove Rowe to leave his comfort zone behind and take on an international role?

"Curiosity," he explained.[3] "If you're curious about the world, where people come from with different perspectives, it leads you to explore." Rowe wanted to carve his own path in the advertising world, though it was daunting to lead local teams in a country where he didn't read or speak the language.

The decision wasn't easy. He worried about leaving his close-knit parents and siblings. "The only time I've ever talked to a therapist was at that time," he shared. Not only did he discover the ease of keeping in touch with FaceTime and other messaging apps, but it made the times with his family so much more meaningful.

His experience in Japan proved transformative in ways he hadn't anticipated. In advertising in the Western world, people are always pushing clients to take risks and move forward quickly. "When I got to Japan, I learned to be more thoughtful." To succeed, he had to slow down, to seek local perspectives to understand the nuances of the culture, or risk making mistakes. "I became a better listener. I had to ask other people's opinions and triangulate to choose the right move. This required a lot of patience, confronting my own self-doubt to recognize my blind spots."

Global advertising work is hard because universal human truths sound shallow unless they're rooted in local culture. Netflix CEO Ted Sarandos has said its programs that were developed for specific local audiences travel better than work developed for a global audience.[4] With such insight, Netflix practices the brand global, adapt local model.

"You've got to go deep," insists Rowe. "You've got to travel, you've got to meet with people and develop relationships. If you can't have honest conversations, you can't get to true insights." This approach is crucial for creating truly effective global campaigns. The process requires a delicate balance of understanding local contexts while identifying overarching human truths that transcend borders.

To gain such insight, Rowe intentionally avoided the expat communities, choosing instead to immerse himself in the local culture.

"Looking back," he reflects, "that was a really good choice because it forced me to learn a lot."

Rowe's global experience led to profound personal growth. Moving to Japan was more than a professional decision—it was "a bit of a self-test," as John describes it. The challenge of running an office in a market so culturally distinct from his own was not just about proving his professional abilities, but also about exploring and redefining his own identity. John emerged with a more expansive understanding of his own potential and capabilities.

"I also met the love of my life in Japan, so it was a very good personal and professional experience."

John Rowe's global career journey exemplifies the transformative power of embracing the complexities of the world beyond one's home market. The relationships he cultivated, the perspectives he gained, and the personal growth he experienced all contributed to his development as a leader.

Where to Start?

People decide to go abroad for a variety of reasons: career and economic opportunities, personal skills development or education, unique experiences, and family. Some people choose to look for a job overseas while others are asked to move abroad by their employers. Businesses, too, can leverage the remote work options available today to hire talent anywhere in the world and build globally minded teams. Two great places to start developing international experience and building skills are working in a global company within your home country and getting an education at a school abroad.

Seek Work, Gain Skills

"I relocated to my company headquarters in Switzerland to advance my career and discovered global opportunities to work with people from all over the world," says Nestlé's Carlota Casellas, reflecting on the pivotal decision that transformed her career.[5]

Leaving behind her life in Barcelona, Casellas encountered not only professional challenges but cultural ones. "In Spain, time is flexible," she explains, "but in Switzerland, punctuality and efficiency are paramount. Whereas Spaniards prioritize leisure time and socializing with family and friends, the Swiss value privacy." The simple gestures and body language she used to communicate in Spain elicited stony reactions in Switzerland, where they value directness and facts.

After nine years of mastering Switzerland's precise and punctual culture, Casellas accepted a promotion that took her even further away—this time to Malaysia. "Moving to Asia introduced me to a world of layered cultures—Malay, Chinese, Indian—each with distinct rhythms, rules, and unspoken codes."

While Switzerland taught her the importance of direct communication and punctuality, Malaysia taught her to slow down, stop, and really listen.

"In Malaysian cultures, harmony is key; decisions are made by consensus, not confrontation. Nonverbal cues are as important as words, so you learn to read between the lines."

The complexity of navigating these cultural landscapes pushed Casellas out of her comfort zone and into discovery. "There's no road map and the sacrifices are real, but you emerge stronger and more adaptable," she says. "Every interaction demands deeper awareness."

The geographic distance only amplified the sense of isolation. "In Switzerland, home felt close, but in Malaysia, I missed my family and friends more than I anticipated." She learned to prepare by studying the cultures and building support systems with other expats and locals alike. She also discovered that her core skills—in marketing, innovation, and digital strategy—were transferable, so she could offer value in return.

"I've come to view the unknown not as something to fear, but as a space filled with uncharted possibilities. Every culture I've lived in has reshaped my perspective, expanding my sense of self."

In the end, working abroad, learning to thrive in new work environments, offers a journey of profound personal growth. For Casellas, that began by joining a multinational company in her native city. For others, it can begin by going abroad to study.

Seek Education, Gain Opportunity

Morin Oluwole's path from her native Nigeria to becoming a leader in luxury and technology across the U.S. and Europe was fueled by ambition and a drive to broaden her worldview.

"I wanted to immerse myself in environments where creativity and technology thrive," she explains.[6] "Moving to California opened doors I never imagined."

After completing her studies at Stanford University and Columbia University, Oluwole began her career at Meta (then Facebook), where she honed her understanding of innovation and global markets. As Meta expanded internationally, she was well-positioned to move to the U.K. and France to develop their luxury business. "Different cultural contexts brought new insights into how digital could transform the luxury experience."

Yet, the transition to France was far from smooth.

"It wasn't just about a new job; it meant untangling the complexities of a new culture," she says. "I was navigating unfamiliar professional and social norms, especially in luxury, where tradition and regional nuances are critical. Learning French from scratch—every meeting, every conversation—stretched my limits."

She also worried about being far from family and the challenge of building a network in a foreign country. And if things didn't go as planned, would it set back her career?

"I overcame those fears by focusing on the opportunities rather than the uncertainties."

That mindset shift was transformative. "I learned to embrace uncertainty, knowing the experience would teach me resilience and adaptability—essential for success in any industry."

Preparation and action were key to overcoming her anxieties. "Researching the business landscape and cultural norms gave me confidence," she says. Seeking advice from mentors who had walked a similar path and building a support system of professionals and friends enriched her experience and helped her navigate the new cultures.

Oluwole focused on her strengths, realizing that her skills were transferable. "While the environment may have been different, the value I brought in digital strategy, luxury marketing, and innovation was still relevant. Instead of worrying about what could go wrong, I saw the experience as an exciting opportunity for growth."

Sure enough, the lessons she learned were profound. "Cultural intelligence was one of the biggest lessons," she reflects. "I had to understand cultural nuances and the local consumer mindset, which made me more flexible and sensitive in my approach to global business. I became comfortable with ambiguity and learned to accept failure."

She also gained a deeper appreciation for the power of global networks. "Collaborating with international teams broadened my perspective on how global businesses function, exposing me to innovative ideas I wouldn't have encountered otherwise. I saw firsthand how cross-border collaboration fuels creativity and innovation."

For those contemplating moving abroad, Morin's advice is simple yet powerful: "Don't let the fear of the unknown hold you back. The growth you'll experience will change you in ways you can't yet see. Leverage your unique perspective while you do your homework, build your support system, and—most importantly—stay open-minded. It's in the discomfort that you'll find the greatest rewards."

Both Oluwole and Casellas embraced the fear of the unknown for what it reveals. They each gained skills and a mindset applicable to any challenge. Professional skills are transferable, so build your strong suit: marketing, digital innovation, engineering, climate finance, sustainable agriculture, etc. And wherever you go, study and immerse yourself in the culture.

BOX 12.1 FIND OPPORTUNITY IN THE COMPLEXITY

Working globally is complicated, so learn to spot the opportunities and use them to your advantage. Time zones create challenges and opportunities. Goldman Sachs' Lisa Shalett explained in Chapter 5 how she differentiated herself by leveraging the time zone in her favor to help her clients understand what happened in foreign markets overnight. When I was working as a global consultant on the U.S. West Coast, I leveraged the time difference to spend quality hours with my children. I rose early in the morning to interact with Europe and worked late in the evening with colleagues in Japan. In between, I worked from home around taking my children to school, playing with them in the afternoons, and finishing dinner and bathtime before jumping on calls with Asia.

Speaking Another Language Is Like Gaining Another Soul

In my case, it was Japan's captivating culture that drew me in. The centuries-old Noh Kyogen theater, with its masked dancers moving and singing in slow, deliberate gestures, mesmerized me. I marveled at how something so ancient could appear so strikingly modern. My fascination led me to study Japanese in college, building on the language skills I had gained as a child in San Francisco attending a French bilingual school and learning Spanish in high school. However, graduating from college at age 21 with a degree in history and a budding interest in journalism, I found myself at a crossroads, unsure how to begin a career with such diverse interests. When an unexpected role arose to work in Japanese television in the country I had admired only from afar, I saw the opportunity to follow both my passions: journalism and Japan.

Over the years I discovered the analytical and narrative practices honed from studying history, along with my cultural and linguistic skills, enabled many global opportunities. Therefore, I believe strongly that those seeking global careers should learn how to think broadly and strategically, while building technical skills, like languages.

Paul Bulcke, the Chairman of Nestlé, the world's largest food and beverage company with operations in nearly 200 countries, emphasizes the significant advantages of multilingual staff.[7] Speaking the local language helps break down barriers, enabling better communication, trust, and overall team effectiveness. It's not just about expressing ideas, but also about understanding emotions and building genuine rapport. Connecting on a more personal level is especially crucial at senior levels where rallying teams behind company goals is crucial.

Many people around the world learn more than one language in school. Unfortunately, English-speaking countries don't prioritize language study as they do math and science. With the explosion of real-time translation options today, some might say learning a language is a waste of time. *Non! Nine! Tidak!* いいえ。 नहीं. *No.* In any language, I disagree. Translation services help immensely with transactions, but learning a language is transformational. Speaking another language teaches us the subjectivity of words and communication, and how to see the unspoken assumptions that color meaning. Nothing replaces how speaking a language opens new worlds, with new opportunities, new relationships, and new ways of seeing and living in the world.

Studies show that bilingual babies are better at recognizing ambiguity, even before learning to walk. In a 2015 study, 16-month-old toddlers were shown two identical toys.[8] One toy was visible to both the child and the speaker, while the other was blocked from the speaker's view. When the speaker asked for a toy, monolingual children randomly picked between the toys, but those exposed to multiple languages consistently chose the toy the speaker could see, distinguishing another's perspective from their own. Before they're even able to connect their own simple words, children who've heard multiple languages understand greater context. Learning a language helps develop greater awareness and objectivity, crucial skills for and benefits of working internationally.

Know Thyself to Understand Others

Developing this awareness is not only about understanding others, but also about gaining a deeper understanding of yourself and your own biases. Having a clear and objective sense of self—recognizing your own strengths, limitations, and cultural assumptions—helps you recognize your subjectivity to adapt more easily to diverse environments.

There are many individual assessments for developing this understanding. In addition to Aperian's GlobeSmart profiles explored in earlier chapters, I have used Myers-Briggs, Enneagram, Insights, and Strength Deployment Inventory (SDI). Each one offers a unique approach to understanding individual and team strengths. In global business, self-awareness is essential for navigating cultural differences and leading with authenticity.

Objectivity is crucial when working internationally, and self-awareness is key to developing it. But building a global career goes further by studying the diverse cultural and professional landscapes you'll encounter. Before taking the leap, it's important to research the necessities.

Do Your Homework

Consider how a company's national culture influences the working experience in ways we may take for granted in our home country. Issues like compensation, vacation, and promotion are often negotiated in many countries. But less obvious considerations like daily work routines, professional relationships, lunch breaks, and even job security vary widely depending on the company's home country. For instance, European firms offer more vacation than most other countries. Salaries are generally highest in the U.S., but there is little vacation, no guaranteed healthcare, and no job security.

While remote work has opened up opportunities to operate from foreign countries, working abroad usually requires a work visa or foreign passport. Securing the right documentation is critical, as is understanding the regulatory and taxation requirements of the country you plan to work in.

Plan ahead for unknowns. I've learned that outlining terms for a possible return *before* you leave is ideal; if things don't go as planned, you've secured your family's return and reduced at least one of the many variables. For instance, while discussing your contract to move overseas, negotiate equal home relocation support if they let you go. I've found myself working abroad with my family when a CEO retired or was fired and the corporate ladder was suddenly pulled out from under me.

Working, traveling, eating exotic foods, and dreaming in a foreign language are amazing experiences that expand your world and awareness, but there is risk involved. Clarify and reduce concerns where possible. It can be tricky, so take measured risks. Focus on what you can control and remember that you and your family will gain invaluable knowledge, skills, and experiences that will shape your future in meaningful ways.

Work–Life Integration

Have Baby, Will Travel

For Fábio Luizari Artoni, the journey from São Paulo to Stockholm was not only a career-defining leap but also a personal adventure that reshaped his worldview. Fascinated by diverse cultural perspectives, Artoni's curiosity wasn't satisfied by books alone. Brazilian companies in 2017 were focused on their large domestic market, so he sought to move abroad for firsthand experience of different cultures and business practices.

"I realized that gaining international experience could enhance my career, allowing me to work with international companies in Brazil or support Brazilian firms in their international ventures," he explains.[9] With his family's enthusiasm and support, he accepted the call via LinkedIn from a U.S. recruiter looking for experience in direct sales.

Along with the excitement came inevitable fears. "My main concerns revolved around my family's adaptation," he admits. Moving to a new country raised questions about how his children—aged eleven, six, and under one—would adjust, not to mention his aging parents, who remained in Brazil. On top of this, he was stepping into a new company with unfamiliar colleagues and without the safety net of an expatriate contract.

The company, Oriflame, was very international, helping the family settle quickly. As his employer helped assure the move and secure a visa, Artoni and his family could immerse themselves in Swedish culture, learning about local customs and values.

For his children who attended local schools, the transition was initially difficult—particularly because English wasn't their home language—but Artoni had read it often took months to adjust.

"The first three months were hard," Artoni recalls, "but we embraced their way of life, engaged in local celebrations, and adopted their values. Immersing the family in Swedish culture was essential for integration. At first, it seemed daunting, but in the end, it was wonderful to experience this adventure together as a family."

At work, one of the most profound lessons Artoni learned was the power of listening. "Whenever I approached a situation through the lens of my Latin American background, discussions didn't go well," he reflects. The ability to step outside his own cultural mindset and evaluate situations from other cultural perspectives became pivotal to his success.

"I learned to put myself in others' shoes, to understand their perspectives, and evaluate situations from their point of view. This shift allowed me to add value to conversations and make better decisions." Artoni became a more open-minded, adaptable leader able to thrive in global environments.

Several years later, the family returned to Brazil, where Artoni became Head of Global Marketing at the Brazilian cosmetics giant, Natura. Even in his own country, he listened more deeply to people of diverse backgrounds, seeing their perspectives not as barriers, but as added value. It took living abroad to gain that mindset. His advice to those considering a move is simple: Give it a go! Overthinking creates unnecessary obstacles. He should know.

"I made this move with three children, including an eight-month-old baby," he explains. "At first, it seemed daunting, but it turned out to be a fantastic experience. Take the plunge and embrace the journey."

Their Happiness Means Our Success

Working internationally opens up opportunities and challenges for the whole family.

With more cultural and gender diversity in the workforce, women are leveraging the flexibility of professional and personal demands. When I was CMO at Shiseido in Japan, our teams traveled frequently to the massive, important Chinese market. Female Japanese managers with kids at home would fly the redeye flight from Tokyo to Beijing for all-day meetings on a Friday and attend working dinners with the local team before flying home late that night to be with their kids over the weekend. Balancing business objectives with family needs, culture-flexing includes navigating different societies' gender norms and expectations.

Men are also finding joy as the "trailing spouse," a real, if dated and demeaning, expression that implies a passive role. In fact, the decision to relocate is usually a joint one, involving mutual support and shared aspirations for adventure and discovery. Both partners are embarking on a significant life change, each with their own challenges and opportunities for personal and professional development.

The saying goes that if the spouse is not happy, the executive won't succeed. Everyone needs to prepare. When I moved to France to run a local marketing team for Nordstrom, both my husband and I were asked to take the Myers-Briggs self-assessment to evaluate our receptivity to change. Many companies provide services to help both the executive and spouse adjust to a new culture, find a place to live, and learn the language. While companies help secure the expatriate's working visa, a spouse cannot work without his/her own. Such corporate support is very helpful in encouraging families to make the leap.

In international relocations, learning extends far beyond classrooms, yet children's formal education remains a top priority for families. If the children are young, you might consider the immersive experience of sending them to local schools. If the children are older and do not speak the local language, many parts of the world offer excellent international schools. These institutions deftly balance teaching local culture with integrating diverse families, providing academic continuity for transient students while fostering a multicultural environment. They not only educate but also serve as community hubs, easing transitions and preparing children for an interconnected world. For many expatriate families, these schools become a crucial anchor, offering stability amidst the flux of international assignments.

Taking children to live abroad provides unforeseen opportunities not only for their individual growth and for the family's communal experience. I gained international leadership advice watching my young children in French schools. Observing them adjust their behaviors formed in the independence of American schools to follow the exacting rules of their imposing French teachers, I too learned to shift my managerial style to be more direct with my teams... And it worked!

While navigating life abroad may seem simpler before settling down, doing so as a family expands the cultural discoveries, stimulates individual growth, and strengthens family bonds. In my opinion, the best ages to move children abroad are between five and thirteen, when the children are old enough to appreciate it and learn the language, the family unit is close, and you can channel pre-adolescent issues into new, long-term experiences. But even with older children, the benefits outweigh the sacrifices.

Teens Take Flight, Family Unites

Moving to a new country with teenagers can be challenging. Beyond the logistics of relocating, parents often worry about how their children will adapt to new schools, make friends, and navigate a foreign environment. Yet, as hotel veteran Sara Kearney discovered, the experience can offer profound rewards for the whole family.

"I was incredibly fortunate to be offered the opportunity to work for an international company early in my career. Living in another country is like opening a portal to unexpected and extremely satisfying surprises and delights," she recalls.[10] Sara didn't set out to build a global career when she started working at a small hotel in New Orleans, Louisiana. Thirty years later, she couldn't imagine her life any other way.

Over her years in global marketing and operations, Sara learned to embrace the unknown. "Keeping an open mind to move from fear to curiosity was key. I developed an insatiable curiosity and passion for learning about culture." So, when she was asked to move with her husband and teenage children to Hong Kong to oversee hotel operations across Asia, the decision came easily.

"My biggest angst," she admitted, "concerned my children. While I knew they would grow tremendously, I worried about how my 14-year-old daughter and 12-year-old son would handle a new school system and make friends in a completely foreign environment."

Drawing on her years of global travel, Sara felt prepared to help her family adjust. She knew immersing themselves in the local culture would help. Both children joined local sports teams, where they made friends and even traveled to many nearby countries for competitions.

There were moments of loneliness and frustration—like struggling to read signs or menus—but overall, the experience forged a stronger family bond. "It built character in all of us," she said, "and deepened our understanding of the importance of a global community."

The timing of their move coincided with the start of the Umbrella Revolution in Hong Kong. "It was an incredible time to be living in Hong Kong and a remarkable learning opportunity for my children." Sara believes her children came away more independent, tolerant, and culturally aware. "They embrace travel as a way to learn about other cultures and to nourish their souls. Plus, they now have friends all over the world!"

Moving with teenagers may feel daunting, but as Kearney's journey shows, the challenges are often outweighed by the lifelong lessons and global perspectives gained. Everyone gains by going abroad, even those who never imagined they would.

Just Do It for Global Growth

Now Vice President of Global Marketing at Google, Marvin Chow's international career was unexpected. When his boss at Nike in the U.S. asked him to relocate to Korea as Marketing Director, Chow was initially skeptical.

"Why?" he recalls. "As the child of immigrants, the goal was always to succeed in America. Why would I choose to leave everything familiar behind?"[11] Yet, what began as a daunting challenge quickly became the most formative chapter of his career both personally and professionally.

Arriving in Seoul, Chow was thrust into an environment where familiar instincts were no longer reliable guides. The cultural divide was more than theoretical; it was visceral.

"Leading in a foreign country forces you to rely less on your gut. You have to ask more questions, gather more information, and carefully discern which insights to trust," he explains. "It was a constant learning curve to navigate not just a new market, but also a new way of thinking."

Between the professional demands and cultural hurdles, Chow suffered his share of imposter syndrome. He had to balance the American sense of urgency and aggressiveness with the Asian desire for consensus. Also, many of the people he led were older and far more experienced in the region. He knew building trust was critical to win over the locals.

Chow learned to lead with curiosity and an open mind. With humility, he embraced local customs. "It's about having a real interest in the food, the music, the language—everything that defines the place. You have to meet people halfway, whether it's debating ideas or doing your part to bridge barriers, small actions can go a long way." This willingness to engage helped Chow forge strong bonds with his team.

Later, Nike moved him to Japan, where language barriers loomed large, so he often relied on fragmented Japanese and using simplified English to get by. But these informal exchanges—raw and unpolished—proved vital. "Those moments of vulnerability, where communication wasn't perfect, actually helped build trust. It brought us closer as a team."

Chow discovered the weight of accountability and, as a result, became very resourceful. In a foreign market, there's no safety net of shared responsibility—success or failure rests squarely on your shoulders. "It's equal parts empowering and terrifying." Leading country teams with limited resources forced him to adopt a "local-first mindset," making every dollar stretch further through creativity and innovation. "It was a crash course in smart marketing."

Chow's time abroad imparted lessons that would stay with him long after he returned to the U.S.: he learned to ask better questions, trust the power of data in unfamiliar settings, and support local teams.

"Being able to experience an entirely new culture, learn a new language and meet incredible people from around the world is a once-in-a-lifetime opportunity that will push you, but you will grow in ways hard to gain even in a global team. The marketing foundation, the skills, and instincts I developed through sheer necessity have done more for my marketing career than any other role."

Chow's advice for those contemplating an international move is clear: "Just do it. My time abroad didn't just refine my career; it reshaped my entire worldview."

People who have worked abroad learn that the unknown is not a place on a map, but a challenge worth exploring.

Summary

- **What is a global career?** A global career involves working across borders and embracing different cultural and business environments that expand your personal and professional horizons. It's more than a job—immersed in unfamiliar settings, you will find an opportunity to discover a new world.
- **Why build a global career?** People pursue global careers for skills development, career advancement, and personal growth. Working abroad broadens your horizons through unique experiences, cultures, and networks, fostering growth in unexpected ways. It enhances cultural intelligence: by increasing your awareness, empathy, and adaptability, and sharpening your listening skills, you'll become a more objective leader with a global mindset.
- **How to launch a global career?** Start by seeking a job in a global company or an education abroad. Build a unique strong suit of transferable skills, do your homework, network, and practice cultural intelligence. Don't let fear hold you back; embrace the discomfort of stepping out of your comfort zone.

The Global Digest

Chapter 12 Takeaways

1. **Curiosity sparks growth:** Let curiosity be your compass. Learning to thrive in foreign cultures leads to professional and personal transformation.
2. **Embrace uncertainty:** See the unknown as an opportunity for growth. Navigating new cultures may push you out of your comfort zone, but this is often where your career takes flight.

3 **Be practical about your path:** Leverage global companies and international educational institutions to kickstart your global career—either locally or abroad.

4 **Preparation reduces risk:** Before packing your bags, take a moment to reflect on who you are and what you hope to achieve, study the foreign culture, secure legal documents, and build a support network of locals and expats.

5 **Build your strong suit of skills:** Your professional expertise—whether in digital innovation, marketing, engineering, or language—has value across cultures, so remember you have a lot to offer as well as much to learn.

6 **Learn a language, gain a soul:** Learning another language transforms our understanding of how we see the world. Beyond bridging communication barriers, it fosters empathy, cultural understanding, and deeper connections.

7 **Smell the roses:** Take time to slow down and observe, engage, and immerse yourself fully in local cultures. Global marketing is only successful when rooted in local insights.

8 **Listen to lead:** Cultural diversity exposes our biases. By actively listening to different perspectives, leaders gain objectivity and flexibility. Cultural intelligence transforms leadership.

9 **Families bond abroad:** International relocations impact the whole family, but shared challenges and adventures abroad foster deeper connections and personal growth for everyone.

10 **Just do it:** Don't overthink an international move; the growth and opportunities far outweigh initial fears and challenges. Take the leap!

References

1 J. Anton (2024) Interviewed by Katherine Melchior Ray, October 18, email

2 D. Rock and H. Grant (2016) Why Diverse Teams Are Smarter, *Harvard Business Review*, November 4. hbr.org/2016/11/why-diverse-teams-are-smarter (archived at https://perma.cc/XU9Y-JXAA)

3 J. Rowe (2024) Interviewed by Katherine Melchior Ray, September 13, GoogleMeet

4 PYMNTS (2024) Netflix Co-CEO: Putting the Audience First Is Key to Authentic Personalization, September 20. www.pymnts.com/subscriptions/2024/netflix-co-ceo-putting-audience-first-is-key-authentic-personalization/ (archived at https://perma.cc/TM9T-KDVQ)

5 C. Casellas (2024) Interviewed by Katherine Melchior Ray, June 13, GoogleMeet; October 9, email

6 M. Oluwole (2024) Interviewed by Katherine Melchior Ray, June 11, GoogleMeet; October 6, email

7 H. Brown and I. Lahiri (2024) The Big Question: Learning Multiple Languages Shows You 'Care', Says Nestlé Chairman, EuroNews, January 8. www.euronews.com/business/2024/01/08/the-big-question-learning-multiple-languages-shows-you-care-says-nestle-chairman (archived at https://perma.cc/UR76-WGVZ)

8 Z. Liberman, A. L. Woodward, B. Keysar, and K. D. Kinzler (2016) Exposure to Multiple Languages Enhances Communication Skills in Infancy, *Developmental Science*, March 21. pmc.ncbi.nlm.nih.gov/articles/PMC5031504/ (archived at https://perma.cc/4PNC-CETT)

9 F. Artoni (2024) Interviewed by Katherine Melchior Ray, June 5, GoogleMeet; October 2, email

10 S. Kearney (2024) Interviewed by Katherine Melchior Ray, July 17, GoogleMeet

11 M. Chow (2024) Interviewed by Katherine Melchior Ray, September 30, email

Conclusion

The Journey Continues

Looking ahead, two significant trends might seem to challenge the core theme of this book: the importance of balancing global brand values with local cultural adaptation, and the need to cultivate a global mindset to do so.

The first is the rise of artificial intelligence (AI). The accelerating pace at which marketing activities like research, analysis, and copywriting are being outsourced to technology might give the impression that we can bypass the work of understanding other cultures, spotting patterns in social fabrics, and collaborating among diverse teams. *Au contraire*, nothing could be further from the truth. While AI is capable of executing certain tasks, it cannot think critically to interpret cultural variables, context, and meaning, or step back to see a bigger picture.[1]

AI is an exceptional area of technology, but narrowly designed to execute specific tasks quickly and efficiently. By gathering information, synthesizing data, and rearranging words, it can generate content and provide direction. Advanced technologies can manage inventory, streamline workflows, and recommend products. However, like any tech offering, the value AI delivers depends on how it is used. Effective results require thoughtful framing and precise prompting, so context becomes even more critical. When guided by the right questions, AI can enhance productivity and creativity, but it relies on humans to provide direction and meaning.

This is why I embrace AI and integrate it into my classes, encouraging students to explore its advantages and recognize its limitations. Despite its capabilities, AI cannot identify universal truths the way humans can because we can make cultural associations and connections. As meaning shifts across context and culture, it takes an informed and flexible human mind to catch subtle clues and feelings to interpret nuanced information correctly. As we increasingly delegate routine tasks to machines, we must also cultivate our humanity—the very skills that make us irreplaceable.

Marketing has always centered on the promise and exchange between a product or service and a customer. From the Silk Road of centuries past to today's digital platforms, the tools and techniques have evolved, but the essence remains unchanged. The spice merchant who counted payment in gleaming gold coins might distrust today's electronic platforms, but he would recognize the timeless art of delivering value. Innovation drives progress and improves efficiency, but true value is created where meaning is felt—in the human experience, shaped by the rich interplay of culture, context, and connection.

The second challenge may come from the markets themselves. The world faces an uncertain future with political landscapes shifting as autocratic leaders gain power in Asia, Eastern Europe, and the U.S. Interconnected economies grapple with trade tariffs, while territorial conflicts disrupt major markets overnight. Meanwhile, our natural world is under siege, as extreme weather events—floods, droughts, and hurricanes—devastate communities. This raises an important question: Could an increasingly fragmented world reject global brands?

We don't believe so. As the world becomes more interconnected with the internet, satellites, and modern transportation, brands have only grown in importance and influence. In a world that often feels chaotic, these brands serve as anchors, offering consistency, reliability, and trust. At their core, global brands represent promises of quality and performance, providing a sense of assurance in unpredictable times. The principle of *brand global, adapt local* will become even more critical. As economies expand and consumer expectations rise, people presume global brands will address their local needs—whether it's the cocoa percentage in a chocolate bar, the operating hours of a jewelry shop, or the preferred options for customer service software.

Ultimately, people spend money where they find meaning. And meaning is born from experiences, emotions, and actions that align with one's values, beliefs, and sense of purpose. Who wants to visit the Champs-Élysées in Paris only to find the same leather goods at the Louis Vuitton store as they would on New York's Fifth Avenue? Today's consumers increasingly crave uniquely local experiences that reflect the surrounding culture. Brands that master the art of local adaptation while staying true to their core identity not only survive—they thrive in the face of fragmentation. We can all learn from Starbucks, which understands that it's not just about serving a cup of coffee, but about delivering experiences that resonate deeply, even for under $10.

As we look forward, it's clear that the rewards of building global brands extend far beyond the business success. The journey of international growth enriches not just the organization but also the individuals leading the way.

Building brands across cultures is as challenging as it is rewarding. Entering unfamiliar markets requires navigating unique cultural preferences and sometimes surprising consumer behaviors. These complexities compel businesses to rethink their offerings and communication strategies to succeed. Brands that go global thrive by staying true to the universality of their promise while thoughtfully adapting it to local cultures. This approach unlocks opportunities for growth, deepens connections with diverse audiences, and strengthens global resilience, creating meaning that transcends borders and forges connections both practical and profound.

The resulting value isn't measured just in market share or profits but in the richness of the perspective gained. Companies become stronger and more flexible; individuals grow professionally and personally—learning to see with fresh eyes, appreciate diverse viewpoints, and understand their place in a global context. Every leader and contributor we spoke with affirmed the immeasurable rewards of this journey. We couldn't agree more. Those global experiences shape who we become.

My family (Katherine) has learned to savor French Mont d'Or cheese during its brief winter season and to "read the air" in choosing to shake hands, kiss on the cheek, or bow. My daughter thrives as a climate investor who speaks six languages, working professionally in three of them and immersing herself in the very markets she supports. My son is completing his PhD in aerospace engineering to improve the interaction between humans and technology and collaborates with his counterparts at science conventions in Europe and Japan. My husband manages a healthcare company with teams working remotely from the U.S., Ukraine, Morocco, Pakistan, and the Philippines. Together, we went global and made it our home, shaping a family culture that blends curiosity, collaboration, and commitment.

As for mine (Nataly), my daughters' childhoods, while still unfolding, have been deeply enriched by international experiences—from receiving beautiful red envelopes embossed with gold foil for Chinese New Year from their teacher in the Boston suburbs, to deciphering the Irish Gaelic in their grandmother's birthday cards. I met my Irish husband in Ecuador and, over the course of our 20-year marriage, we've led two highly global careers. Today, he leads engineering for a company in Copenhagen, managing teams across Mexico, Chile, Brazil, Argentina, Colombia, Spain, Denmark, and Bulgaria. This global life has shaped us as professionals and as parents, opening our eyes to aspects of society we might never have otherwise appreciated. It's never too soon—or too late—to experience more of what the world has to offer.

Brand global, adapt local is not just a business imperative—it's about fostering connections, cultivating empathy, and embracing the shared humanity that unites us across the vast diversity of our world. It's a way to create value that lasts far beyond the bottom line, shaping a more connected and compassionate global community.

Let's Connect

The world is vast, diverse, and beautiful. Learning that how we see and interpret it is not the only truth, but a partial view, may be hard at first. But when we learn to recognize our subjectivity, we gain countless new perspectives to grow immeasurably. Cultural intelligence helps expand that view to see, understand, and embrace different perspectives. We learn from both the answer and the asking. We can literally see more angles. Feel more emotions. Appreciate more unique aspects of others. And become more ourselves.

Our greatest satisfaction comes not only from the experiences we've shared in building business opportunities, diverse teams, and families across continents and nationalities, but from passing them onto others. Through that and teaching students at UC Berkeley Haas and Middlebury, we have helped countless people—young professionals and mid-career leaders alike—build their own journeys. If you liked this book, if you learned something, and if you want to hear more, please let us know. We are happy to connect.

For More Information

Katherine Melchior Ray

Website: katherinemelchiorray.com/

LinkedIn: www.linkedin.com/in/katherinemelchiorray/

Cultural Crossroads: katherinemelchiorray.substack.com/

Contact: kmelchiorray@gmail.com

Nataly Kelly

Website: borntobeglobal.com/

LinkedIn: www.linkedin.com/in/natalykelly/

Contact: nataly@borntobeglobal.com

Reference

1 C. Hofacker (2024) Analyzing AI, Aerospace America, January 2024. aerospaceamerica.aiaa.org/departments/analyzing-ai/ (archived at https://perma.cc/C8UY-X2PP)

INDEX

Note: Page numbers in *italics* refer to figures.

More from Kogan Page

ISBN: 9781398610088

ISBN: 9781398618992

ISBN: 9781398618572

ISBN: 9781398611627

www.koganpage.com

KoganPage

Printed and bound by CPI Group (UK) Ltd, Croydon, CR0 4YY

17/09/2026

14964327-0001